Global governance and the United Nations system

D1279381

Global governance and the United Nations system

Edited by Volker Rittberger

United Nations University Press

TOKYO · NEW YORK · PARIS

United Nations University Press
The United Nations University, 53-70, Jingumae 5-chome,
Shibuya-ku, Tokyo, 150-8925, Japan
Tel: +81-3-3499-2811   Fax: +81-3-3406-7345
E-mail: sales@hq.unu.edu
http://www.unu.edu

United Nations University Office in North America
2 United Nations Plaza, Room DC2-2050–2058, New York, NY 10016, USA
Tel: +1-212-963-6387   Fax: +1-212-371-9454
E-mail: unuona@igc.apc.org

United Nations University Press is the publishing division of the United Nations
University.

Cover design by Jean-Marie Antenen

Printed in the United States of America

UNUP-1075
ISBN 92-808-1075-8

Library of Congress Cataloging-in-Publication Data

Global governance and the United Nations system / edited by Volker
Rittberger.
    p.   cm.
Includes bibliographical references and index.
ISBN 92-808-1075-8
1. International organization. 2. United Nations. I. Rittberger, Volker,
1941–
JZ5566.4   .G58   2001
341.23—dc21   2001007540

969444

Contents

List of tables and figures

Note on measurements

In this volume:

1 billion = 1,000 million
1 trillion = 1,000 billion
1 tonne   = 1,000 kg
1 ton   = 2,240 lb
$1   = one US dollar

Foreword

In 1995, the United Nations celebrated its fiftieth anniversary. As a tribute to this anniversary the United Nations University (UNU) launched the project "The United Nations System in the Twenty-first Century." This long-term study, divided into five key issue areas (peace and security, economic development, environment, human dignity, and governance), has a main focus on (and underlying question regarding) how global international institutions can adapt to the requirements of the twenty-first century.

In 1998, we started work on the subproject "Global Governance and the United Nations" and tried to determine how the UN system might cope with the apparent need for institutional adaptation and reform. The starting point of the research was the fundamental changes in the global system. The end of the cold war and the bipolar system, on the one hand, and the growing number of resourceful private actors in the international arena – such as transnational corporations (TNCs) or non-governmental organizations (I/NGOs) – on the other, point to the beginning of the end of the (Westphalian) international system with its territorially rooted borderlines and nation-states. Since the new transnational actors are able to act in, and take advantage of, a twilight zone of uncoordinated national legal orders, there is a need to fill the gaps in public coordination and control by international institutions, which otherwise run the risk of losing their legitimacy.

The present volume represents the output of a collaborative venture by nine scholars with very different cultural backgrounds from all over the world. The main focus in this volume is the prospect of global governance based on the UN system. Briefly summarized, global governance (in contrast to international governance) refers to the decreased salience of states and the increased involvement of non-state actors in norm- and rule-setting processes and compliance monitoring. Moreover, global governance refers to multilevel governance which includes not only levels of public policy-making beyond the nation-state but also the subnational (i.e. regional or local) levels.

This book examines the development from international to global governance basically looking at the fundamental change of actors, agendas, and collective decision-making as well as at the UN system in the world of the twenty-first century. Governance, the authors argue, faces three different challenges at the turn of the century (i.e. the revolution in information and communication technologies, the processes of globalization, and the end of the cold war and of bipolarity) leading to serious governance gaps (jurisdictional, operational, incentive, and participatory gaps) with which existing international governance systems cannot cope adequately and which prompt a multifaceted move toward global governance.

The contributors to this volume discuss the various aspects of this transformation, extrapolate its trends, and provide suggestions about possible and desirable forms of global governance. Starting with some general reflections, chapter 1 gives an overview of the debate, discusses the transformation from international to global governance, and ends with an analysis and evaluation of the emergence of global governance. In this context, chapters 1 and 2 try to highlight several key questions, such as the roles of states, intergovernmental organizations (in particular the UN system), and non-state actors – market forces as well as civil society actors – in a future world order. Will they cooperate in global governance systems and, if so, how? To what extent will states still be able to attain their governance goals, such as providing security, protection, and social welfare? Chapter 3 seeks to determine whether international institutions at the regional level, such as security communities, are more effective in achieving governance goals for the peoples of their respective regions. Chapters 4 and 5 explore the changing nature of non-state actors such as I/NGOs or business corporations, especially in their function as addressees of rules and as rule makers, and pay attention to the increasing political salience of these actors. The author of chapter 6 asks whether a democratic world republic is the ethically desirable and justifiable model of global governance. Finally, chapter 7 addresses the crucial question of how social justice can be attained or furthered by a transition from existing international governance systems to global governance. Altogether, this volume offers a wide-ranging analysis of world-order problems at the beginning of the twenty-first century.

After the cooperation of scholars from a variety of academic and cultural backgrounds had been secured, the first draft chapters were prepared for, and discussed at, an authors' workshop in Paris, 13–14 October 1999, convened on the premises of UNESCO, sponsored by the European Office of the UNU, and coordinated by the Centre for International Relations of the University of Tübingen, Germany. This joining of forces permitted a smoothly run workshop and contributed to a very satisfactory outcome.

In March 2001, the editor and some of the contributors presented their work at the annual meeting of the International Studies Association (panel: "Cooperation in Governance: Civil Society and International Organizations") in Chicago. The presentations to this panel and the subsequent discussions made possible further scrutiny of the work by a highly competent and interested academic audience. This provided very useful input before we put the final touches to our chapters.

A project such as this, with the contributors hailing from all over the world, presents a great challenge to the authors, to the editor, and, of course, to the sponsor of the project. Thus, many thanks are due to Dr Albrecht Schnabel and the staff of the UNU headquarters, who were strongly supportive of this project throughout. It is also my pleasure to acknowledge with gratitude the generous funding received from the UNU for this project.

Members of the academic staff of the Centre for International Relations of Tübingen University also contributed substantively to the success of this project. Hans Seidenstücker was untiring in taking notes at the workshop in Paris. The provision of his excellent summaries of our discussions constituted a very valuable service and was appreciated by all members of the team. Tanja Brühl took charge of the project coordination in Tübingen: she made sure that we did not miss deadlines, that the Paris workshop ran smoothly, and that the contributors received substantive and timely feedback on the various drafts of their chapters. She also proved to be an able collaborator on the introductory chapter of the book. Klaus Stodick transformed many of the manuscripts into readable form and checked the copy-editor's queries.

A final word of thanks goes to the United Nations University Press and its editorial staff, in particular Janet Boileau and Gareth Johnston, who have been an unfailing source of encouragement and support. Heather Russell has been a most helpful copy-editor, doing her best for those authors whose mother tongue is not English and contributing in many ways to making this volume a readable and authoritative book. Many others have also contributed to its completion; although it is impossible to mention every single person who has helped in one way or another, I do wish to thank them all.

Volker Rittberger
Tübingen, Germany, September 2001

1

From international to global governance: Actors, collective decision-making, and the United Nations in the world of the twenty-first century

Tanja Brühl and Volker Rittberger

The central challenge we face today is to ensure that globalization becomes a
positive force for all the world's people, instead of leaving billions of them
behind in squalor
Kofi Annan 2000: 6

Introduction: Why discuss global governance?

Secretary-General Kofi Annan identifies in his millennium report to the United Nations some of the pressing challenges that the world's peoples face and that fall within the UN ambit. He proposes new initiatives (such as a disaster-response initiative or a health internetwork) and enumerates priorities that people should address (such as to halve, by 2015, the proportion of the world's people with an income of less than one dollar a day). Kofi Annan states that "all these proposals are set in the context of globalization, which is transforming the world as we enter the twenty-first century" (Annan 2000: 6).

The Secretary-General is not alone in referring to globalization as a challenge to, and driving force for change of, existing international governance systems. It is widely accepted that globalization not only alters the relationship between governments and market forces but also has important implications for the identities and activities of transnational social actors (Lynch 1998). Thus, instead of states only, a triad of actors

1

comprising (1) states and intergovernmental organizations (IGOs), (2) market forces and (3) civil society actors play important roles in existing international and evolving global governance.

International governance is the output of a non-hierarchical network of interlocking international (mostly, but not exclusively, governmental) institutions which regulate the behaviour of states and other international actors in different issue areas of world politics (Rittberger 2000: 198). *Global* governance is the output of a non-hierarchical network of international *and transnational* institutions: not only IGOs and international regimes but also transnational regimes are regulating actors' behaviour. In contrast to international governance, global governance is characterized by the decreased salience of states and the increased involvement of non-state actors in norm- and rule-setting processes and compliance monitoring. In addition, global governance is equated with multilevel governance, meaning that governance takes place not only at the national and the international level (such as in international governance) but also at the subnational, regional, and local levels. Whereas, in international governance, the addressees and the makers of norms and rules are states and other intergovernmental institutions, non-state actors (in addition to states and intergovernmental institutions) are both the addressees and the makers of norms and rules in global governance.

International governance, which has grown in the past 150 years, particularly after the Second World War, is confronted by three different challenges leading to governance gaps with which international governance systems cannot cope adequately and which, arguably, prompt a move toward global governance. First, the technological revolution, especially in information and communication technologies, not only has been a precondition of globalization but also enables, *inter alia*, citizens and non-governmental organizations (NGOs) to enter the stage of world politics. Owing to this technological revolution (especially the Internet), these new actors can gather and process information more easily and rapidly and are able to formulate more timely and persuasive political appraisals. In addition, the Internet is helpful in distributing individuals' and non-state actors' statements instantaneously and inexpensively around the world.

Second (and most important), globalization has altered the relationships within the triad of actors. In order to govern effectively (i.e. to fulfil the several tasks of governance [see below]) it is necessary, first, to ensure a well-balanced relationship within the triad of actors and, second, to make it possible for these actors to participate in governance processes adequately and equitably.

Furthermore, globalization, which has accelerated since the 1990s, has given rise to heated arguments about the distribution of gains and losses resulting from it. Today, most observers agree that there is no basis for an over-optimistic assessment of the impact of globalization. Instead of a steady increase and a fair distribution of wealth, we notice an ever-widening gap between rich and poor people in industrialized and developing countries alike (UNDP 1999). Reducing, or even closing, this gap by working toward a more equitable balance between shareholders and stakeholders in the world economy (and the national economies) is one of the formidable tasks of governance at the national, international, and global levels.

The third challenge to international governance has been the end of the cold war as a historical turning point that has enlarged the scope of action of all actors in the triad mentioned above. For example, global institutions such as the UN system have no longer been blocked by the vetoes of one or both of the two superpowers. International organizations of the UN system, such as the World Trade Organization, have been given expanded jurisdiction and are tested in their capabilities by their own success. In a similar vein, the remarkable growth of peace-keeping operations in the 1990s has exacerbated the UN budgetary predicament. Finally, the emergence of "new wars" (Kaldor 1999) and the spread of "old wars" make it more difficult for the United Nations to fulfil its task of maintaining peace.

Although these three challenges (technological revolution, globalization, and the end of the cold war) differ considerably in character, they are all contributing to, first, the emergence of *new problems or governance tasks*, such as regulating the uses of the Internet and ensuring security of information; in addition, existing governance tasks, such as the new quality of intrastate conflicts or the increasing disparities within and among nations, have become more pressing. Second, *new actors* have entered the world stage as a result of these three challenges. This heterogeneous set of new actors includes, *inter alia*, transnational corporations (TNCs) and business associations, as well as transnational social movement organizations (TSMOs) (Smith, Chattfield, and Pagnucco 1997), transnational advocacy networks (cf. Keck and Sikkink 1998), and other coalitions of NGOs capable of running transnational political campaigns (cf. Boli and Thomas 1999).

Existing international governance systems fail to respond to these new problems and to deal adequately with the new actors' aspirations. Therefore, demands for more effective and responsive governance systems have arisen. International governance is reacting to this need by transforming itself (cf. Commission on Global Governance 1995; Messner and Nuscheler 1996, 1997). In order to design more effective and responsive governance systems, it is an important task for both policy makers and scholars to analyse the ongoing transformation of governance and, as far as possible, to recommend what governance on a global scale could (or, even, should) look like. This book tries to contribute to these analyses by addressing several key questions.

The most important question is about the roles that states, IGOs such as the United Nations, and non-state actors will play in a future world order. Will they cooperate in global governance systems and, if so, how? To what extent will states still be able to attain their governance goals, such as providing security, protection, and social welfare (see Zürn, chap. 2)? Are international institutions at the regional level, such as security communities, more effective in providing security for the peoples of their respective regions? If that is the case, how can security communities be promoted where they do not yet exist (see Peou, chap. 3)? Non-state actors, such as NGOs or business corporations, seem to be increasingly important in the evolving global governance systems, both as addressees of rules and as rule makers. Thus, governing arrangements beyond the state require adjustments such that global governance resting on the triad of actors (states and IGOs; market forces; civil society actors) can substitute for international governance. To what extent can IGOs influence or even regulate these non-state actors, especially the activities of market forces (see Higgott, chap. 4)? How do NGOs interact with, or even participate in, the policy-making process of intergovernmental institutions (see Tussie and Riggirozzi, chap. 5)? In addition to studying these specific questions, some more general considerations are in order. How can global governance best be organized in order to improve on the attainment of governance goals? Is a democratic world republic the best model of global governance (see Höffe, chap. 6)? Last but not least, how can social justice be attained or furthered by a transition from international governance systems to global governance (see Tandon, chap. 7)?

In this chapter, we present some general reflections on international as well as global governance. First, we analyse international governance as it has taken shape in the past and sketch the three challenges that have contributed, and are contributing, to its current transformation. Thereafter, the deficiencies of international governance are highlighted. Next, the emergence of global governance at the beginning of the twenty-first century is analysed and evaluated. In the concluding section, we provide an overview of the book's content.

International governance at the end of the twentieth century

Before the structure and the main actors of international governance in the form in which it has existed up to the end of the twentieth century are analysed, it is necessary first to clarify the notion of governance.

The term *governance* refers to purposive systems of rules or normative orders apart from the regularities (natural orders) emerging from unrestricted interactions of self-interested actors in a state of anarchy. This implies that the actors recognize the existence of certain obligations and feel compelled, for whatever reason, to fulfil them (Mayer, Rittberger, and Zürn 1993: 393). In other words, "governance is order plus intentionality" (Rosenau 1992: 5). Governance includes the existence of a political process which "involves building consensus, or obtaining the consent or acquiescence necessary to carry out a programme, in an arena where many different interests are in play" (Hewitt de Alcántara 1998: 105).

Governance is sometimes confounded with government, although these are different concepts. The term *government* refers to formal institutions that are part of hierarchical norm- and rule-setting, monitoring of compliance with rules, and rule enforcement. Governments have the power both to make binding decisions and to enforce them; thus, governments may allocate values authoritatively (Stoker 1998: 17), although not without limitations in regard to ends and means. In contrast, *governance* is more encompassing than government (Rosenau 1992: 4). As "the capacity to get things done" (Czempiel 1992: 250), governance may take different forms: whereas at the state level it is mostly exercised by governments (governance *by* governments), above this level it needs to take the form of governance *with* (multiple) governments or governance *without* governments. The latter is defined as the exclusive regulation of social behaviour in an issue area by non-state actors, and is based on normative institutions involving a stable pattern of behaviour of a given number of actors in recurring situations. So far, governance without governments does not seem to play a paramount role in world politics, although the amount of "private regulations" is increasing (Cutler, Haufler, and Porter 1999). In comparison, governance with (multiple) governments (or, to be more specific, governance without a world government, but with national governments and international institutions) is defined as governance by both states and non-state actors. Although institutions of hierarchical norm- and rule-setting (governments) are involved in this form of governance, non-hierarchical norm- and rule-setting is predominant (Zürn 1998: 169–170).

It has been mentioned that governance is a purposive mechanism that is steering social systems towards their goals (Rosenau 1999: 296). These governance goals are neither constant nor exogenously determined, but, rather, are time and place specific. Governance goals are at the same time "normative goods" (as they are generally regarded as valuable and desirable) and "functional goods" (as the non-attainment of one or more of these objectives may, in the long run, lead to political crisis) (Zürn, chap. 2). However, there is no consensus on the content of core governance goals. In a narrow sense, there are three main goals of governance, mostly pursued by governments on the state level: these are (1) to provide the population with physical security, (2) to guarantee the stable reproduction of their natural environment, and (3) to ensure their livelihood, i.e. the production and distribution of needed goods and services. In a broader and more differentiated sense, core governance goals encompass (1) security in its defence function (safeguarding the population and the territory in question against the risk of war in general) and its protective function (safeguarding individuals against the risk of crime and the destruction of the environment). Furthermore, governance is expected to provide (2) legal certainty (rule of law) and (3) channels of participation and to produce a symbolic system of reference and the communicative infrastructure within which a sense of collective civil society can develop. Finally, a goal of governance is (4) to correct inequalities that result from markets (Zürn, chap. 2).

As long as national governments were able to attain these core governance goals independently ("governance by governments"), the need for international governance was not pressing (Rittberger 2000: 192). Owing to several factors, however, the ability as well as the willingness of the separate states to pursue these governance goals on their own has constantly decreased. The experience of the economic depression of the 1930s, of the Second World War and the cold war, as well as the decolonization of the third world, have enhanced the states' readiness or capability to cooperate and have thus strengthened the demand for international governance. In addition, international interdependence has intensified as a result of the extending exchanges and transactions among individuals and collective actors. Therefore, individual states, more often than not, cannot handle the problems arising from interdependence (or, to be more precise, from the costly effects of these interactions and transactions) independently (Keohane and Nye 1977, 1987). As a result of interdependence (and of constraints on autonomous decision-making resulting from interdependence sensitivity and vulnerability), the need for political regulations "beyond the nation-state" has increased dramatically (Mayer, Rittberger, and Zürn 1993: 393). This has prompted the states to consider the option of pooling or delegating sovereignty more frequently. Sovereignty is pooled when governmental decisions are made by common voting procedures other than unanimity; sovereignty is delegated when supranational organs are permitted to take certain decisions autonomously, without an intervening interstate vote or unilateral veto (Moravcsik 1998: 67). Delegating sovereignty rarely takes place in world politics, because most states do not readily accept an authority above themselves. Thus, delegating sovereignty may be observed more often in regional integration schemes, such as the European Union (EU). Here, the European Commission enjoys the right of initiative in most areas of legislation coming under the jurisdiction of the EU, and to a more limited extent in external trade and accession negotiations. In world politics, the establishment of international courts, such as the International Court of Justice or the future International Criminal Court, are a result of delegating sovereignty. In contrast, pooling sovereignty is more frequent, as, for instance, in the main UN organs including even the Security Council, where decisions are taken by common voting procedures other than unanimity.

In general, the demand for international cooperation and international governance has increased during the last decades. Since the 1950s, and even more so since the 1970s, this demand has contributed to the establishment of international institutions in general and of IGOs and international regimes in particular (see Rittberger 1995: 72; Beisheim et al. 1999: 325–353). In addition, already existing international institutions have constantly gained higher attention and importance. These IGOs and international regimes have become part and parcel of the international system ("regulated anarchy," cf. Rittberger and Zürn 1990) and have constrained the states' behaviour. Although most international institutions have been predominantly intergovernmental, governments still have played an outstanding role in international governance. In comparison to "governance by governments" at the state level, however, international governance is less backed by formal authority, since most international institutions do not have strong monitoring, let alone enforcement mechanisms.

The following section highlights the challenges to international governance more closely.

Three challenges to international governance

The technological revolution

Over the last twenty years, a revolution in information and communication as well as in transportation technologies has taken place. This revolution has at least three different dimensions: first, the capacity of information and communication technologies has increased in qualitative as well as quantitative terms; second, common limitations in space and time have been progressively overcome, thus dramatically enhancing connections between peoples and places; third, existing information and communication technologies have been much more effectively connected and integrated in the last decades, thus stimulating the growing practice of "computer matching" (Frissen 1997: 112–115).

The technological revolution – and, with it, the heightened availability of information and communication channels, especially through the Internet – challenge national governments as well as international governance in at least four different ways:

- The progress in information and communication technology increases, in particular, non-state actors' ability to influence international politics.
- International negotiations change drastically, owing to the increased availability of information.
- The concept of citizenship is being transformed following technological developments contributing to the skill revolution.
- The Internet, being governed (mostly) by private authority, is one of the new realms of governance without governments.

Reduced transaction costs, as well as a minimized time lag, simplify communication between different actors around the globe. This enables, for instance, civil society actors to build up transnational alliances, to formulate joint statements, and to develop joint strategies in regard to issues of common interest, thus exerting influence on international political processes. By opening the public dialogue to citizens all over the world, the Internet is contributing to the establishment of more egalitarian international relations. This democratizing effect in the sense of giving voice to individual opinions in international processes, however, does not hold for *all* citizens, since in some states the openness of the Internet and its public accessibility is under state control (Shapiro 1999: 24).

At least three examples illustrate the enhanced international political role of international NGOs [(I)NGOs] arising from the achievements of the technological revolution. First, the International Campaign to Ban Landmines (ICBL), launched in October 1992 in New York City, has been extremely successful in building public awareness and contributing to the political resolve necessary to bring about a landmine ban (cf. Cameron, Tomlin, and Lawson 1998). As an outcome of the Ottawa Process, 122 states signed a treaty banning the use, production, stockpiling, and transfer of antipersonnel mines. The ICBL, which was awarded the Nobel Peace Prize in 1997, consists of more than 1,200 (I)NGOs in some 60 countries around the world. It united national and international initiatives to achieve its goal. Since the ICBL operated without a secretariat, member organizations were free to pursue the campaign's goals as it best fitted their respective mandates and resources (Williams and Goose 1998: 22). Thus, communication among the member organizations was highly important. Although two members of the coordination committee of the ICBL observe that "a bit of mythology has developed surrounding the ICBL and its reliance on electronic mail" (ibid.), they admit that the use of new media has had a major impact on the ability of member organizations from diverse cultures to exchange information and develop integrated political strategies. In particular, communication with campaigners in developing countries was improved by electronic mail (e-mail), and it did allow the campaign to share information, jointly to develop strategies more effectively, and jointly to plan major activities and conferences (ibid. 24). Without the technological revolution, these (I)NGOs could never have worked so closely together.

The second example of effective collaboration of (I)NGOs from all over the world that is based on using new technologies is the NGO Coalition for an International Criminal Court (CICC). This Coalition consists of over 800 (I)NGOs. Its main purpose has been to advocate the establishment of an effective, just and independent International Criminal Court (ICC). In order to attain this goal, the Coalition is maintaining a World Wide Web site and e-mail lists to facilitate the exchange of (I)NGOs' and experts' documentation and information about the ICC negotiations and the ad hoc War Crimes Tribunals in Arusha and the Hague between both non-state and state actors. Certainly, the compilation and distribution of reports on governments' positions concerning key issues during the ICC negotiations in Rome was among the most effective actions undertaken by the CICC. Publishing national "votes" and stances in regard to certain proposals kept the delegations, (I)NGOs, and the press informed about which positions were supported by the different countries, and thereby pinpointed where additional lobbying by (I)NGOs was necessary (Pace and Thieroff 1999: 395).

The third "success story" of (I)NGOs' activities that influenced world politics is the "Anti-MAI campaign". More than 600 (I)NGOs in more than 50 states defeated a Multilateral Agreement on Investment (MAI) by the world's 29 richest states. The talks between the members of the Organization for Economic Co-operation and Development (OECD) in Paris eventually broke down after the draft agreement had been published by the international NGO network and, as a result of adverse publicity, key member states such as France changed their positions and withdrew from the negotiations (cf. Smythe 2000).

Apart from (I)NGOs, IGOs also profit from these enhanced communication possibilities. Via the Internet, the public can easily be informed of their tasks and programmes. Furthermore, both knowledge of, and compliance with, international norms (such as the protection of human rights or of the human environment) can be improved considerably, since civil society actors can refer to these norms and demand their states' compliance with them (cf. Keck and Sikkink 1998).

At first, one might conclude that the technological revolution moves the international system in the direction of being more democratic by providing better access to information and by enhancing communication flows (cf. Gellner and von Korff 1998). On further appraisal, however, it appears equally true that the recent technological achievements may also have some negative effects on access to, and dissemination of, communication. The most important argument against the democratic qualities of contemporary information technology (IT) is, of course, that only a small (though growing) part of the world's population has access to and knowledge of it. Whereas in the OECD countries in 1998 approximately 255 personal computers and 37.86 Internet hosts per 1,000 people existed, there were only 0.26 Internet hosts per 1,000 people in developing countries (the number of personal computers was negligible). In comparison, the number of personal computers per 1,000 people (12 and 15) in the Arab states and East Asia was considerable (UNDP 1999: 201). In January 2000, 72 per cent of all Internet hosts were located in the United States but only 3 per cent in the developing countries (Afeman 2000: 430). This problem has entered UN discussion under the heading of the "digital divide." In his millennium report, Secretary-General Kofi Annan observes that the problem arises for various reasons: these include lack of resources and skills, inadequate basic infrastructure, illiteracy and lack of language training, and concerns about privacy and content (Annan 2000: 34). Thus, he announced two "bridges over the digital divide": the first is the Health InterNetwork for developing countries, which will establish and operate 10,000 on-line sites in hospitals and public health facilities throughout the developing countries in order to provide access to up-to-date health and medical information; second, the United Nations Information Technology Service (UNITeS) will train groups of people in developing countries in the use of IT. Although both initiatives certainly are a step in the right direction, they will probably not be able positively to bridge the "digital divide."

The second aspect of the challenge to international governance deriving from the technological revolution refers to international negotiations which, as a result of the heightened availability of information, have undergone profound changes. As is generally assumed, even important and far-reaching decisions often have to be made through a haze of uncertainty (Young 1994: 101–102). These informational gaps not only impair adequate assessment of the problem given but also make it difficult to find an acceptable – let alone optimal – solution. Additional information, of course, reduces this uncertainty. On the other hand, new and supplementary information may complicate a situation even further, as the number of possible arguments in favour of, or against, a policy increases and the spectrum of outcomes widens. Thus, the surplus of information may foster the decision makers' uncertainty with regard to their individual preferences instead of allaying it, and negotiations may become prolonged rather than eased and curtailed. Some authors suggest that the pace of technological progress not only influences the time-frame of international negotiations but also has even outstripped governments' ability to structure political processes and make use of the new technologies (Reinicke and Deng 2000: 2).

The third aspect of this challenge to international governance is on a "micro-level": the technological revolution is contributing to a transformation of citizenship due to the skill revolution. Skill revolution means that people have become "increasingly more competent in assessing where they fit in international affairs and how their behavior can be aggregated into significant collective outcomes" (Rosenau 1997: 58–59). The effects of the skill revolution are not necessarily positive in terms of leading to the evolution of globally shared values or a less self-centred and more humane mankind; on the contrary, the skill revolution also leads "to more selfish conduct, in which the welfare of larger systems is ignored" (Rosenau 1995: 4). It has both widened and narrowed people's consciousness and thus has altered the concept of citizenship. "In some parts of the world people have raised their sights above the nation-state and shifted their responsiveness to authority 'upward' to transnational or supranational entities; others have shifted in a 'downward' direction and become responsive to their subgroups ..." (Rosenau 1995: 4).

Another, fourth, aspect of the challenge to international governance posed by the technological revolution is provided by the Internet as a realm largely governed by private authority. In the late 1980s, the US Department of Defense and the US National Science Foundation began to privatize the Internet. Originally designed for the exchange of military data, the Internet was mostly used by university researchers, government scientists, and outside computer engineers before the late 1980s. Ever since, commercial interest in the Internet has constantly been growing. Although, initially, it was used mainly by private business to offer infrastructural services, it was soon conquered by commercial providers who offered Internet access to a large group of private and commercial users (Spar 1999: 34). Though anarchy in the Internet probably has to be tolerated to a certain extent, many users demand a stricter regulation of conduct. Their arguments for a higher degree of control in the Internet are (a) that serious business has to be based on a set of fundamental rules (i.e. reliability and predictability), and (b) that the amount of information with "objectionable content"[1] (i.e. pornographic, violent, blasphemous, dissident, or hate-mongering) should be reduced drastically. Thus, a new governance task, namely to regulate the uses of the Internet and to assure security and safety of the information infrastructure, has arisen (Florini 2000: 21).

So far, international governance has failed to establish these rules. The initiative of regulating the Internet could be taken by separate national governments according to their own legislative traditions and specific national interests, if the uses of the Internet could be confined to national territories. This, however, is not entirely feasible, owing to the Internet's decentralized technical structure. Neither would international organizations be capable of governing the Internet, since the processes of reaching agreements and making decisions on an international level run much too slowly to match the rapid-fire rate of technological change (Spar 1999: 47). Thus, the private sector has been prompted to develop the rules for regulating its conduct all by itself. An example of this self-coordination of private actors is the Internet Corporation for Assigned Names and Numbers (ICANN), the technical coordination body for the Internet. Created in October 1998 by a broad coalition of the Internet's business, technical, and academic user communities, ICANN has assumed responsibility for a set of tasks, such as coordinating the assignment of Internet domain names and protocol parameters. ICANN is an example for the establishment of private authority (Cutler, Haufler, and Porter 1999), where non-governmental entities tilt the delicate balance between the private sector and government closer to the side of the former (Spar 1999: 32).

To sum up, the technological revolution has had both positive and negative consequences. On the one hand, the Internet in particular contributes to strengthening democratizing trends by enabling citizens and civil society actors around the world to participate in public dialogues. On the other hand, the Internet facilitates the dissemination of objectionable information and may also be utilized by criminal and terrorist organizations. Because of the decentralized structure of the Internet, both traditional methods of exercising jurisdictional authority (by national governments and international governance) and alternative models of cooperation among international information disseminators are faced with the risk of failure in regulating the use (and the content) of the global information flows (Hurley and Mayer-Schönberger 2000). In addition, the technological revolution increases the capacity of non-state actors relative to states to take part in international political processes, thus creating a much larger number of players in the international system (Florini 2000: 21).

Globalization

Globalization has become a "fashionable concept" (Hirst and Thompson 1996: 1), although there is neither a consensus definition nor a common understanding of the sources and consequences of globalization (Beisheim and Walter 1997: 153). Thus, Richard Higgott asserts that globalization is "the most over-used and under-specified concept since the end of the Cold War" (see Higgott, chap. 4 as well as Devetak and Higgott 1999: 483).

In general, there are two major ways of defining the concept of globalization.[2] In a narrow sense, globalization denotes a continuous process of increasing cross-border economic flows, both "financial and real,"[3] which are conducive to greater economic interdependence among formerly distinct national economies (Reinicke 1998: 6). It can thus be defined more precisely as the "tendency towards international economic integration, liberalization and financial deregulation beyond the sovereignty of the territorial state" (Higgott, chap. 4). In this context, globalization is interchangeable with economic interdependence. This implies that globalization is not an entirely new phenomenon, for economic interdependence among states has been observed as a characteristic of the international system since the beginning of the 1970s (and may date even further back, as some authors claim, e.g. Hirst and Thompson 1996).[4] As interstate and transnational interactions and exchange relationships have accelerated since the 1970s and 1980s, interdependence has deepened.

In its broader sense, the term globalization is not restricted to the mechanisms of cross-border *economic* transactions. Instead, it means the extension of cross-border *societal* exchanges and transactions (Zürn 1995: 141)[5] in a wide range of non-economic areas such as communication and culture (interaction of signs and symbols), mobility (transboundary movement of persons), security (exchange of, or jointly produced, threats), and environment (exchange of pollutants and the joint production of environmental risks) (Beisheim et al. 1999; Walter, Dreher, and Beisheim 1997; Zürn 1998: 73–95) as well. Globalization thus denotes the "widening, deepening and speeding up of worldwide interconnectedness in all types of contemporary social life, from the cultural to the criminal, the financial to the spiritual" (Held et al. 1999a: 2). It is not restricted to the economic realm, but includes a general accumulation of links across the world's major regions and across many domains of social activity (Held et al. 1999b: 483). In that broader sense, globalization has a historical dimension (Keohane and Nye 2000a). Probably the oldest form of globalization is environmental: "[C]limate change has affected the ebb and flow of human populations for millions of years" (Keohane and Nye 2000b: 3). Globalization in a military context dates from the times of Alexander the Great's expeditions of 2,300 years ago (ibid.: 4). These different dimensions of globalization have appeared and disappeared again over the centuries. These historical manifestations of globalization can be characterized as "thin" globalization. For example, the Silk Road provided an economic and cultural link between ancient Europe and Asia, but the road was plied by a small group of traders and the goods primarily had a direct impact on a small group of consumers along the road only (ibid.: 7). In comparison, today's globalization is "thick," being more both intensive and extensive.

As mentioned above, theoretical approaches to globalization differ widely and there is no consensus yet whether globalization is indeed a *global* or rather a *regional* or *interregional* phenomenon. Whereas some scholars suggest that globalization mostly, though not exclusively, takes place among the OECD countries (see e.g. Zürn, chap. 2), others claim that it has a worldwide effect. Robert Cox, for example, observes that globalization "implies a progressive integration of all people into the world economy ... [and] implies, in consequence, an increasing homogenisation of global culture, with the development of common patterns of consumption and common aspirations as to the nature of the 'good life'" (Cox 1997: xxii).

It is important to note that globalization, in all cases mentioned, has emerged not accidentally but as the result of political strategies of the world's leading states, aiming at the "neo-liberal" goal of establishing an advantageous political–economic order on both the national and the global level (cf. Higgott, chap. 4). Deregulation, economic liberalization, and privatization are preconditions of globalization that have been implemented first in the United States ("Reaganomics") and Great Britain ("Thatcherism") (cf. Altvater and Mahnkopf 1996; Scherrer 1999). Thus, the shift from state intervention to market self-rule, the so-called "retreat of the state," has been in large part the consequence of governmental policies in leading OECD countries (Strange 1996: 44). Apart from the national governments mentioned above, intergovernmental organizations, such as the International Monetary Fund (IMF) and the World Bank, have for some time played a major role in supporting globalization since their work has been determined by the same principles, namely deregulation, liberalization, and privatization (see Higgott, chap. 4 for the Washington Consensus).

Globalization depends on commonly accepted norms and rules that ensure competition, such as "rules of property," "rules of exchange," and "rules of enforcement" (Spar 1999: 32). More generally speaking, the market as an institution is dependent on a set of external (i.e. non-market) institutions such as property rights or public mass education in order to function effectively and efficiently. Without non-market mechanisms to coordinate collective action, these public goods tend to be underproduced. Therefore, it is important for the functioning of market economies that the provision of these public goods is ensured (Kaul, Grunberg, and Stern 1999a: xx). Some specialized agencies of the United Nations (such as the World Trade Organization [WTO] or the World Intellectual Property Organization [WIPO]) contribute to the establishment and protection of this kind of stable (commercial) order by providing, maintaining, and usefully extending the "soft infrastructure" (Zacher 1999: 6). In general, however, the output of international norms and regulations to ensure the provision of these public goods on a global scale has not kept pace with the rising demand for them (Väyrynen 1999).

Globalization challenges international governance systems in at least three ways. First, it tends to contribute to a widening of the gap between rich and poor, which indicates that international governance systems fail to attain one of the primary goals of governance, i.e. to provide for social welfare. Second, owing to deregulation, economic liberalization, and privatization, transboundary market forces (most importantly, TNCs) are increasingly participating in international affairs. As a consequence, the balance within the triad of inter- and transnational actors has changed and needs to be (re-)adjusted. Third, civil society actors react to this failure of international governance and to the changed balance within the triad by forming alliances and protesting against this development and other unwelcome effects of globalization (cf. Nye 2000).

Social welfare on the global level has become an increasingly important governance task in the era of globalization. At first glance, this statement may surprise, as it has been widely believed that globalization would open up new opportunities and increase the welfare of all peoples. Some analysts point out that free trade has contributed to improving the world economic situation in the last decades (e.g. WTO 2000). The per capita incomes, for instance, have more than tripled as global gross domestic product (GDP) increased nine times in the past 50 years; the share of people enjoying "medium human development" had risen from 55 per cent in 1975 to 66 per cent in 1997 (UNDP 1998: 25). At the same time, however, the gap between poor and rich, both worldwide and within states, has not narrowed but has widened: the top fifth part of the world population in the richest states capture 82 per cent of the expanding exports and 68 per cent of foreign direct investment; the bottom fifth capture hardly more than 1 per cent (UNDP 1998: 31). The difference between the incomes of the richest and poorest states has grown from 35:1 in 1950 to 71:1 in 1992 (UNDP 1999: 6). Formulating and implementing appropriate policy responses to contain these gaps seems to be imperative, especially because citizens of states generally referred to as "winners of globalization" also suffer from its negative effects. In the United States and the United Kingdom, the inequality of income distribution, measured by the Gini coefficient,[6] has risen by a rate of more than 16 per cent from the 1980s to the early 1990s (UNDP 1999: 6; cf. also Tandon, chap. 8; Stewart and Berry 1999). Countering the negative effects of globalization by appropriate public policy, and thus preventing global social disparities from progressing even further, seems to be one of the foremost tasks of governance. Nevertheless, existing international governance systems have not been able to redistribute wealth or to provide compensatory mechanisms that underwrite social cohesion (Devetak and Higgott 1999: 488).

The second aspect of the challenge to international governance systems resulting from globalization is the altered relationship between business actors and states (cf. Higgott and Phillips 2000). Owing to deregulation, economic liberalization, and privatization on both the national and the international level, not only the number of TNCs but also their influence in world politics has risen. Today, TNCs control financial capital, technology, employment, and natural resources to an unprecedented extent. Their transnational production has grown in scale, scope, and intensity (Cutler, Haufler, and Porter 1999: 14). TNCs use their power resources in world politics both by trying to influence governmental and intergovernmental policy-making and by cooperating with other market actors: private actors are increasingly involved in authoritative decision-making that was previously the prerogative of national governments or intergovernmental institutions. For instance, TNCs have displayed a remarkable prominence in the Uruguay Round negotiations of the GATT. Besides TNCs' activities in trade negotiations, they play a prominent role in environmental and even security issues (ibid.: 16). Additionally, they have intensified their cooperation with other market competitors. The result of this "interfirm cooperation" is the establishment of private authority over transnational affairs (ibid.). This "industry self-regulation" seeks to attain four major aims: these are (1) to establish international standards to increase efficiency in global transactions; (2) to ensure the security of these transactions; (3) to maintain industry autonomy by pre-empting or preventing government regulation; and (4) to respond to societal demands and expectations of appropriate corporate behaviour ("good corporate citizenship") (Haufler 2000: 126). In order to reach these goals, industries agree to international standard regimes (such as those initiated and monitored by the International Organization for Standardization) or to codes of conduct (such as the Responsible Care programme) (cf. Haufler 2000).

The protests of civil society groups against the negative effects of globalization highlight another aspect of this challenge to international governance. The civil protests have coalesced in an "antiglobalization movement", a heterogeneous network of (among others) labour unions, environmentalists, and churches. Lory Wallach, one of the organizers of the protests in Seattle, summarizes the common ground of the movement members as follows:

• All of them query "the democratic deficit in the global economy," which tends to undermine the credibility and legitimacy of international (economic) institutions.

- They all "feel directly damaged by the actual outcomes of the status quo, albeit in different ways" (Wallach 2000: 47).

Protest activities of civil society groups at important international conferences have attracted an unexpected amount of public attention. When the "No New Round Turnaround" campaign organized the protests at the WTO meeting in Seattle 1999, neither the city administration nor the police were in the least prepared for the number of participants. One year later, in Prague 2000, the officials were already expecting mass demonstrations to accompany the IMF and World Bank Annual Meeting, and the UN Millennium Summit in New York City in fall 2000 brought about protest activities of civil society groups as well. The so-called "S8 Mobilization campaign" demanded a "truly democratic United Nations" and queried the role of global business in world affairs, especially in the UN system (Crosette 2000: 4). These joint activities of heterogeneous civil society groups have been described as "globalization-from-below" (Falk 1999: 131; cf. Mittelman 2000: 26; Tussie and Riggirozzi, chap. 5).

These three aspects of globalization – the widening gap between poor and rich and the growing relevance of both market forces and civil society actors – profoundly alter the states' performance in international governance systems. Nation-states have lost their position as the paramount loci of governance, yet they continue to play a significant role in the evolving global governance (see Zürn, chap. 2; Messner 1998; for a detailed discussion see also the sections on the limits of international governance systems and towards global governance, pp. 19–35).

The end of the cold war

The main problems of international politics in the cold war period with regard to governance systems can be summarized as (1) unstable cooperation between East and West at best and conflict brinkmanship at worst, and (2) the dramatically reduced scope of action of most international organizations, especially the UN system.

With the end of the cold war, the structure of the international system began to change. This transformation challenged the international governance systems in several ways. Most importantly, bipolarity no longer limited the international organizations' scope of action, as a consequence of which they succeeded in gaining greater salience in world politics. After the Security Council's ability to act ceased to be blocked by the antagonism of the two superpowers, the way to peaceful conflict management seemed to be open (cf. Betts 1994). Thus, in the early 1990s, an extraordinary increase in the number of peace-keeping operations can be observed: whereas the United Nations initiated no more than 15 peace-keeping operations in the long period between 1945 and 1989, the Security Council authorized 18 between 1989 and 1994 alone (Peou chap. 3).[7] The intensified action of the Security Council is a result of the re-definition of what is seen as a threat to peace, breach of peace, or act of aggression according to Article 39 of the UN Charter, and of a revised notion of what is considered to be sovereign national activity (Doyle 1998: 4).

This remarkable new trend has caused two major difficulties, however: first, the deployment of troops acceptable to all conflict parties has become increasingly problematic (Armstrong, Lloyd, and Redmond 1996: 130); second, the apparently endless demand for peace-keeping has compounded the United Nation's financial problems. The expenditure for peace-keeping operations rose from 31.04 per cent of the total budget in 1990 to 49.92 per cent in 1997. At the same time, the budgetary short-fall due to unpaid contributions by several member states, above all the United States, amounted to about US$3 billion in 2000.

In addition to being confronted with these two difficulties, the United Nations faces novel, grave obstacles to fulfilling its task of maintaining international peace and security. This results from the fact that the fea-tures of war have changed drastically in the last decades. Today, most wars are intrastate instead of interstate (Hippler 1999: 422; cf. also Rohl-off and Schindler 2000). In the 1980s and 1990s, this new kind of war evolved especially in Africa, the Balkans, and in the south of the former Soviet Union (Daase 1999; Kaldor 1999). "New wars" differ from "old wars" with regard to their goals and the methods of warfare, and in the way that they are financed. Whereas "old wars" served geopolitical or ideological goals, most "new wars" are concerned with identity politics (national, clan, religious, or linguistic identity). New warfare draws on the experience of both guerrilla warfare and counter-insurgency: the military units combine different groups with a decentralized organization. In old, conventional wars, battles were the decisive encounters: here, the actors were typically vertically organized units. The war economies of "old wars" were centralized and autarchic; in "new wars," they are de-centralized and heavily dependent on external resources (Kaldor 1999: 6–8).

So far, the United Nations has failed to prevent (sometimes, even to mitigate or speedily to terminate) these "new wars." This is partly due to the constraints of institutional mechanisms: they were created in order to deal with "old wars" and are thus less capable of handling this new kind of armed conflict effectively (cf. Ropers and Debiel 1995). Thus, it might be helpful to include new actors in conflict-resolution mecha-nisms. Since "unofficial actors," such as NGO representatives or citizens' groups (so-called Track Two diplomacy), nowadays perform a range of supplemental or parallel functions to the official interstate relations

(Track One diplomacy), they may help to improve relationships between different actors at various levels and among different individuals and groups. However, up to now Track One and Track Two diplomacy have not been coordinated adequately. The United Nations should thus consider establishing such coordinating mechanisms (Rasmussen 1997: 43; cf. Zartman 1999) or to react otherwise by adapting its institutional structure to the new characteristics of war.

In addition to this institutional adaptation of the United Nations to the "new wars," the United Nations should rethink its "paradigm of intervention." The limited effectiveness of some UN missions, such as those in Congo, Somalia, and the former Yugoslavia, suggests the need for a new approach in peace-keeping (cf. Mockaitis 1999). A new "paradigm of intervention" should take into account, *inter alia*, the fact that, more often than not, a consent of the parties is missing (Annan 1998b: 172). Thus, a consensus as to what the ultimate goals of a mission shall be is even more important. The United Nations appears to be the agency of choice for developing and implementing this new "paradigm of intervention," as it has conducted peace missions of various kinds for the half-century of its existence (Mockaitis 1999: 138).

Limits of international governance systems

The (non-)attainment of governance goals at the end of the twentieth century

In the previous sections, three different challenges (technological revolution, globalization, and the end of the cold war) to international governance systems have been outlined. Under these altered circumstances, the effectiveness of the present international governance system, which is part of governance legitimacy, turns out to be insufficient in at least two regards.

First, it has been suggested that new governance tasks have arisen – such as, for instance, the regulation of the Internet. In addition, long-term problems have grown more pressing. Today's international governance systems have not been able adequately to meet these demands on their policy-making capabilities. This is especially true for "trans-sovereign problems" (Cusimano 2000), i.e. problems extending across state borders in an almost uncontrollable way. Examples are environmental threats, refugee flows, nuclear smuggling, or international criminal activities. In the last decades, the number and extent of these problems have clearly risen.

Second, new actors have entered the world stage and other non-territorial actors, such as international (governmental and non-governmental) organizations, have multiplied. The examples of the ICBL, the NGO CICC, and the Anti-MAI campaign show that non-state actors' exertion of influence on international politics is facilitated by the achievements of the technological revolution. Additionally, the influence of transnational corporations and business associations on world politics has risen as a result of deregulation, economic liberalization, and privatization.

A critical assessment of the work of international governance systems clearly demonstrates that they fail to deal adequately with these new problems and the new actors' aspirations. Thus, the attainment of governance goals by international governance systems, in which states play a paramount role, seems to be extremely difficult, if not impossible.

1. The defence function of governance (safeguarding a certain population and territory against the risk of war) cannot be sufficiently fulfilled by most states. In many regions of the world, people are suffering from war. With the number of wars having increased since the end of the cold war, the number of people affected by war has multiplied correspondingly (Peou, chap. 3). Furthermore, most states are even less able to fulfil their protective function adequately (safeguarding individuals against the risks of crime and destruction of the environment) as global "evils" (e.g. terrorism, drugs, diseases) cross borders more easily. The most prominent examples of this type of transnational security problem are terrorist organizations and transnational criminal organizations (cf. Rittberger, Schrade, and Schwarzer 1999; Williams and Savona 1996; Williams 1999).

2. The important governance goal of ensuring legal certainty (rule of law) cannot generally be fulfilled. This is most obviously demonstrated by states such as Somalia and Sierra Leone. With the number of "failed states" having increased in the last decades, this governance goal is even less likely to be met in many regions of the world than ever before.[8]

3. Many citizens criticize their limited opportunities to participate in, or at least to influence, public policy-making as insufficient (see below).

4. Finally, the growing gap between rich and poor, both all over the world and within individual states, shows that the governance goal of correcting socio-economic disparities that result from the functioning of markets also cannot generally be attained.

The continual non-attainment of governance goals by international governance systems calls for more effective governance systems. As a consequence of the limitations of international governance systems, efforts to overcome them will orient themselves towards global governance. In order to develop concepts of more effective and responsive governance

Table 1.1 Limits of international governance systems

Output legitimacy	Input legitimacy
Jurisdictional gap	Participatory gap
Operational gap	
Incentive gap	

systems, the causes for the failure of international governance systems to attain governance goals must be analysed in more detail.

Four governance gaps undermine the governance systems' legitimacy

The failure of international governance systems to attain their governance goals, and thus the reduction of their legitimacy, mainly originates from four governance gaps. As the following section suggests, these four gaps considerably impair the capacity of international governance systems to deal with urgent problems (output dimension of legitimacy) and impede some actors' opportunities to participate in public policy-making (input dimension of legitimacy) (table 1.1).

The previous sections have indicated that the attainment of governance goals by international governance systems has become increasingly difficult. This is particularly true for transsovereign problems. This lack of effectiveness has been referred to as the governance systems' reduced output legitimacy (Zürn 2000: 184; Scharpf 1998a; cf. also Keohane and Nye 2000c). In general, output legitimacy is achieved or maintained whenever "collectively binding decisions ... serve the common interest of the constituency" (Scharpf 1998b: 3). Obviously, international governance systems have not been sufficiently effective in dealing with existing problems and have thus failed, for the most part, to achieve output legitimacy.

Three major governance gaps have contributed to the undermining of the output legitimacy of international governance systems, as follows.

1. *A jurisdictional gap* (Kaul, Grunberg, and Stern 1999a: xxvi): Even though many political challenges are global today, public policy-making is still predominantly national in both focus and scope. The most prominent example of this kind of border-crossing or globally relevant problems are the transsovereign problems already mentioned above, e.g. environmental degradation. Global threats such as the greenhouse effect, for example, cannot effectively be countered by uncoordinated national policies and thus call for a global climate policy to regulate the behaviour of all states as well as non-state actors.

2. *An operational gap*: Policy makers and public institutions lack the policy-relevant information and analysis as well as the necessary policy instruments to respond to the daunting complexity of policy issues (Reinicke and Deng 2000: vii). This is especially true in environmental politics. Since clear-cut causal chains are rare in this issue area, decision-making is often impeded by informational uncertainty. Furthermore, the management of current problems is often interrupted by the advent of even more pressing new ecological problems. To meet these requirements, a permanent process of learning and adjustment is necessary (Brühl and Simonis 2000: 8). Therefore, scientific experts as well as NGOs play an important part in the processes of decision-making in this issue area by providing scientific analysis, transforming it into policy-relevant knowledge, and proposing adequate policy responses.

3. *An incentive gap* (Kaul, Grunberg, and Stern 1999a: xxvi): Since international cooperation has become more salient in international relations, the implementation of international agreements has become essential. Today, the operational follow-up of international agreements remains underdeveloped; moral suasion, or shaming, frequently is the only mechanism available to induce states to comply with international obligations (Kaul, Grunberg, and Stern 1999b: 451). This compliance problem makes it difficult for international institutions (as parts of the existing international governance systems and evolving global governance) to contribute effectively to the attainment of governance goals as they continue to depend on the willingness of individual states to implement international regulations.

In addition to these three governance gaps, which undermine the output legitimacy of international governance systems, a fourth, *participatory* gap has opened up (Reinicke and Deng 2000: viii; Kaul, Grunberg, and Stern 1999a: xxvi). As more and more public policies are made by or within international institutions, the general public or particular stakeholders are frequently excluded from their deliberations and decisions. Thus, input legitimacy is reduced as well (cf. Kohler-Koch 1998).[9] Input legitimacy is given when collectively binding decisions derive from the constituents' active consent (Scharpf 1998a: 85). Participation and consent thus are essential elements of input legitimacy (Rittberger 2000: 210). The addressees' acceptance of norms and rules as binding hinges on their participation in creating and implementing them. According to Seymour Martin Lipset (1960: 79), effective governance depends both on the invention of beneficial solutions to pressing social needs and on general access to the political process. The subjects' loyalty can be obtained only by preserving their right to participate actively in political decision-making processes. Input legitimacy may be undermined by several factors: (1) new social forces with the power to revolt against the established order are denied access to the political process; or (2) participation is devalued for recognized actors who still have sufficient power to hamper a smooth functioning of the governance system (Rittberger 2000: 210). In both cases, these actors feel deprived of their part in influencing rule creation and rule management affecting their interests. Being kept away from the political process, they tend to ignore the established order whenever feasible.

From the vantage point of a state-centric approach focusing on the horizontal self-coordination of sovereign states, input legitimacy of international governance systems is not likely to be undermined as long as states remain the dominant actors in world politics (Young 1994: 99–100). The participation of states' representatives in institutional bargaining mechanisms is ensured by the fact that these bargaining processes themselves are structured by a consensus rule. Owing to the principle of state sovereignty, no state can be bound to certain norms and rules against its consent; generally acceptable solutions for collective-action problems thus have to be formulated. The consensus rule for international negotiations therefore guarantees mutually acceptable results in processes of horizontal self-coordination of states, i.e. international governance systems (Rittberger 2000: 211).

However, international governance systems have increasingly come under pressure on both theoretical and practical grounds. The difficulties derive from at least two basic developments. First, owing to the ever-expanding and ever-deepening transnational connections, national governments are successively losing their monopoly of representing their societies in international political processes. As suggested in the previous sections, influential new actors with a growing ability to affect the authoritative allocation of values have emerged in the global arena. These new actors challenge the input legitimacy of purely intergovernmental policy-making (Rittberger 2000: 212). Second, as a result of the growing need for international or global solutions for formerly national problems, the subjects of democratic states, having minimal influence on the processes of collective decision-making on the international level, feel increasingly alienated from the political process (cf. Scharpf 1993).

The United Nations may serve to underpin this argument. Like other international institutions, the UN system is state-centric. Even if the governments of the member states are elected democratically (and many of them are not), the input legitimacy of public policy-making within these institutions is rather low because of the distance between decision makers and the people affected by these decisions (Bienen, Rittberger, and Wagner 1998). "The Peoples of the United Nations," to which the opening paragraph of the UN Charter refers, have had few, if any promising avenues open to them for making themselves heard by the UN policy-making bodies.

Towards global governance

Finding ways to close these governance gaps is one of the most prominent tasks of politicians and political scientists. In this section, we first present three different models of international or global governance. In terms of desirability and feasibility, however, only one model remains. We then outline and discuss some reform proposals and the ongoing change in global governance, such as the opening of the UN system towards non-state actors. To conclude this section, we ask whether these changes are contributing to more effective and legitimate global governance.

Three models of global governance

With the end of the cold war as a historical turning point that had triggered a moment of euphoria (Young 1997: 273), a discussion about the future structure(s) of world politics has begun. In the first years after the end of bipolarity, the discussion centred on the question of whether the world would be structured in a uni-, tri-, or multipolar way. Since then the main emphasis of the discussion has changed, and more general questions are being asked, such as what effective global governance looks like and, in particular, whether hierarchical or non-hierarchical governance systems are more effective and legitimate.

At least three different models of global governance can be distinguished. Whereas protagonists of a hierarchical model argue that a world state (or at least a hegemonic power) would be necessary to ensure the effectiveness and legitimacy of global governance, advocates of a non-hierarchical governance system suggest that horizontal self-coordination would suffice to achieve effective and legitimate global governance just as well as, or even better than, the hierarchical models (cf. Rittberger, Mogler, and Zangl 1997; Rittberger 2000).

Authoritative coordination by a world state

The first model associates global governance with various conceptions of a world state. Advocates of this model hold that mutual respect for norms and rules cannot be expected under conditions of anarchy. As long as states have to worry about their national integrity and as long as they are afraid that others will break their promises, cooperation and joint institution-building will be the exception in world politics. Following this line of reasoning, the mutual fear of being attacked or exploited by others can be effectively reduced only by installing a "Leviathan," – i.e. by creating a central authority with the capacity to make and enforce norms and rules. Only if it is commonly realized that the benefits of rule-breaking are outweighed by the inescapable negative sanctions that it provokes, can states risk relying on public institutions that are designed to manage collective-action problems or the problem of distributing the gains from cooperation. With "Leviathan" on their side, no other state will dare to exploit them.

However, as long as rational actors pursue their interests in an anarchical environment, they are trapped in a state of insecurity about their survival and well-being. In such a situation every state has to take care of itself and to base its strategies on worst-case scenarios. Therefore, nobody expects others to abide by rules that are not sanctioned by a power that keeps them all in awe. The basic idea underlying the model of the world state is thus that rational actors (even when their interests are not strictly opposed to one another) are unable to cooperate unless their freedom of action is restrained by a central authority above them. At the same time, the creation of a central authority would fundamentally alter the structure of the international system. The anarchically organized society of sovereign states would cease to exist and would give way to a centralized, though multinational, polity where the monopoly of the legitimate use of force is vested in a supranational institution possessing the requisite powers of governing.

The emergence of a world state is sometimes conceived of via analogy with the process of state-building in post-medieval Europe. According to German sociologist Norbert Elias (1976), there were two crucial elements driving the civilizing process that involved the formation of the territorial state: the first was the increased interdependence among social actors as a result of extended exchange relations and the second was the monopolization of the legitimate use of physical force. During this civilizing process, humans learned to control their innate drives and subordinated themselves to, or internalized, norms and rules of social conduct. The monopolization of the means of physical force that has accompanied the formation of modern states reflects, according to Elias, a general process toward concentrating the control over the means of physical force in world history. Consequently, one might expect a similar development to occur at the international level. At the end of this process, the concept and the function of the modern state would find its replication on a global scale.

The world state does not need to have a centralized structure with a unitary world government that governs by centralized "top-down" mechanisms. In contrast, one could also think of the world state organized according to the principle of subsidiarity (cf. Höffe 1997). Large intermediary regional units of continental or subcontinental size could be the basis of a world state (Höffe, chap. 7; cf. also Höffe 1999). A world republic would be governed by a federal world government. The scope of a world state's tasks is limited to issues that cannot be dealt with by the individual state. The federal world republic thus does deny the state's authority (Höffe, chap. 7).

Although a world state may be most effective in ensuring compliance with international norms and rules, it may not be feasible or desirable. As to the feasibility of this model, one is left to wonder whether there is any sign of a world people or citizenry in the making. In addition, nothing indicates that the United Nations or another institution will be transformed into a world federal government at any time in the near future (Falk 1995: 6). As to the desirability of a world state, one has to contemplate the prospect of creating a world state requiring, by definition, the establishment of a worldwide legal monopoly of physical force, which could be accomplished only by restraining powerfully various forces of local and national resistance against this project of global governance.

Hierarchical though not authoritative coordination: Governance under the hegemonic umbrella

The second model of global governance also assumes that compliance can be achieved only through a hierarchical sanctioning power. International governance under the hegemonic umbrella substitutes the world state by a hegemon, i.e. a very powerful state that might be considered a functional equivalent to a supranational authority (Lake 1993). Owing to the overwhelming power resources that it controls, the hegemon has the means to create international norms and rules and to secure compliance with them. These norms and rules are tailored to the interests of their maker; however, the particular national interests of the hegemon, to a great extent, converge with the interests of the system (Waltz 1979: 189). The subordination of other states to the hegemonic order, and their compliance with the rules that constitute this order, is guaranteed by the superior power of the hegemon. However, this power-based explanation is just one side of the coin: non-hegemonic states can also have an interest in fostering a hegemonic order, because it provides benefits, such as economic gains and security, for them.

According to this model, the effectiveness of international institutions is held hostage to the hegemon's continuing ability to maintain order. The model of hegemonic governance implies hierarchy, but the hegemon is not equivalent to a world (or regional) government. The hegemonic system is still composed of sovereign states. The hegemonic order most likely could, and would, cover only a much smaller range of international activities, leaving those (global or regional) cooperation problems un-attended that are not vital from the point of view of the hegemon. An-other difference between the hegemonic order and the world state model is that a hegemonic order can, but need not, be global.

Governance under the hegemonic umbrella is not desirable because hegemony is a temporary phenomenon (although one that, according to some theories, recurs in a cyclical manner). This type of governance sys-tem would be unstable, and the rise and fall of hegemons does not take place without major conflicts (or, sometimes, even wars) in world poli-tics. Therefore, the model plays a minor role in discussions on future governance systems, even though it attracted much attention in the early 1990s (Group of Lisbon 1996).

Order as a result of horizontal self-coordination: Governance without world government

The third model, governance without world government, does not as-sume that the effectiveness of international institutions depends, in one way or another, on hierarchical rule-making and rule-enforcement, and therefore, on the concentration of the means of physical force on the global level. As a consequence, the civilizing process, with its concomi-tant growth of transactions and interdependencies, may continue without some monopoly of physical force emerging on the world scene. Indeed, increasing interdependence, especially mutual vulnerability, improves the prospects for horizontal self-coordination by and among equals (Keohane 1993: 35).

In this model, the coordination of international activities is affected by states agreeing, for their mutual benefit, upon norms and rules to guide their future behaviour and to create mechanisms which make compliance with these rules and norms possible (i.e. in each actor's self-interest). One of the premises of this model is that rational actors are assumed to be aware of the fact that, under circumstances that are increasingly pre-sent in today's world, collective action will lead to outcomes which are individually, let alone collectively, preferable to the results of unilateral action. To break an agreement will necessarily entail a loss of reputation as a reliable partner. A reputation of untrustworthiness would exclude a government from future cooperative ventures. Thus, one could expect that the higher the density of international transactions in an issue-area and the longer the shadow of the future, the more likely is the establish-ment and the maintenance of international institutions if collective-action problems arise and persist.

This third model varies with regard to its state-centrism. Some scholars argue that nation-states will remain the most important actors (Cox 1997: xvi). According to this notion, governance without world government is more or less the same as the model of international governance that was predominant in the late twentieth century, in which states and intergovernmental institutions attempt to regulate the behaviour of states and other international actors. Others predict that states will disaggregate over time into separate, functionally distinct parts, and that these parts will network with their counterparts abroad, thus creating a dense web of relations that constitute a transnational order (Slaughter 1997: 185). This model is even more far-reaching than global governance as defined at the beginning of this article, since it suggests that states remain important, though not paramount, actors in evolving global governance.

Research shows that governance without governments is widespread in industrially developed societies. The model proved to be quite helpful in understanding the success and the failure of attempts at institution-building in both military and political-economic relations (Axelrod and Keohane 1985: 227; Young 1989: 375; Zürn 1992: 505–506). In addition, governance without world government is entirely suitable to close the governance gaps discussed in the previous section. As long as states (and non-state actors) recognize that problems and conflicts can best be regulated through cooperation, governance legitimacy in its output dimension is likely to be secured. To be more precise, the jurisdictional gap is closed as transsovereign problems are dealt with through international or transnational institutions. The incentive gap is narrowed because states are interested in complying with international norms and rules (at least as long as they consider that existing problems could best be dealt with at the international level). The operational gap is narrowed inasmuch as non-state actors play an important role in this governance model, thereby bringing their knowledge and resources to bear on the international and transnational policy-making processes. In addition, the participatory gap is also narrowed since non-state actors, such as civil society groups, have access to (or are even participants in) decision-making bodies. In sum, this model is desirable as well as feasible.

From international to global governance

The three models depicted in the previous section are not currently implemented, nor can any one of them serve as an outline for the future. Current international governance and evolving global governance have to be regarded, rather, as a patchwork of heterogeneous elements deriving from governance under the hegemomic umbrella (e.g. in security communities, cf. Peou, chap. 3) as well as governance without world government (e.g. international regimes). As governance without world government appears to be the most desirable and feasible of possible governance models, it is discussed in this section in more detail.

To gain a foothold in the future, global governance will have to overcome the governance gaps (jurisdictional, operational, incentive, and participatory gaps) that curtailed the effectiveness and legitimacy of twentieth-century international governance systems. However, there is no general consensus about how these gaps can and should be narrowed or even closed. Several reform proposals, especially concerning the structures and functions of international organizations have been put forward.[10] The following section summarizes these reform proposals and discusses the prospects of these reform endeavours. As the UN system plays a central role in global governance, we especially focus on its contributions to the closure of the governance gaps.

Closing the jurisdictional gap

The jurisdictional gap results from the discrepancy between a globalizing world and separate national units of policy-making. Although it is generally acknowledged that international or transsovereign problems are most effectively handled on the international level, national policy makers in many countries still partly recoil from institutionalized international cooperation (Kaul, Grunberg, and Stern 1999b: 467).

In general, there are three conceivable ways of closing the jurisdictional gap (cf. Kaul, Grunberg, and Stern 1999b: 466–478).

1. To ensure an acceptable solution to pressing global problems, all decision-making could be transferred to the international or global level. This *modus operandi* would call for the establishment of a world state or global governance under the hegemonic umbrella. As suggested in the section on the three models of global governance, however, neither of these two governance models is feasible or desirable.
2. All decision-making could be transferred back to the state level. There is no need for international regulation unless global "evils" cross state borders and collective action problems need to be solved. In the twenty-first century, however, such a perspective seems to be highly unrealistic as interactions and transactions between international actors have never been more lively than today.
3. A so-called "jurisdictional loop" "that runs from the national to the international and back to the national – by way of several intermediate levels, regional and subregional" could be established (Kaul, Grunberg, and Stern 1999b: 466).

This kind of loop is sometimes equated with global governance (cf. e.g. Commission on Global Governance 1995). Whereas in international governance the most important loci of governance have been the states (and intergovernmental institutions), in global governance other actors on different levels, such as local, subregional, and regional, influence public policy-making as well. The actors' relevance and influence varies with the issue-area and topic. Global governance thus is a wide-ranging dynamic process of complex interactive decision-making which is subject to continuous development according to the frequently changing circumstances (ibid). In some cases, there might be "scope for principles such as subsidiarity, in which decisions are taken as close as possible to the level at which they can be effectively implemented" (ibid. 5; cf. Messner 1998; Messner and Nuscheler 1997).[11] In these networks of actors and institutions, however, individual states will remain salient participants since they still have "the capacity to raise taxes [and] the ability to hurl force at enemies" (Held et al. 1999: 495). Yet, one may also think of states as "sandwiches between global forces and local demands" (ibid.; cf. Messner 1998; Zürn 1998).

In these networks, the UN system can play a leading role. "With its universality, it is the only forum where the governments of the world come together on an equal footing and on a regular basis to try to resolve the world's most pressing problems" (Commission on Global Governance 1995: 6). To narrow the jurisdictional gap, the United Nations may extend its cooperation with regional organizations; it would, thereby, contribute to putting the principle of subsidiarity on a firm basis.

Strengthening the regional organizations' role in the UN system, and in world politics in general, is frequently proposed by scholars (cf. for the issue area peace and security Peou, chap. 3) as well as diplomats. As early as 1992, former UN Secretary-General Boutros Boutros-Ghali already acknowledged this necessity in his "Agenda for Peace," and the current Secretary-General Kofi Annan has repeatedly confirmed Boutros-Ghali's view (e.g. Annan 2000).

However, a "regionalization" of the United Nations has not yet taken place and is not very likely to occur in the near future. One reason is that there are few regional organizations that can be considered "acceptable" regional counterparts of the UN system with regard to their effectiveness and legitimacy (cf. Peou, chap. 3). Even if more effective and legitimate regional organizations existed, establishing a division of labour between them and the United Nations would be problematic.[12]

Closing the operational gap

In the last decades, a profound lack of necessary information, analysis, and policy instruments has prevented policy makers and public institutions from responding effectively to the daunting complexity of policy issues (Reinicke et al. 2000: vii).

By working more closely together with non-state actors, policy makers could narrow the operational gap. Global public-policy (GPP) networks, or public–private partnerships (PPP) in general, may help to bridge the operational gap (Reinicke and Deng 2000).[13] These (trisectoral) networks connect individuals and institutions with common interests across borders and different sectors of activity: these include local, national, and regional governments, transnational corporations, and other business actors, as well as their associations and civil society. This wide range of members from different backgrounds enables the networks to collect a wide range of information and expertise and thus to provide "a more complete picture of particular policy issues and giving voice to previously unheard groups" (Reinicke and Deng 2000: viii).

The United Nations has recognized the usefulness of global public policy networks. In his millennium report, Secretary-General Kofi Annan refers to centralized hierarchies of governance as anachronistic in the world of the twenty-first century, "an outmoded remnant of the nineteenth century mindset" (Annan 2000: 13). He points out that effective governance can be achieved only by the widening of participation possibilities as well as of accountability; the United Nations "must be opened up further for the participation of the many actors whose contributions are essential to managing the path of globalization" (ibid). The United Nations could serve as the platform for global public policy networks, thus playing an intermediatory role between states, business, and civil society. By facilitating the emergence of these networks and contributing to their effective operation, the United Nations will increase its own effectiveness and credibility (Reinicke and Deng 2000: 78).

Since the 1990s, the United Nations and its specialized agencies have been active in such networks (e.g. the World Commission on Dams, which presented its guidelines for dam-building in November 2000, or the Roll-Back Malaria Initiative, initiated by the World Health Organization). These networks differ in the topics with which they are dealing. All GPP networks, however, share the function of developing and disseminating knowledge that is crucial for addressing transnational challenges. Thereby, they successfully contribute to the closure (or at least the narrowing) of the operational gap (ibid. 93).

The most prominent example of a public–private partnership in the making is the Global Compact between business and the United Nations. In the past, Secretary-General Kofi Annan and his team have emphasized that they consider UN–corporate partnerships a promising new way to gain political and financial support for the United Nations. In his declaration of the Global Compact's basic guidelines, he challenged business leaders to help achieve the realization of nine UN core principles in the areas of environment, labour, and human rights within their corporate domains. These principles derive from the Universal Declaration of Human Rights, from the Rio Declaration of the UN Conference on Environment and Development, and from the Four Fundamental Principles and Rights at Work adopted at the World Economic and Social Summit in Copenhagen in 1997 and reaffirmed by the International Labour Organization in 1999.[14] The Global Compact serves as a frame of reference to stimulate best practices and to bring about convergence around universally acknowledged values (Kell and Ruggie 1999; Paul 2001). It was formally launched at a meeting of almost fifty corporations, the International Chamber of Commerce, the World Business Council for Sustainable Development, and some NGOs (e.g. Amnesty International, WWF International) at UN headquarters on 26 July 2000.

The major aim of the Global Compact is to strengthen the "social pillars" upon which every market, including the global market, depends. It seeks to facilitate the tension-free functioning of the global markets and to overcome (or at least to mitigate) resistance to globalization. By entering a partnership with business actors, the United Nations may additionally attain both informational and even financial support, and thus narrow its operational gap.[15]

NGO activists have harshly attacked the Global Compact.[16] They criticize especially its lack of monitoring and sanctioning mechanisms. In particular, they point out that there is no independent agency to collect information about the signatory corporations' compliance with the nine UN principles. At present, apart from an annual report of their progress and the problems in implementing the UN guidelines posted on the Global Compact website, member corporations do not have any obligations. Corporations may simply pay lip service to the Global Compact's objectives (cf. Paul 2001). In spite of the Global Compact's deficits as it is currently set up, however, public–private partnerships in general are – and will remain – a promising medium for contributing to the closure of the UN system's operational gap.

Closing the incentive gap

Global governance has been defined as the output of non-hierarchical networks of international and transnational regimes. To work effectively, global governance is strictly dependent on the performance of these institutions. An incentive gap (i.e. a malfunctioning of the operational follow-up of international agreements) severely threatens this effectiveness. A primary task among the efforts towards the establishment of global governance is thus the closure of the incentive gap.

The closure of the incentive gap (i.e. the establishment of effective compliance mechanisms) can be achieved by different strategies. As a first step, institutions may enhance compliance in a cooperative, problem-solving approach (Chayes and Chayes 1995: 3). This approach is based on the assumption that non-compliance frequently does not derive from a conscious decision to disregard norms and rules but from the member states' inability to abide by them, as well as from a certain incomprehensibility of the norms and rules themselves (ibid. 22). "Active management," i.e. capacity building, dispute settlement, and the adaptation and modification of norms set forth in treaties, may thus be a useful tool for improving compliance (ibid. 197). The actors' efforts towards complete fulfilment of their obligations can be effectively supported and organized by institutions (ibid. 227).

The ozone regime, for instance, has implemented this managerial strategy for enhancing compliance. If a member state fails to comply with the Montreal Protocol's rules, the Implementation Committee submits recommendations to the Meeting of the Parties to agree on suitable measures. Hitherto, the Implementation Committee has mostly recommended offers of assistance to non-complying states. The Russian Federation, for example, received additional funding through the Global Environmental Facility in order to speed up the conversion of chlorofluorocarbon (CFC)-production facilities (Brühl 1999).

If the managerial model of compliance does not positively influence the actors' behaviour, a second measure of closing the incentive gap is required – namely, authoritative dispute settlement. Compliance with the agreed norms and rules can be enhanced by hauling deviant actors before a court of law or a body akin to it. In fact, more and more international institutions tend to establish specific compliance mechanisms based on judicial or quasi-judicial dispute-settlement procedures, thus taking an important (though not universal) step towards the legalization of world politics. Legalization is defined as "the degree to which rules are obligatory, the precision of those rules, and the delegation of some functions and interpretation, monitoring, and implementation to third parties" (Goldstein et al. 2000: 387). "Legalized institutions" adopt precise rules and delegate authority to a neutral entity for implementation of the agreed rules (ibid.). Typically, compliance in these legalized institutions is higher than that in non-legalized institutions.

The WTO is an example of such a legalized institution. WTO members have agreed that, if they believe that a state is violating the WTO's rules, the Dispute Settlement Body (DSB) will deal with these violations on the basis of clearly defined rules with definite timetables for reaching a decision. Once a decision has been handed down, the DSB also has the power to authorize retaliation against a state that does not comply with a ruling. Since 1995, the DSB has authorized five suspensions of trade concessions.

The majority of international and transnational institutions have not yet implemented an adequate compliance follow-up. In institutions without any compliance follow-up, such as the climate-change regime, agreements on at least one or another compliance mechanism will be necessary to ensure an effective follow-up.

Closing the participatory gap

The participatory gap emerged from the primarily state-centric orientation of international governance. As state-centric international institutions were still crucial to international governance systems at the end of the twentieth century, non-state actors have been kept at arms' length from decision-making. Both NGOs and intergovernmental organizations have criticized this fact, the latter having finally recognized the important function of NGOs (both advocacy and service organizations) in formulating and implementing international public policies (Rittberger and Breitmeier 2000; cf. Tussie and Riggirozzi, chap. 5).

Numerous proposals to expand the role of non-state actors in global governance have been made, including, for instance, the establishment of a Second UN Assembly.[17] Apart from certain differences in both electoral mode and general mandate of a possible Second Assembly, all proposals aim at strengthening the role of societal actors in the United Nations. In contrast to the present diplomatic UN representation, members of a Second Assembly would be accountable not to their governments but to their popular constituencies. Furthermore, any national group of deputies would represent their polity in its political, social, and cultural diversity (Bienen, Rittberger, and Wagner 1998: 297). The distance between rulers and addressees of public policies would thus be minimized.

Because of its all-encompassing nature, a complete implementation of this reform proposal is not very likely. Less far-reaching reforms of the participation of civil society actors in international institutions, however, already have been implemented and even more are to come. Most international organizations have initiated a process of opening-up toward NGOs (Tussie and Riggirozzi, chap. 5); thereby, they are adapting their internal structures and processes to meet the challenges to their legitimacy.

The relationship between the United Nations and NGOs has been changeable, especially in the course of the cold war and its periods of rising and decreasing tension. With the waning of the cold war, NGOs have gained more influence in the UN system (Tussie and Rigirozzi, chap. 5). Starting from the International Conference on Environment and Development in Rio in 1992, NGOs have been more actively involved in world conferences than ever before: they were granted observer status and even active participation in most of the negotiations. However, the UN system's willingness to open up during the 1990s went far beyond the area of world conferences. In 1996, the UN Economic and Social Council (ECOSOC) adopted a resolution (Res. 31/1996) that redefines the criteria for NGOs to be accredited to the ECOSOC. This resolution is the first to take into account the full diversity of NGOs at different political levels. Thus, apart from (I)NGOs, regional, national, and subregional NGOs can be accredited to the ECOSOC as well. Moreover, various specialized agencies and special programmes have granted greater access to NGOs.

During the last decade, arrangements for consultations with NGOs have been revised, improved, and extended across the UN system, allowing NGOs decisively to influence international political debates. The notion that the United Nations obviously profits from the involvement of NGOs, especially in agenda setting and implementation, is confirmed by Secretary-General Kofi Annan who observes that the advantages of the increased NGO participation cannot be overestimated (Annan 1998a).

Although the revision of the UN system's arrangements for NGO participation will narrow the participatory gap, the efforts will not be sufficient to close it. There are two reasons for this. First, the different bodies of the United Nations still vary in their openness towards NGOs. Diana Tussie and Maria Pia Riggirozzi suggest that the differences in international organizations' openness relate to the functional performance of these institutions (chap. 5). They argue that what they term service organizations, e.g. the World Bank, are more open toward civil society actors than those that they term forum organizations, e.g. the UN General Assembly. Second, for closing (or narrowing) the participatory gap, balanced representation of the global civil society in international organizations is necessary; this calls for the incorporation of southern NGOs in addition to northern NGOs. Ngaire Woods (2001: 97) suggests that (particularly) transnational NGOs with their predominantly northern membership distort the inequalities of power and influence in world politics even further: these NGOs are only adding yet another channel of influence to those people and governments who already are powerfully represented.

Closing the participatory gap thus remains an important objective for the UN system for a long time to come.

Overview of the content of this volume

We have suggested that international governance is confronted by three different challenges: these are the revolution in information and communication technology, globalization, and the end of the cold war. As a consequence, new problems have arisen and a variety of non-state actors have entered the world political stage. For international governance systems, the attainment of governance goals has become increasingly difficult. Their failure results from four major gaps that have opened up – the jurisdictional, operational, incentive, and participatory gaps. Owing to these gaps, governance legitimacy in its output and input dimensions is reduced. The limitations of the effectiveness and legitimacy of international governance systems call for the establishment of more adequate governance systems, i.e. global governance. Although several proposals for narrowing (or even closing) the four governance gaps have been made, none of them has yet been implemented, apart from minor adjustments of the United Nations and its associated international organizations.

Whereas this chapter serves to outline the major trends of the transformation of governance beyond the nation-state, the following chapters analyse the shift from international to global governance in more detail. The authors discuss the various aspects of this transformation, extrapolate its trends, and provide suggestions about possible forms of global governance.

In chapter 2, Michael Zürn investigates the political systems in the national and postnational constellation. Political systems in the national constellation are characterized by a convergence of recognition, resources, and the realization of governance goals in one political organization, the nation-state. In a globalizing, or denationalizing, world this convergence of the three dimensions of a political system in one political organization dissolves and a new multilevel system of governance takes shape. Governance in the postnational constellation will approximate complex arrangements between governing institutions "with and without national governments." In the postnational constellation the attainment of the governance goals of security and the rule of law will be at least as likely as in the national constellation. However, the governance goals of providing effective participation channels and social welfare will be much more difficult to attain.

In chapter 3, Sorpong Peou claims that international peace and stability cannot be attained by the UN system alone. Regional security communities could help the United Nations to promote peace and stability. "Stable" security communities are defined as those whose members develop dependable mutual expectations of peaceful change. Today, variations in regional stability and peace can be observed: North America and Western Europe have become the most stable regions, whereas non-Western regions have proved to be far less effective in maintaining stable peace than their Western counterparts. The variation in regional stability and peace follows from the fact that regions and their member states do not meet equally the conditions that are considered essential for building security communities. These conditions encompass democratic performance of the member states, the presence of a democratic leader in the security community which possesses adequate material capabilities for effective democratic intervention, experience of the member states in managing conflicts, and membership size of the security community.

In chapter 4, Richard Higgott discusses the relationship between globalization and governance. In the 1980s and early 1990s the Washington Consensus (WC), with its buzzwords "liberalization," "deregulation," and "privatization," has governed international economic thinking and practice. As a result, financial markets have expanded rapidly. The financial crises of 1997 have made policy makers aware of the need to rethink the relationship between the market and the state. As a result of rigorous debates about the policy successes and failures of the WC, a Post-Washington Consensus (PWC) is emerging and has added another set of buzzwords – such as "civil society," "social capital," "capacity building," or "transparency," to the WC. In short, the PWC is an attempt to embed and humanize globalization institutionally. Therefore, the major financial and economic international organizations and regimes will be a potentially greater source of the promotion of social justice than they have been in the past.

In chapter 5, Diana Tussie and Maria Pia Riggirozzi examine the relationship of different IGOs and (I)NGOs. The former are found to be increasingly open toward civil society actors. The authors suggest that the variation in openness depends on an IGO being more like a forum or a service organization. This distinction relates to the way in which IGOs perform their function. Service organizations, exemplified by the international financial institutions, provide specific in-country services and disburse funds to "clients." These service organizations were first in broadening their collaboration with NGOs. Forum organizations are established to provide a venue or framework for negotiations and collective decision-making, ranging from consultations to binding commitments. These organizations, such as the UN General Assembly or the WTO, are still less open towards NGOs. Governments of member states are the main actors, leaving civil society organizations with a secondary role in the process of negotiations and decision-making.

In chapter 6, Otfried Höffe develops the core ideas of a subsidiary and federal world republic, arguing that such a world republic is the adequate response to the challenges of globalization. The world republic needs to rely on the constitutive principle of federalism, since "only a federalist unity can be a morally dictated and legitimate world republic." In this scheme, the individual states remain responsible for enforcing the law. The territorial states have the rank of first-order states, while the world republic is no more than a second-order or (where there are intermediary polities at the continental or subcontinental level) even a third-order state. Citizenship in the world republic is therefore understood as complementary citizenship. Global civil rights do not take the place of national civil rights, but the former supplement the latter.

In chapter 7, Yash Tandon examines to what degree existing international governance conforms to criteria of social justice. This provocative chapter consists of three parts. First, Tandon observes that the contemporary world is "pathological": it is ruled by profits, as, for instance, "health is subordinated to the demands of profit" or the protection of plants takes precedence over the protection of human lives. Second, the author presents and discusses three different conceptions of justice: "justice as fairness" (Rawls), "justice as charity," and "justice as welfare." Finally, he asks which of the wide variety of actors on the world political stage are able and willing to pursue social justice. Since neither northern nor southern states nor TNCs are purveyors of justice, only civil society organizations can be relied upon to be agents of the Rawlsian concept of "justice as fairness."

Notes

1. However, it is important to note that, to a certain extent, additional information at a certain time or in a certain context may be harmful, and at another time and place this same increment of information may have a neutral or even beneficial effect (Hurley and Mayer-Schönberger 2000).
2. Since the main purpose of this section is to discuss the challenges posed by globalization to international governance, and not the analysis of globalization itself, we refer only to the two extreme views on globalization. For a more differentiated view see Held et al. (1999a: 2–16).
3. For data and analysis cf. Albert et al. (1999).
4. Robert O. Keohane and Joseph S. Nye, Jr (2000a: 105) distinguish globalization and interdependence. According to these authors, globalization, first, refers to networks of connections rather than single linkages and, second, includes multicontinental distances, not simply regional networks. (For their concept and analysis on interdependence see Keohane and Nye 1977, 1987.)
5. These scholars prefer the term "denationalization" to "globalization," as the latter is mostly understood as a process resulting in a status of globality. Because most transboundary interactions take place within the OECD world, and not on a global level, "globalization" appears to be a misnomer. "Denationalization," in contrast, refers only to the extension of societal transactions beyond the national level, no matter what the actual scope of the transactions (see Zürn, chap. 4; Zürn 1998; Beisheim et al. 1999).
6. A value of 0 signifies perfect equality; a value of 1, perfect inequality. The world Gini coefficient deteriorated slightly from 0.63 in 1988 to 0.66 in 1993. In the Russian Federation, the Gini coefficient rose markedly from 0.24 to 0.48 between 1987–1988 and 1993–1995 (UNDP 1999: 6).
7. However, in the second half of the 1990s the UN started to wane in global influence. The number of Blue Helmets decreased to 27,000 in 2000 after it had peaked in 1993, when 80,000 peace-keepers were deployed (Peou, chap. 3).
8. Kalevi J. Holsti (1996: 119) defines "failed states" as follows: "Leaders become increasingly isolated and inhabit make-believe worlds concocted by their cronies and dwindling sycophants. Government institutions no longer function except perhaps in the capital city. The tasks of governance, to the extent that they are performed at all, devolve to warlords, clan chiefs, who are well armed. The state retains the fig leaf of sov-

ereignty for external purposes, but domestic life is organized around local politics. The national army ... disintegrates into local racketeering, or hires itself out to local rulers."

9. Input legitimacy is more difficult to achieve in international governance than in governance by national governments, because neither an international public nor a transnational collective identity has yet come into existence (cf. Brock 1998; Wolf 2000: 213–242; Zürn 2000: 192).

10. In his Presidential Address to the American Political Science Association, Robert Keohane (2001: 3), for instance, has proposed that each political institution in global governance needs to meet the three criteria of accountability, participation, and persuasion. We discuss these criteria under the headings of closing the jurisdictional gap (accountability), the participation gap (participation and accountability), and the incentive gap (persuasion).

11. At first glance, this idea looks very promising but its further analysis shows that it remains unclear who is to decide on the appropriate level of public policy-making in distinct areas (cf. Brand et al. 2000, also Mürle 1998). For a different point of view see Höffe (1997).

12. In addition, UN member states apparently do not favour implementing far-reaching reforms in general. This reluctant attitude is indicated by their recurrent inability to agree on less important reform proposals. Thus, the closure of all governance gaps will be difficult to achieve. For different UN reform proposals cf. Alger 1998; Hüfner and Martens 2000. Whereas most of the far-reaching reform proposals have not been implemented, Kofi Annan has implemented a "Quiet Revolution" (Annan 1998a) by reforming the UN Secretariat.

13. Global public policy (GPP) networks are one set of arrangements of public–private partnerships. GPP networks are institutional innovations as not only do they combine the "voluntary energy and legitimacy of the civil society sector with the financial muscle and interest of business and the enforcement and rule-making power and coordination and capacity-building skills of states and international organization," but also they create new knowledge as consensus emerges over often contentious issues. They thus ensure constant learning of all participants (Reinicke and Deng 2000: 29–30).

14. The Secretary-General asked the business community to support and respect the following:

    1. The Universal Declaration of Human Rights (1948) Principle 1 (protection of international human rights within their sphere of influence) and Principle 2 (make sure their own corporations are not complicit in human rights abuses).

    2. The Declaration of the International Labour Organization on fundamental principles and rights at work Principle 3 (guarantee freedom of association and the effective recognition of the right to collective bargaining), Principle 4 (support the elimination of all forms of forced and compulsory labour), Principle 5 (assist the effective abolition of child labour), and Principle 6 (support the elimination of discrimination in respect of employment and occupation).

    3. The Rio Declaration of the UN Conference in Environment and Development (1992) Principle 7 (support a precautionary approach to environmental challenges), Principle 8 (undertake initiatives to promote greater environmental responsibility), and Principle 9 (encourage the development and diffusion of environmentally friendly technologies).

15. Cf. the modalities of the guidelines "Cooperation between the United Nations and Business Community" issued by the Secretary-General of the United Nations, 17 July 2000.

16. "Think-tank NGOs" such as the Transnational Resource and Action Center have published various short articles on this topic, cf. Paul (2001). Other NGOs have written a

"coalition letter" to Kofi Annan [www.corpwatch.org/trac/globalization/blast1tr.html] (23.11.2000).

17. For an overview of these reform proposals see Bienen, Rittberger, and Wagner (1998).

REFERENCES

Afeman, Uwe. 2000. "Internet and Developing Countries B Pros and Cons." *Nord–Süd Aktuell* 14(3): 430–452.

Albert, Mathias, Lothar Brock, Stephan Hessler, Ulrich Menzel, and Jürgen Neyer. 1999. *Die Neue Weltwirtschaft. Entstofflichung und Entgrenzung der Ökonomie.* Frankfurt/M: Suhrkamp.

Alger, Chadwick F. 1998. "Conclusion: The Potential of the United Nations System." In: *The Future of the United Nations System: Potential for the Twenty-First Century*, ed. Chadwick F. Alger. Tokyo: United Nations University Press, 409–429.

Altvater, Elmar, and Birgit Mahnkopf. 1996. *Grenzen der Globalisierung. Ökonomie, Ökologie und Politik in der Weltgesellschaft.* Münster: Westfälisches Dampfboot.

Annan, Kofi. 1998a. Report of the Secretary-General: Arrangements and Practices for the Interaction of Non-governmental Organizations in all Activities of the United Nations System. (A/53/170). July 10, 1998.

Annan, Kofi. 1998b. "Challenges of the New Peacekeeping." In: *Peacemaking and Peacekeeping for the New Century*, eds Otunnu, Olara A. and Michael W. Doyle. Lanham, MD: Rowman and Littlefield, 169–188.

Annan, Kofi. 2000. *"We the People." The Role of the United Nations in the 21st Century.* New York: United Nations.

Armstrong, David, Lorna Lloyd, and John Redmond. 1996. *From Versailles to Maastricht. International Organizations in the Twenty-first Century.* New York: Macmillan.

Axelrod, Robert and Robert O. Keohane. 1985. "Achieving Cooperation under Anarchy. Strategies and Institutions." *World Politics* 38(1): 226–254.

Beisheim, Marianne and Gregor Walter. 1997. "'Globalisierung' – Kinderkrankheiten eines Konzepts." *Zeitschrift für Internationale Beziehungen* 4(1): 153–180.

Beisheim, Marianne, Sabine Dreher, Gregor Walter, Bernhard Zangl, and Michael Zürn. 1999. *Im Zeitalter der Globalisierung? Thesen und Daten zur gesellschaftlichen und politischen Denationalisierung.* Baden-Baden: Nomos.

Betts, Richard K., ed. 1994. *Conflict after the Cold War. Arguments on Causes of War and Peace.* New York: Macmillan.

Bienen, Derk, Volker Rittberger, and Wolfgang Wagner. 1998. "Democracy in the United Nations System. Cosmopolitan and Communitarian Principles." In: *Re-Imagining Political Community. Studies in Cosmopolitan Democracy*, eds Daniele Archibugi, David Held, and Martin Köhler. Cambridge: Polity Press, 287–308.

Boli, John and George M. Thomas, eds. 1999. *Constructing World Culture. In-*

ternational Non-Governmental Organizations since 1875. Stanford, CA: Stanford University Press.

Brand, Ulrich, Achim Brunnengräber, Lutz Schrader, Christian Stock, and Peter Wahl. 2000. *Global Governance. Alternativen zur neoliberalen Globalisierung?* Münster: Westfälisches Dampfboot.

Brock, Lothar. 1998. "Die Grenzen der Demokratie: Selbstbestimmung im Kontext des globalen Strukturwandels und des sich wandelnden Verhältnisses zwischen Markt und Staat." In: *Regieren in entgrenzten Räumen*, ed. Beate Kohler-Koch. Opladen: Westdeutscher Verlag (PVS Sonderheft 29), 271–292.

Brühl, Tanja. 1999. "Zahnlose Tiger? Mechanismen der Rechtsdurchsetzung in der internationalen Umweltpolitik." In: *Belohnen, Beschämen, Bestrafen. Globale Vereinbarungen und ihre Durchsetzung*, ed. World Economy, Ecology and Development (WEED). Bonn: WEED, 21–27.

Brühl, Tanja and Udo E. Simonis. 2000. *World Ecology and Global Environmental Governance.* Berlin: WZB paper FS II 01-402.

Cameron, Maxwell A., Brian W. Tomlin, and Bob Lawson, eds. 1998. *To Walk without Fear. The Global Movement to Ban Landmines.* Oxford: Oxford University Press.

Chayes, Abram and Antonia Handler Chayes. 1995. *The New Sovereignty: Compliance with International Regulatory Agreements.* Cambridge, MA: Harvard University Press.

Commission on Global Governance. 1995. *Towards the Global Neighbourhood. The Report of the Commission on Global Governance.* Oxford: Oxford University Press.

Cox, Robert W. 1997. "Introduction." In: *The New Realism. Perspectives on Multilateralism and World Order*, ed. Robert W. Cox. Tokyo: United Nations University Press, xv–xxx.

Crosette, Barbara. 2000. "Globalization Battle Moves to UN." *International Herald Tribune* 4 September, 4.

Cusimano, Maryann K. 2000. "Beyond Sovereignty. The Rise of Transsovereign Problems." In: *Beyond Sovereignty. Issues for a Global Agenda*, ed. Maryann K. Cusimano. Boston, MA: Bedford/St Martin's, 1–40.

Cutler, A. Claire, Virginia Haufler, and Tony Porter. 1999. "Private Authority and International Affairs." In: *Private Authority and International Affairs*, eds A. Claire Cutler, Virginia Haufler, and Tony Porter. Albany, NY: State University of New York Press, 3–28.

Czempiel, Ernst Otto. 1992. "Governance and Democratization." In: *Governance without Government. Order and Change in World Politics*, eds James N. Rosenau and Ernst Otto Czempiel. Cambridge: Cambridge University Press, 250–271.

Daase, Christopher. 1999. *Kleine Kriege B Große Wirkung. Wie unkonventionelle Kriegsführung die internationale Politik verändert.* Baden-Baden: Nomos.

Devetak, Richard and Richard Higgott. 1999. "Justice Unbound? Globalization, States and the Transformation of the Social Bound." *International Affairs* 75(3): 483–498.

Doyle, Michael W. 1998. "Introduction: Discovering the Limits and Potential of

Peacekeeping." In: *Peacemaking and Peacekeeping for the New Century*, eds Olara A. Otunnu and Michael W. Doyle. Lanham, MD: Rowman and Littlefield, 1–21.

Elias, Norbert. 1976. *Über den Prozeß der Zivilisation. Soziogenetische und psychogenetische Untersuchungen* (2 vols). Frankfurt/M: Suhrkamp.

Falk, Richard. 1995. *On Humane Governance: Toward a New Global Politics. The World Order Models Report of the Global Civilization Initiative.* Cambridge: Polity Press.

Falk, Richard. 1999. *Predatory Globalization. A Critique.* Cambridge: Polity Press.

Florini, Ann M. 2000. "Who Does What? Collective Action and the Changing Nature of Authority." In: *Non-State Actors and Authority in the Global System*, eds Richard A. Higgott, Geoffrey R. D. Underhill, and Andreas Bieler. London: Routledge, 15–31.

Frissen, Paul. 1997. "The Virtual State: Postmodernisation, Information and Public Administration." In: *The Governance of Cyberspace. Politics, Technology, and Global Restructuring*, ed. Brian D. Loader. London: Routledge, 111–125.

Gellner, Winand and Fritz von Korff, eds. 1998. *Demokratie und Internet.* Baden-Baden: Nomos.

Goldstein, Judith, Miles Kahler, Robert O. Keohane, and Anne-Marie Slaughter. 2000. "Introduction: Legalization and World Politics." In: *International Organization* (special issue, eds Judith Goldstein, Miles Kahler, Robert O. Keohane, and Anne-Marie Slaughter) 54(3): 385–399.

Group of Lisbon. 1996. *Limits of Competition.* Cambridge, MA: MIT Press.

Haufler, Virginia. 2000. "Private Sector International Regimes." In: *Non State Actors and Authority in the Global System*, eds Richard A. Higgott, Geoffrey R. D. Underhill, and Andreas Bieler. London: Routledge, 121–137.

Held, David, Anthony McGrew, David Goldblatt, and Jonathan Perraton. 1999a. *Global Transformation. Politics, Economics and Culture.* Cambridge: Polity Press.

Held, David, Anthony McGrew, David Goldblatt, and Jonathan Perraton. 1999b. "Globalization." *Global Governance* 5(4): 483–496.

Hewitt de Alcántara, Cynthia. 1998. "Uses and Abuses of the Concept of Governance." *International Social Science Journal* 50(115): 105–113.

Higgott, Richard and Nicola Phillips. 2000. "After Triumphalism: The Limits of Liberalisation in Asia and Latin America." *Review of International Studies* 26(3): 359–380.

Hippler, Jochen. 1999. "Konflikte und Krisenprävention." In: *Globale Trends 2000. Fakten, Analysen, Prognosen*, eds Ingomar Hauchler, Dirk Messner, and Franz Nuscheler. Frankfurt/M: Fischer, 421–438.

Hirst, Paul and Grahame Thompson. 1996. *Globalization in Question. The International Economy and the Possibilities of Governance.* Cambridge: Polity Press.

Höffe, Otfried. 1997. "Subsidiarität als Gesellschafts- und Staatsprinzip." *Schweizerische Zeitschrift für Politikwissenschaft* (special edition: *Subsidiäres Staatshandeln*) 3(3): 259–290.

Höffe, Otfried. 1999. *Demokratie im Zeitalter der Globalisierung.* München: C.H. Beck.

Holsti, Kalevi J. 1996. *The State, War, and the State of War.* Cambridge: Cambridge University Press.

Hüfner, Klaus and Jens Martens. 2000. *UNO-Reform zwischen Utopie und Realität. Vorschläge zum Wirtschafts- und Sozialbereich der Vereinten Nationen.* Frankfurt/M: Peter Lang.

Hurley, Deborah and Viktor Mayer-Schönberger. 2000. "Information Policy and Governance." In: *Governance in a Globalized World*, eds Joseph N. Nye and John D. Donahue. Washington, DC: Brookings Institution Press, 330–346.

Kaldor, Mary. 1999. *New and Old Wars. Organized Violence in a Global Era.* Cambridge: Polity Press.

Kaul, Inge, Isabelle Grunberg, and Marc A. Stern. 1999a. "Introduction." In: *Global Public Goods. International Cooperation in the 21st Century*, eds Inge Kaul, Isabelle Grunberg, and Marc A. Stern. Tokyo: United Nations University Press, xix–xxxviii.

Kaul, Inge, Isabelle Grunberg, and Marc A. Stern. 1999b. "Conclusion: Global Public Goods. Concepts, Policies and Strategies." In: *Global Public Goods. International Cooperation in the Twenty-first Century*, eds Inge Kaul, Isabelle Grunberg, and Marc A. Stern. Tokyo: United Nations University Press, 450–507.

Keck, Margaret E. and Kathryn Sikkink, eds. 1998. *Activists Beyond Borders: Advocacy Networks in International Politics.* Ithaca, NY: Cornell University Press.

Kell, Georg and John Gerard Ruggie. 1999. "Global Markets and Social Legitimacy: The Case of the 'Global Compact'." Paper Presented at an International Conference on Governing the Public Domain Beyond the Era of the Washington Consensus? Redrawing the Link Between the State and the Market. York University, Toronto, Canada, November 4–6.

Keohane, Robert O. 1993. "The Analysis of International Regimes – Towards a European–American Research Programme." In: *Regime Theory and International Relations*, eds Volker Rittberger and Peter Mayer. Oxford: Clarendon Press, 23–45.

Keohane, Robert O. 2001. "Governance in a Partially Globalized World. Presidential Address, American Political Science Association, 2000." *American Political Science Review* 95(2): 1–15.

Keohane, Robert O. and Joseph S. Nye, Jr. 1977. *Power and Interdependence. World Politics in Transition.* Boston, MA: Little, Brown.

Keohane, Robert O. and Joseph S. Nye, Jr. 1987. "'Power and Interdependence' Revisited." *International Organization* 41(4): 725–753.

Keohane, Robert O. and Joseph S. Nye, Jr. 2000a. "Globalization: What's New? What's Not? (And So What?)." *Foreign Policy* 118: 104–119.

Keohane, Robert O. and Joseph S. Nye, Jr. 2000b. "Introduction." In: *Governance in a Globalizing World*, eds Joseph S. Nye, Jr and John D. Donahue. Washington, DC: Brookings Institution, 1–40.

Keohane, Robert O. and Joseph S. Nye, Jr. 2000c. "The Club Model of Multilateral Cooperation and Problems of Democracy." Paper Prepared for the American Political Science Association Meeting, Washington, DC, August 31–September 3.

Lake, David A. 1993. "Leadership, Hegemony, and the International Economy. Naked Emperor or Tattered Monarch with Potential?" *International Studies Quarterly* 37(4): 459–489.

Lipset, Seymour Martin. 1960. *Political Man. The Social Bases of Politics*. London: Heinemann.

Lynch, Cecelia. 1998. "Social Movements and the Problem of Globalization." *Alternatives* 23(2): 149–173.

Mayer, Peter, Volker Rittberger, and Michael Zürn. 1993. "Regime Theory. State of the Art and Perspectives." In: *Regime Theory and International Relations*, ed. Volker Rittberger. Oxford: Clarendon Press, 391–430.

Messner, Dirk. 1998. "Die Transformation von Staat und Politik im Globalisierungsprozeß." In: *Die Zukunft des Staates und der Politik: Möglichkeiten und Grenzen der politischen Steuerung in der Weltgesellschaft*, ed. Dirk Messner. Bonn: Dietz, 14–43.

Messner, Dirk and Franz Nuscheler. 1996. "Global Governance. Organisationselemente und Säulen einer Weltordnungspolitik." In: *Weltkonferenzen und Weltberichte. Ein Wegweiser durch die internationale Diskussion*, eds Dirk Messner and Franz Nuscheler. Bonn: Dietz, 12–36.

Messner, Dirk and Franz Nuscheler. 1997. "Global Governance. Herausforderungen an der Schwelle zum 21. Jahrhundert." In: *Frieden machen*, ed. Dieter Senghaas. Frankfurt/M: Suhrkamp, 337–361.

Mittelman, James H. 2000. *The Globalization Syndrome. Transformation and Resistance*. Princeton, NJ: Princeton University Press.

Mockaitis, Thomas R. 1999. *Peace Operations and Intrastate Conflict. The Sword or the Olive Branch?* Westport, CT: Praeger.

Moravcsik, Andrew. 1998. *The Choice for Europe: Social Purpose and State Power from Messina to Maastricht*. Ithaca, NY: Cornell University Press.

Mürle, Holger. 1998. *Global Governance. Literaturbericht und Forschungsfragen. INEF-Report 32/1998*. Duisburg: Institut für Entwicklung und Frieden.

Nye, Joseph. 2000. "Take Globalization Protests Seriously." *International Herald Tribune*, 10 November 2000, 25–26.

Pace, William R. and Mark Thieroff. 1999. "Participation of Non-Governmental Organizations." In: *The International Criminal Court. The Making of the Rome Statute. Issues, Negotiations, Results*, ed. Roy S. Lee. London: Kluwer Law International, 391–398.

Paul, James A. 2001. "Der Weg zum Global Compact: Multinationale Unternehmen und die Vereinten Nationen." In: *Die Privatisierung der Weltpolitik. Entstaatlichung und Kommerzialisierung im Globalisierungskontext*, eds Tanja Brühl, Tobias Debiel, Brigitte Hamm, Hartwig Hummel, and Jens Martens. Bonn: Dietz, 104–129.

Rasmussen, J. Lewis. 1997. "Peacemaking in the Twenty-First Century: New Rules, New Roles, New Actors." In: *Peacemaking in International Conflict. Methods and Technique*, eds William I. Zartman and J. Lewis Rasmussen. Washington, DC: United States Institute of Peace Press, 23–49.

Reinicke, Wolfgang H. 1998. *Global Public Policy: Governing Without Government*? Washington, DC: Brookings.

Reinicke, Wolfgang H. and Francis Deng, eds with Jan Martin Witte, Thorsten Benner, Beth Withaker, and John Gershman. 2000. *Critical Choices. The United Nations, Networks and the Future of Global Governance*. Ottawa: International Development Research Center.

Rittberger, Volker (with the assistance of Bernhard Zangl). 1995. *Internationale Organisationen. Politik und Geschichte*, 2nd edn. Opladen: Leske & Budrich.

Rittberger, Volker. 2000. "Globalisierung und der Wandel der Staatenwelt. Die Welt regieren ohne Weltstaat." In: *Vom ewigen Frieden und vom Wohlstand der Nationen*, ed. Ulrich Menzel. Frankfurt/M: Suhrkamp, 188–218.

Rittberger, Volker and Helmut Breitmeier. 2000. "Environmental NGOs in an Emerging Global Civil Society." In: *Global Environment in the Twenty-First Century: Prospects for International Cooperation*, ed. Pamela Chasek. Tokyo: United Nations University Press, 130–163.

Rittberger, Volker, Martin Mogler, and Bernhard Zangl. 1997. *Vereinte Nationen und Weltordnung: Zivilisierung der internationalen Politik*? Opladen: Leske & Budrich.

Rittberger, Volker, Christina Schrade, and Daniela Schwarzer. 1999. "Introduction: Transnational Civil Society and the Quest for Security." In: *International Security Management and the United Nations*, eds Muthiah Alagappa and Takashi Inoguchi. Tokyo: United Nations University Press, 109–138.

Rittberger, Volker and Michael Zürn. 1990. "Towards Regulated Anarchy in East–West Relations." In: *International Regimes in East–West Politics*, ed. Volker Rittberger. London: Pinter, 9–63.

Rohloff, Christoph and Hardi Schindler. 2000. "Mit weniger Gewalt in die Zukunft. Debatten und Befunde aus der empirischen Friedens- und Konfliktforschung." *Die Friedens-Warte* 74(3–4): 289–308.

Ropers, Norbert and Tobias Debiel, eds. 1995. *Friedliche Konfliktbearbeitung in der Staaten- und Gesellschaftswelt (Eine Welt 13)*. Bonn: Stiftung Entwicklung und Frieden.

Rosenau, James N. 1992. "Governance, Order, and Change in World Politics." In: *Governance without Government. Order and Change in World Politics*, eds James Rosenau and Ernst-Otto Czempiel. Cambridge: Cambridge University Press, 1–29.

Rosenau, James N. 1995. "Changing Capacities of Citizens, 1945–1995." In: *Issues in Global Governance. Papers Written for the Commission on Global Governance*. London: Kluwer Law International, 1–57.

Rosenau, James N. 1997. *Along the Domestic–Foreign Frontier: Exploring Governance in a Turbulent World*. Cambridge: Cambridge University Press.

Rosenau, James N. 1999. "Toward an Ontology of Global Governance." In: *Approaches to Global Governance Theory*, eds Martin Hewson and Timothy Sinclair. Albany, NY: State University of New York Press, 287–301.

Scharpf, Fritz W. 1993. "Legitimationsprobleme der Globalisierung. Regieren in Verhandlungssystemen." In: *Regieren im 21. Jahrhundert. Zwischen Globalisierung und Regionalisierung*, eds Carl Böhret and Göttrik Wewer. Opladen: Leske & Budrich, 165–185.

Scharpf, Fritz W. 1998a. "Demokratische Politik in der internationalisierten Ökonomie." In: *Demokratie – eine Kultur des Westens? 20. Wissenschaftlicher Kongreß der Deutschen Vereinigung für Politische Wissenschaft*, ed. Michael Greven. Opladen: Leske & Budrich, 81–103.

Scharpf, Fritz W. 1998b. "Interdependence and Democratic Legitimation, Working Paper 98/2." Cologne: Max Planck Institute for the Study of Societies.

Scherrer, Christoph 1999. *Globalisierung wider Willen? Die Durchsetzung liberaler Außenwirtschaftspolitik in den USA*. Berlin: Edition Sigma.

Shapiro, Andrew L. 1999. "The Internet." *Foreign Policy* 115, 14–27.

Slaughter, Ann-Marie. 1997. "The Real New World Order." *Foreign Affairs* 76(5): 183–197.

Smith, Jackie, Charles Chatfield, and Ron Pagnucco, eds. 1997. *Transnational Social Movements and Global Politics. Solidarity Beyond the State*. Syracuse, NY: Syracuse University Press.

Smythe, Elizabeth. 2000. "State Authority and Investment Security. Non-State Actors and the Negotiation of the Multilateral Agreement on Investment at the OECD." In: *Non-State Actors and Authority in the Global System*, eds Richard A. Higgott, Geoffrey R. D. Underhill, and Andreas Bieler. London: Routledge, 74–90.

Spar, Debora L. 1999. "Lost in (Cyber)space: The Private Role of Online Commerce." In: *Private Authority and International Affairs*, eds A. Claire Cutler, Virginia Haufler, and Tony Porter. Albany, NY: State University of New York Press, 31–51.

Stewart, Frances and Albert Berry. 1999. "Globalization, Liberalization, and Inequality." In: *Inequality, Globalization, and World Politics*, eds Andrew Hurrell and Ngaire Woods. Oxford: Oxford University Press, 150–186.

Stoker, Gerry. 1998. "Governance as Theory: Five Propositions." *International Social Science Journal* 50(155): 17–28.

Strange, Susan. 1996. *The Retreat of the State. The Diffusion of Power in World Economy*. Cambridge: Cambridge University Press.

United Nations Development Programme. 1998. *The Human Development Report 1999*. New York: United Nations.

United Nations Development Programme. 1999. *The Human Development Report 2000*. New York: United Nations.

Väyrynen, Raimo. 1999. "Norms, Compliance, and Enforcement in Global Governance." In: *Globalization and Global Governance*, ed. Raimo Väyrynen. Lanham, MD: Rowman & Littlefield, 25–46.

Wallach, Lory. 2000. "Lorys' War, Foreign Policy Interview." *Foreign Policy* 118, 28–57.

Walter, Gregor, Sabine Dreher, and Marianne Beisheim. 1997. "Globalization Processes in the G-7." *Global Society* 13(3): 229–255.

Waltz, Kenneth. 1979. *Theory of International Politics*. New York: McGraw-Hill.

Williams, Jody and Stephen Goose. 1998. "The International Campaign to Ban Landmines." In: *To Walk Without Fear. The Global Movement to Ban Landmines*, eds Maxwell A. Cameron, Robert J. Lawson, and Brian W. Tomlin. Oxford: Oxford University Press, 20–47.

Williams, Phil. 1999. "The Dark Side of Global Civil Society: The Role and Impact of Transnational Criminal Organizations as a Threat to International Security." In: *International Security Management and the United Nations*, eds Muthiah Alagappa and Takashi Inoguchi. Tokyo: United Nations University Press, 173–209.

Williams, Phil and Ernesto U. Savona, eds. 1996. *The United Nations and Transnational Organized Crime*. Ilford: Frank Cass.

Wolf, Klaus Dieter. 2000. *Die Neue Staatsräson – Zwischenstaatliche Kooperation als Demokratieproblem in der Weltgesellschaft. Plädoyer für eine geordnete Entstaatlichung des Regierens jenseits des Staates.* Baden-Baden: Nomos.

Woods, Ngaire. 2001. "Making the IMF and the World Bank More Accountable." *International Affairs* 77(1): 83–100.

World Trade Organization. 2000. "Trade, Income Disparity and Poverty." In: *Special Studies 5*, eds Dan Ben-David, Hakan Nordström, and L. Alan Winters. Geneva: World Trade Organization.

Young, Oran. 1989. "The Politics of International Regime Formation." *International Organization* 43(3): 349–376.

Young, Oran R. 1994. *International Governance. Protecting the Environment in a Stateless Society.* Ithaca, NY: Cornell University Press.

Young, Oran R. 1997. "Global Governance. Toward a Theory of Decentralized World Order." In: *Global Governance. Drawing Insights from the Environmental Experience*, ed. Oran R. Young. Cambridge, MA: MIT Press, 273–299.

Zacher, Mark W. 1999. *The United Nations and Global Commerce*. New York: United Nations Department of Public Information.

Zartman, I. William. 1999. "Intervening to Prevent State Collapse: The Role of the United Nations." In: *Multilateral Diplomacy and the United Nations Today*, eds James P. Muldoon, Jr, JoAnn Fagot Aviel, Richard Reitano, and Earl Sullivan. Boulder, CO: Westview Press, 68–77.

Zürn, Michael. 1992. *Interessen und Institutionen in der internationalen Politik. Grundlegung und Anwendung des situationsstrukturellen Ansatzes.* Opladen: Leske & Budrich.

Zürn, Michael. 1995. "The Challenge of Globalization and Individualization. A View from Europe." In: *Whose World Order? Uneven Globalization and the End of the Cold War*, eds Hans-Henrik Holm and Georg Sorensen. Boulder, CO: Westview Press, 137–163.

Zürn, Michael. 1998. *Regieren jenseits des Nationalstaates. Globalisierung und Denationalisierung als Chance.* Frankfurt/M.: Suhrkamp.

Zürn, Michael. 2000. "Democratic Governance Beyond the Nation-State. The EU and Other International Institutions." *European Journal of International Relations* 6(2): 183–221.

2

Political systems in the postnational constellation: Societal denationalization and multilevel governance[1]

Michael Zürn

Introduction

The uneasy debate about the declining or reinforced sovereign nation-state did not last very long. Whereas hyper-globalists saw the coming global age as one with global enterprises, global civil society, the dominance of market relations, and no place for sovereign states, globalization sceptics pointed to the rise of trading blocs, economies less interdependent than 100 years before, and state executives more autonomous than ever. More sophisticated analyses acknowledge significant changes, yet expect them to lead to a relocation, reconstitution, or transformation of sovereignty[2] and the role of the nation-state.[3] Most of these efforts are, however, deficient in at least one respect: they focus exclusively on a state or national political system without seeing them as part of a more encompassing constellation. This focus leads to conclusions that, for instance, there are "core aspects of the institution of sovereignty which remain unchanged and there are core aspects of the institution which have changed dramatically over time" (Sørensen 1999: 591). While it is true that sovereignty and the modern nation-state cannot be understood by focusing on only one aspect, a thorough understanding needs to take into account not only different aspects but also the *relationship* between different aspects of political systems and how this relationship constitutes different overall constellations. Along this line, my aim is to put forward a relational understanding in a changing – from national to postnational

48

– constellation of political systems. Moreover, debates about appropriate conceptual tools (about *assumptions*) for understanding the role of the state in global governance should be geared towards the development of *hypotheses* about observable outcomes in international relations and global politics. In this chapter, some expectations about the impact of the changing overall constellation on governance are developed against the background of the conceptualization of postnational political systems.

The argument, in a nutshell, is that political systems consist of three dimensions – recognition, resources, and the realization of governance goals. Political systems in the national constellation were characterized by a convergence of all these three Rs in one political organization – that is, the nation-state. This national constellation was bound together by the congruence of social and political spaces. In a denationalizing world with a relative strengthening of cross-border compared with within-border transactions and the emergence of new social spaces, the convergence of the dimensions of political systems in one political organization dissolves and a new governance architecture arises. To the extent that we move towards such a postnational constellation with multilevel governance, the provision of public goods will change significantly, casting doubts on the capacity to manage the problems that we are expected to face in the new century. I proceed in four steps:

1. In the next section (pp. 50–57) my aim is to develop a multidimensional notion of the sovereign state that binds it to the national constellation and, thereby, to demonstrate that it was only the interplay of a number of dimensions of political systems, all of them converging on the national level, that made the sovereign nation-state possible.
2. With the sharp rise in the number of societal transactions crossing national borders, this national constellation faces a fundamental challenge to which, however, political actors respond by making deliberate choices rather than merely yielding to external pressures as hyper-globalists would like us to believe. The section on pp. 57–70 therefore sketches the challenges of, and the political responses to, "societal denationalization" (a term that I prefer to "globalization").
3. Societal denationalization and political responses to it may eventually lead to a "postnational constellation". Although it is impossible to comprehend this postnational constellation in detail today (its shape is by no means determined and is more likely to be the outcome of political struggles), I attempt in the section on pages 70–74 to sketch the architecture of multilevel political systems by highlighting and extrapolating some empirical trends.
4. In the final section (pp. 74–76) I reflect on the extent to which the attainment of governance goals will be possible in the future.

Analysis of current trends			Extrapolation of trends	Hypotheses about the future
Societal denationa-lization →	Challenges for national capacity to govern →	Political responses →	Postnational constellation of statehood →	Postnational capacity to govern

Figure 2.1 Steps in the argument

Two notes of caution must be added. First, parts of the argument in this contribution refer to the future and thus cannot easily be tested against observations about the past and present world. The different steps in the argument follow three different modes of reasoning: the first step is based on an analysis of current trends; in a next step these trends are extrapolated; finally, hypotheses are developed about the outcomes that this extrapolated world will produce (see figure 2.1). Needless to say, it therefore contains elements of (I hope) informed speculation.

Second, the focus of this contribution is limited to governance in the world of the Organization for Economic Co-operation and Development (OECD). It is this area in the world where the nation-state has been fully developed and where denationalization processes are most significant. The notion of a postnational governance system in the OECD world therefore does not preclude struggles in other parts of the world to develop a nation-state in the first place. In doing so, they may repeat many of the merits and the sufferings of nationalization that first took place in Western Europe in the eighteenth and nineteenth centuries. In these especially troubled parts of the world, an understanding of future political developments must take into account both aspirations for nation-building at the periphery *and* the impacts of a postnational constellation in the centre.[4]

Political systems in the national constellation

"Political system" is a more general concept than "sovereign nation-state." At all times (and in all societies), norms, rules, and procedures have been developed by which social control and conflict management have been exerted (see e.g. Wesel 1997). Moreover, the norms, rules, and procedures that govern societies have always been in specific relationships with each other so that they together represent institutional arrangements or architectures. Any one of these institutional arrangements for the governance of societies systematically favours certain outcomes over others and thus establishes rule and authority. A political system, defined as the overall arrangement that establishes rule in a given society, is a permanent feature of all societies. Political systems, however, vary significantly over time and space as to the source of legitimacy of the rules, the making of the rules, the social purpose for which the rules are employed, and the means and instruments through which the rules are enforced. The specific constellation or interplay of these aspects of political systems is often used to characterize concrete manifestations of it. The sovereign nation-state can be described on the basis of three dimensions, all of which converge at the national level.

The first dimension is *recognition*, which is the normative basis for modern political systems. The most important component of this dimension is the principle of *sovereignty* – that is "the supreme legal authority of the nation to give and enforce the law within a certain territory and, in consequence, independence from the authority of any other nation and equality with it under international law" (Morgenthau 1967: 305). From a historical perspective, sovereignty is attributed by other states. It was recognition as an international legal subject which ultimately made a political organization a state. "Sovereignty, in the end, is status – the vindication of the state's existence as a member of the international system" (Chayes and Chayes 1995: 27). Although elements of sovereignty had already de facto evolved to a significant degree from the fifteenth century on, it became formally recognized only through the Westphalian treaties. Furthermore, it took a further 300 years before the world was completely compartmentalized into different sovereign states, each given exclusive property rights for a certain territory, and before powerful threats such as pirates and mercenaries lost significance in such transnational spaces as the open sea (Thomson 1994).[5]

Only later on, mainly in the eighteenth and nineteenth centuries with the rise of *nationalism*, was external recognition supplemented by internal recognition of the territorial state as the legitimate and necessary organizational form of a political community that defined itself as a nation.[6] It is in this process that ordinary people began "... to allot recognition to the conceptual existence of the state at all" (Nettl 1968: 566). The territorial state thus became a nation-state. Although the territorial state was able to build upon protonational cultures and communities, at the same time it contributed to the rise of national identities through harmonization policies and the symbolic representation of "imagined communities" (Anderson 1991). As a result of this, the notion prevailed according to which national boundaries and territorial state boundaries have to coincide (Gellner 1991). Legitimacy, defined as a generalized perception that a given political organization is desirable or appropriate

within some socially constructed sphere,[7] increasingly depended on both
successful policies (output legitimacy) and proper procedures for participation in policy-making (input legitimacy). In sum, "sovereignty is the
recognition by internal and external actors that the state has the exclusive authority to intervene coercively in activities within its territory"
(Thomson 1995: 219).

The second dimension is that of *resources*. Recognition is contingent
upon both material and normative prerequisites. States would certainly
not have prevailed without a material basis – that is, the underlying
resources. A state's authority is recognized by others "when [it] has
achieved the capability to defend its authority against domestic and international challenges" (Thomson 1995: 220). Fundamental to the development of this capability is the process of the monopolization of force.
A royal monopoly of force prevailed as a result of fierce competition
between different power holders, first in France and in England. This
monopolization of force was accompanied by a tax-raising monopoly
through which, in turn, the monopoly of force could be defended against
aggressors from within and outside the controlled territory (Elias 1976;
Tilly 1985; Giddens 1985).

Third, is the dimension of the *attainment of goals*. Perhaps the most
fundamental dimension of modern political systems is the notion of an
organization that is *public* and thus exists to *deliver goods* for the people
who are part of this organization (see Reus-Smit 1997). It is the Parson-
ian category of goal attainment that is central here. Thus, sovereign
states were for a long time linked to the capacity of the state to govern
effectively. Only later was the people's right to self-determination disconnected from effective governance. As late as 1946, the British Government refused to give up its colonies at short notice, with the argument
that these countries lacked effective states that were able to pursue public goods. The British Government was able to cite the League of Nations, which restricted the right to state-building by establishing criteria
for the "capacity for independence." In 1960, however, the United Nations passed a resolution that the right to self-determination did not depend on the existence of the ability to govern: "Inadequacy of political,
economic, social or educational preparedness should never serve as a pretext for delaying independence."[8] Subsequently, "quasi-states" emerged,
which owed their existence primarily to recognition and assistance by
other states and international organizations, but did not conform to the
notion of a complete political system, including the ability to deliver the
goods of governance effectively.[9]

What, then, are these goals of governance? At first sight we must agree
with Dieter Grimm (1994: 771) that "every area of life open to human
influence has also been the target of state activity." However, a second

look reveals that in various academic disciplines and discourses – be they normative or empirical – there are, despite partially divergent terminology, surprisingly similar notions of the general goals of governance.[10] These different perspectives can be integrated using the following formula. Modern political systems must have four objectives:

1. *Security*. The security goal is primarily related to safeguarding the population and the territory in question against the risk of war in general (defence function) and the provision of internal protection, i.e. safeguarding individuals against the risk of crimes and the destruction of the environment (protective function). In this sense, reducing external and internal threats to the security of human beings and their environment is one of the core goals of governance.

2. *Rule of law*. Governance is expected to provide legal certainty – defined as norms and their applications that are public, relatively stable, consistent, and prospective – and legal equity, i.e. the principle that like cases are treated alike (see e.g. Böckenförde 1969). Whereas the rule of law as a general principle applies to all kinds of issue areas, it is especially important in the economic sphere where it helps to make markets possible (North 1981). Moreover, the political meaning of the principle of the rule of law is directed against the arbitrary use of political power and the violation of human rights in general.

3. *Identity and channels of participation*. Governance is expected to (re)produce a symbolic system of reference and the communicative infrastructure within which a sense of collective civil identity can develop. Against this background a public sphere can develop and channels of participation in collective decision-making can be established.

4. *Social welfare*. The social welfare goal refers to market corrections through which the effects of economic crises are reduced and social inequalities at least contained. Encouraging economic growth and curbing social inequalities by state interventions with a view to fostering general material prosperity seems to be a major goal of modern political systems.

These four objectives are "normative goods," as they are regarded by most people – at least in the Western world – as valuable and desirable; at the same time, they are "functional goods," as in the long run the non-attainability of one or more of these objectives may lead to political crisis. Functionality and normativity are here bound together to the extent that the goals of governance necessarily do have a normative status and thus affect recognition.

To be sure, the *goals of governance*[11] are not constant or exogenously determined; they are time-specific and space-specific. Governance goals have clearly expanded (and only occasionally shrunk) in the course of history. This expansion of governance goals was accompanied by a growth of the state apparatus, reflecting the national constellation. In spite of revolutions, counter-revolutions, and restoration, and in spite of devastating civil and international wars, the expansion of state activities and the size of the state apparatus happened to be more or less linear. In the early sixteenth century, at the beginning of the absolutist period in France, around 12,000 people – that is, 0.0006 per cent of the total population of around 20 million – were state servants (cf. Braudel 1992: 549). This proportion grew to around 1.25 per cent in 1905 (i.e. 500,000 employees with a population of around 40 million; cf. Hobsbawm 1992: 99) and to well over 20 per cent in 1980 (Bruder and Dose 1992: 277). Simultaneously, the goals of state activities expanded. Only the post-Second World War welfare states aimed at a full set of governance goals including security, legal certainty, channels of participation, and social welfare. In the sixteenth and seventeenth centuries, the early *absolutist territorial state* (an ideal type of which is represented by absolutist France under Louis XIV) focused on internal and external security as the major goal of governance. The *constitutional nation-state* (ideal type: England during the Regency period of the Hanoverians) established the rule of law and thus provided the legal certainty that made a surge in economic growth and efficiency possible in the eighteenth century. The nineteenth century saw the rise of political communities that increasingly developed a sense of collective identity and demanded more participation in public decision-making. As a result, the *liberal-democratic state* (ideal type: the United States during the presidency of Woodrow Wilson) came to the fore. Finally, significant state intervention in market processes to reduce crisis-proneness of the economy and to increase social security (ideal type: the Scandinavian states) led to the *welfare state* in the course of the twentieth century. It is thus clear that governance goals are not static; they change over time, are partially discursively constructed, partially reflective of interest and power constellations, and in fact have increased in number.

The fully developed modern nation-state of the twentieth century can thus be grasped as a three-dimensional political constellation containing the following:

1. A legitimate monopoly of force, which is needed to maintain internal autonomy and which determines the size of the territory in which it can collect taxes (*resources*);
2. Recognition by other states – at least in principle – on the basis of minimum constitutional standards as well as recognition by the national society (*recognition*);
3. A minimum degree of public-interest orientation (*goals of governance*).

Although these three dimensions of modern political systems, in general terms, need not necessarily converge in *one* political organization, the *nation-state* (as one historically specific manifestation) represents a configuration in which each dimension supports the other by converging in one organization. Recognition depends upon the attainment of goals; the attainment of goals depends upon the availability of resources; and the availability of resources depends upon recognition.

The nation-state as the dominant political system of modern times, however, depends on a contextual condition. It is based on a high level of congruence between social and political spaces. The congruence of national society and nation-state is thus the socio-economic and sociocultural prerequisite for the "national constellation," in which all three dimensions of political systems converge in one political organization. It is in this respect that globalization or societal denationalization challenges the national constellation. A growing incongruence of social and political spaces undermines the cohesion of the national constellation as a whole. To be sure, sovereignty, as the legal concept expressing external recognition, has always been analytically distinct from the effectiveness of governance and the state's resources. Although within the national constellation these dimensions are interdependent, they can none the less be analytically separated. In this respect, Robert O. Keohane (1993: 93) is correct in stating that the "problem that international interdependence poses in the first instance for governments is not that it directly threatens their formal sovereignty or even their autonomy, but that it calls into questions their effectiveness." However, the qualifying "in the first instance" is of the utmost significance here. Purely formal sovereignty in the absence of material resources and a governing capacity is always extremely precarious.

Two clarifications are required. First, the fully developed modern nation-state described above represents an *ideal type*. States in the real world show significant variance when it comes to the degree to which recognition, resources, and the realization of governance goals are developed. There have been, and still are, so-called nation-states that do not even qualify as such, according to the above criteria. There have been states ridden by civil war that were still acknowledged without question by other states (for instance, America in the American Civil War). There have been states whose monopoly of force was exploited more or less exclusively for private purposes without any direct danger to the monopoly of force or to the recognition of the state as such by other states (for instance, Rhodesia in the initial period of White minority government). There are also states with internal autonomy and a certain degree of public-interest orientation without broad international acceptance (for instance, Taiwan since Chiang Ching-kuo). Finally, there are states that do badly on all three counts, as so-called *failed states* amply demonstrate. However, these deviations have been perceived and discussed as deficits and problems for modern states in all such cases. The *nation-state* has been characterized by the convergence of a monopoly of force, internal and external recognition, and policies displaying a public-interest orientation in one political organization, even if in specific cases this has only been an approximation – and sometimes not even that. In this sense, the nation-state differs taxonomically from other types of political systems such as empires, city-states and city-associations (such as the Hanseatic League) that had emerged in the Dark Ages but as political systems proved inferior to the territorial state and, by extension, the nation-state.

Second, one reason for the superiority of the nation-state over other institutional alternatives has arguably been its capacity to realize governance goals more effectively (see Spruyt 1994). Employing a concept of political systems, which contains the notion of goal attainment and thus ascribes a public-interest orientation to nation-states, invites criticism. Klaus Dieter Wolf (2000) argues that this perspective naïvely conceptualizes the nation-state as a problem-solving agency for the good of the society writ large.[12] For a number of reasons, however, the emphasis on the governance goals does not necessarily imply such a benign conception of the state and modern political systems, respectively. To begin with, governance goals are – as already mentioned – discursively constructed and the result of political struggles. Hence, governance goals reflect social asymmetries and thus a social purpose that must not be identical with the current state of normative political theory.[13] There is no question that economic actors often play a privileged role in the construction of governance goals. Economic actors are even more privileged when it comes to decision-making about the realization of these goals. The policies carried out, therefore, to a large extent indeed reflect the needs of the economy (which are not always identical with those of the society in general) and the particular interests of powerful economic actors (Lindblom 1977; Offe 1973). Moreover, the linkage of the definition of modern political systems with a minimum of public-interest orientation does not imply that the agents who act in the name of the state – the executive and the administration – must be altruists; of course, they are not – as is amply proved by endless tales of abuse of official authority by dignitaries in any number of states. Nor, finally, does the linkage of the definition of modern political systems with a minimum of public-interest orientation imply that the autonomous political organization as such – the political–administrative system and the political class as a whole – does not have interests of its own. Of course, it does have such interests: it is especially interested in maximizing its resources and in securing the monopoly of force, and thus maintaining a high degree of autonomy from society and other states (see Wolf 2000). However, these agents of the political systems are embedded in an institutional structure that is to some extent bound to the public interest. This institutional "interest of the state in itself" (Offe 1975) is related to the attainment of governance goals, to the stated purpose of the organization.[14] The state thus consists of executives, a political–administrative system (political class plus upper bureaucracy), and a larger institutional structure with inscribed governance goals. These three components together determine and balance out the "interests of states." State behaviour and governmental activities are thus driven by these state interests, the needs of the economy, and the particular interests of powerful economic actors, as well as the societal interests that are reflected in the governance goals. In this sense, the public-interest orientation of the nation-state is by no means dominant; it is only one dimension of it – albeit a necessary one – as it is of political systems in a more general sense.

In sum, the three dimensions of modern political systems are synergetic as long as social and political spaces are congruent. The national constellation is a configuration with mutually supportive elements that could persist in a world in which political and social spaces were congruent. It is, therefore, not sufficient to diagnose that, in the age of societal denationalization, the governing capacity of the nation-state decreases whereas formal sovereignty in the form of recognition by other states remains untouched. On the contrary, it is necessary to ask questions that take into account the interdependence of the three dimensions of modern political systems in a context in which the congruence of social and political spaces becomes fainter. What elements of the nation-state are challenged through societal denationalization and what kind of political responses can be observed (see the next section)? What could a multi-level system of governance look like (see pp. 70–74)? What does this mean for the goals of governance – that is, security, the rule of law, legitimacy, and social welfare (see pp. 74–76)?

Challenges of, and responses to, denationalization

The term "societal denationalization" is preferable to "globalization" for a number of reasons. First, the term "societal denationalization" does not convey a problematic notion of absolute de-bordering and takes into account that the relative intensification of many cross-border transactions has taken place only within the OECD world:[15] 84 per cent of world trade is transacted between countries inhabited by approximately 28 per cent of the world population. This OECD focus is even more evident if one looks at foreign direct investments: over 91 per cent of all foreign direct investments between 1980 and 1991 went to OECD countries and the ten most important threshold countries (Hirst and Thompson 1996: 67).[16] Communication flows indicate a similar concentration in OECD countries. A world map showing the distribution of Internet connections is particularly informative: it shows that even within the OECD world there are clear gravitational centres, the borders of which, however, do not coincide with national borders. Even in the USA there are extensive networks only along the two coastlines, which also include parts of Canada (see Beisheim et al. 1999: 65). Second, the "placeboundedness" of social transactions has not been transformed by what many call globalization. Sassen (1998) correctly asks why, after all, if knowledge workers can telecommute so easily, so many of the world's desktops are to be found in a few square kilometres in New York, Tokyo, London, and a few other places? Space and the borders of spaces will remain of significance in the coming age. Third, the concept of denationalization as it is used here distinguishes between interactions that regulation (societal denationalization) and actual regulation beyond the nation-state (political denationalization, see pages 62–70) and thus leaves room for studying their interactive effects. A notion of globalization that includes societal and political processes is too compound to be of any analytical use.[17]

Societal denationalization can thus be defined as the extension of social spaces, which are constituted by dense transactions, beyond national borders without being necessarily global in scope. Even though the scope of most of these cross-border transactions is, indeed, not global, they still cause a problem for national governance simply because the social space to be governed is no longer exclusively national. The degree of societal denationalization can be operationalized as the extent of cross-border transactions relative to transactions taking place within national borders. Social transactions take place whenever goods, services, and capital (constituting the issue area of economy), threats (force), pollutants (environment), signs (communication), or persons (mobility) are exchanged or commonly produced. An empirical investigation carried out against the background of this conceptualization shows that societal denationalization is not a uniform process but, rather, a jagged one that differs notably among issue areas, countries, and over time.[18]

Among the large OECD countries, societal denationalization, defined in terms of a growing significance of cross-border transactions, is most pronounced in Great Britain and Germany, and less so in the United States and Japan. Societal denationalization is in some areas as weak as assumed by sceptics. International telephone calls, for instance, do not exceed 2 per cent of all calls in any of the large OECD countries. In other areas, social transactions are already completely denationalized, especially in the consumption of cultural goods such as movies (motion pictures) (with over 90 per cent of imports). Societal denationalization is not a linear development; it has been taking place in mild forms since the 1950s. Accelerated denationalization first occurred in the 1960s with the massive deployment of nuclear weapons in the issue area of force. From the 1970s on, the growth of cross-border exchanges accelerated with respect to goods and capital, information, travel, migration, and regional environmental risks. Surprisingly, the growth of some of these exchange processes levelled off for a few years in the 1980s. Veritable denationalization thrusts, however, occurred in a number of very specific issue areas just as the growth in cross-border exchanges slowed down. The most notable developments took place with respect to global financial markets, global environmental dangers, the Internet, and organized crime. The common feature of all these more recent developments is that they concern the *integrated production* of goods and bads, rather than the mere *exchange* of goods and bads across national borders.

The causes of societal denationalization are of minor interest in our context. Although it is undoubtedly true that certain policies implemented by the United States and the United Kingdom, especially the lifting of capital controls, accelerated economic denationalization (see Helleiner 1994), it is also true that the current state of affairs was neither designed nor planned by anybody. It is the interaction between unilateral national policies, the institutionalization of a liberal economic order after the Second World War, and the development of new technologies – especially in communication and transportation – that made societal denationalization possible but also strongly emergent as a force that constitutes challenges and triggers responses.

Challenges

Seen in this way, societal denationalization undermines the national constellation. The most significant impact of societal denationalization is on the capacity of the nation-state to achieve governance goals, since effective governance depends upon the *spatial congruence* of political regulations with socially integrated areas. National governments, which are still bound by the old borders, can no longer project their policy-making capacity over the whole territory, which confines social problems (Reinicke 1998: 65). Consequently, the shift of boundaries of socially integrated areas – i.e. the place where there is some critical shift in the relative density of social transactions (see Deutsch 1969: 99) – requires an adaptation of political institutions if regulations are to remain effective. One can distinguish, again in rough historical order, four specific challenges through which the nation-state's achievement of governance goals may be diminished as a result of denationalization.

First, as national borders no longer encompass sufficient territory to function as sufficiently large markets for big companies, all national regulations that have a protective impact are challenged. Each national regulation that is not harmonized at the international level separates markets and creates a barrier for the efficient development, pursuit, and sale of goods and services. In a world in which the barriers between different markets are dissolving, research and development costs rise and product cycles shorten. Larger markets and unhindered cooperation with other enterprises are then seen as essential to remain competitive. In other words, in a denationalized world the "static efficiency costs of closure" increase (Frieden and Rogowski 1996: 35). For instance, all over the world, car manufacturers import parts that amount to over 50 per cent of the overall value of the end-product. If, owing to tariffs, these imports are more expensive in one country than in another country with a liberal trade policy, the former manufacturer will be at a significant comparative disadvantage and will press for liberalization. As another example, the nationally organized and protected organizations for post and telecommunications companies (PTTs) experienced increasing pressures from the 1980s on, when private multinational corporations (MNCs) wanted to reorganize their internal communications at the best possible value. To the extent that the relative proportion of communication costs increased, MNCs were no longer willing to accept and pay for the inefficiencies of national PTT companies. The MNCs finally succeeded in obtaining the dissolution of national monopolies in the telecommunications market. In general, economic integration will create further demands for overcoming the disadvantages of political segmentation in order to maximize the gains from economic exchange by harmonizing national policies or by common rules that prohibit nation-state intervention. These demands are due to *efficiency pressures* and express a desire for non-discrimination in the markets.

Second, political regulations may have little impact if they cover only parts of the relevant social space. A national regulation by Australia alone can do little to prevent rising cancer rates due to the depletion of atmospheric ozone. Along the same lines, Germany – for good reasons – has more severe restrictions on the distribution of racist propaganda material than many other countries. However, if someone residing in the United States feeds such material into the Internet, authorities in Germany cannot legally prohibit, let alone effectively prevent, these activities. Moreover, even the best defence policy would be of little help to China in the defence of the integrity of their south-west border if India and Pakistan engaged in a nuclear exchange. The resulting drop in *efficacy of national regulatory policies* resulting from the discrepancies between social and political spaces has given rise to demands for the coordination of regulatory policies at the international level.

Third, a regulation that does not apply to all social actors within an integrated social space can be counter-productive. In particular, policies that create costs for the production of goods may turn out to be self-defeating for the competitiveness of the area to which the policy applies. In this vein, manufacturers' associations all over the industrialized world complain at every opportunity that the social and environmental costs of production are too high. According to them, wages, social policies, environmental regulations, and corporate taxes need to be cut. Against this background, the widespread fear of a race-to-the-bottom in national social and environmental standard-setting is not surprising.[19] In the national context, this challenge benefits especially those groups that do not favour cost-intensive market-correcting or redistributive policies. On the other hand, groups in favour of redistributive policies will demand the establishment of international norms to avoid the *race-to-the-bottom dynamics*.

Fourth, effective participation in the national constellation depends on the spatial congruence between the rulers (the *state agents*) and the ruled (the national *society*).[20] Yet this notion becomes problematic as soon as the nature of the pertinent moral and political community is contested, as happens in the course of societal denationalization (see Held 1995). The rise of cross-border transactions damages the normative dignity of state borders and national identities (Schmalz-Bruns 1998: 372). If there is no *input congruence*, then a group affected by a decision but not participating in its making can be considered as being subject to extra-national determination rather than being nationally self-determined. This new form of foreign determination tends to be symmetrical and is based on manifold transborder externalities. The decisions of the British and German governments in the 1960s and 1970s, for example, not to implement certain environmental protection measures, led to acid lakes and high fish mortality in Scandinavia. Nevertheless, the Swedish fishermen were not in a position to participate even via representatives in public will-formation and decision-making in Great Britain or Germany. Against this background, demands for the enlargement of moral and political communities arise, so that the interests of all those who are affected by such decisions have an opportunity to participate in their making (*distribution of participation channels*).

The challenges involved in denationalization, and the types of policy mainly affected (at the national level) or demanded (at the international level) are listed in table 2.1.

Table 2.1 Challenges involved in denationalization

Challenge to effectiveness of national policies	Type of policy mainly affected/ demanded[a]	Example
Efficiency	Regulative/market-making policy	Protectionist policies
Efficacy	Regulative/regulative policy	Environmental policies
Race-to-the-bottom	Redistributive/regulative policy[b]	Welfare policies
Input-incongruence	Distributive policy[c]	Risk regulation

a. The policy that is affected is at the national level, whereas the policy that is demanded is at the international level.
b. It is frequently sufficient to employ a regulative policy at the international level (e.g. minimum social standards) to retain re-distributive policies at the national level. See Leibfried and Pierson (1995) and Zürn (1998a: 342–344).
c. It is a distributive policy in so far as the distribution of participation rights and channels are concerned.

Responses

These challenges to the effectiveness of national policies in attaining governance goals do not directly translate into a decline of the nation-state. The challenges are serious, yet the outcome is largely determined by political choices. Governments and other political organizations can respond to these challenges in a number of different ways. First, they may passively await the decline in effectiveness of national policies, partly because they favour the institutional status quo, partly because they can use international pressure as a pretext for furthering their own domestic goals such as deregulation. Second, regionalist parties may push for decentralization of, or even secession from, nation-states in order to exploit as flexibly as possible the opportunities offered in the denationalized environment. The rise of the Lega Nord and the revival of the Scottish National Party as well as the Parti Québécois can be related to economic and cultural denationalization and thus be interpreted as a fragmentative political response. Third, governments and other political organizations may aim at developing integrative political responses to denationalization. The incongruence between national regulations and denationalized areas of social transactions calls into question the very capacity of the nation-state to provide goods that made it successful in the first place. In this predicament, national governments and transnational actors may endeavour to regain control by establishing international and transnational or even supranational regimes, networks, and organizations for the coordination and harmonization of their policies – i.e. to set up governance systems beyond the nation-state. It is this third response to societal denationalization that may be labelled political denationalization and needs to be explored more closely here.

In general terms, governance is distinct from anarchy – the unrestricted interplay of actors driven by self-interest – in that social actors recognize the existence of obligations and feel compelled to honour them by their behaviour. Governance refers to purposive systems of norms and rules[21] and thus goals are constitutive for governance. Governance in modernity has best been provided within the nation-state by a government that claimed a monopoly of legitimate force and thus ruled by hierarchical orders. Governance took the form of *governance by government.*

The form of governance needs, however, to be distinguished from goal attainment. The goals of governance can be provided by a government, but also by governance with or without governments. All forms of governance beyond the nation-state lack a central authority or a "world state" equipped with a legitimate monopoly of the use of force.[22] Thus, governance beyond the nation-state cannot take the form of governance by government; rather, it needs to be a form of governance with governments such as we see it in international institutions, or governance without government as in transnational institutions, or supranational governance. In spite of the absence of governance by government, governance beyond the nation-state has developed significantly over the last decades. The sum of all institutional arrangements beyond the nation-state makes up regional or global governance systems. The interplay of different forms of governance beyond the nation-state can produce polities of a new quality, as attested by the European Multi-Level Governance System.[23]

Governance with governments

Governance with many governments regulates, through intergovernmental agreements, state and non-state activities, the effects of which extend beyond national borders. The United Nations system as a whole symbolizes governance with governments, which consists essentially of three components. Central to governance with many governments are *international regimes*, defined as social institutions consisting of agreed-upon and publicly announced principles, norms, rules, procedures, and programmes that govern the interactions of actors in specific issue areas. As such, regimes contain specific regulations and give rise to recognized social practices in international society.[24] Regimes comprise both substantive and procedural rules and are thus distinct from mere *intergovernmental networks*, which frequently include only procedural rules. Such networks meet on a regular basis and may develop coordinated responses to specific situations, but they do not govern behaviour in a certain issue area for a prolonged period of time.[25] Other components of international governance are *international organizations* that are material entities and can be the infrastructure for both international regimes and intergovernmental networks.[26] Any of these components of international governance beyond the nation-state can be regional or global in scope. The United Nations system is the most important element of governance with governments, comprising formal international organizations (above all, the United Nations), a number of intergovernmental networks, and numerous UN-based international regimes.

A first measure of the extent of governance with governments is the number of international governmental organizations (IGOs). Until the early 1980s this figure grew continuously to a total of 378, reflecting the permanent growth in the importance of cross-border transactions. In the late 1980s, as the growth of some cross-border transactions slowed down, the overall number of international organizations declined rapidly to less than three hundred. Only recently has the number of international organizations begun to increase again. Currently, the number of IGOs is still below the 1980 figure, unless IGO emanations are included.[27]

The number of international organizations is only a very rough measure of the development of international governance. It is easily conceivable that a relatively constant number of IGOs has produced a higher regulatory output and thus strengthened international governance. Indeed, the overall number of multilateral treaties deposited at the United Nations has grown in a linear fashion from less than 150 in 1960 to well over 400 in 1998. The same applies to the annual ratification of multilateral treaties (Hirschi, Serdült, and Widmer 1999: 40). This remarkable growth pattern is replicated on the level of different issue areas. The number of new international environmental treaties and agreements has grown continuously since the beginning of the century: whereas, until the 1970s, on average every 5 years brought about 5 treaties, this number has grown to about 25 from the 1980s on (see Beisheim et al. 1999: 351). A very similar pattern applies to the development of new international economic treaties and agreements (Beisheim et al. 1999: 353). In the field of culture and communication, the regulatory output of existing international regimes, such as the International Telecommunication Union (ITU)-based telecommunication regime, again shows steady growth up until the 1980s.[28] This pattern differs slightly only in the field of international security. The regulatory output of the nuclear non-proliferation regime and the Security Council showed no clear pattern for a long time and was rather erratic. Since the end of the 1980s, however, the number of Security Council resolutions has grown dramatically. This applies also to conventions and declarations on the protection of human rights (Beisheim et al. 1999: 343–347).

The rise of international agreements is accompanied by a growing

intensity of transgovernmental relations.[29] Different state agencies –
regulatory agencies, courts, executives, and increasingly also legislatures
– are networking with their counterparts abroad. Learning from counterparts can be considered to be the major goal of these transgovernmental exchanges. Ann-Marie Slaughter, who sees this development as
the most significant for understanding the new world order, describes its
core very well:

> ... the preferred instrument of cooperation is the memorandum of understand-
> ing, in which two or more regulatory agencies set forth and initial terms for an
> ongoing relationship. Such memorandums are not treaties; they do not engage
> the executive or the legislature in negotiations, deliberation, or signature. Rather,
> they are good-faith agreements, affirming ties between regulators' agencies based
> on their like-minded commitment to getting results. (Slaughter 1997: 190)

At first sight, the quantitative rise of governance with many governments does not seem to affect the national constellation in qualitative
terms. The *constitutional principles* of the Westphalian system of sovereign states are intergovernmental in that states represented by their governments recognize each other as sovereign states, thus laying the ground
for international society (see Bull 1977). However, a closer look reveals
two anomalies. First, the rise of issue-area specific international regimes
has – in addition to elements of the recognition dimension of political
systems – moved parts of the governance dimension of political systems
to the international level. The international recognition to govern in a
given territory, which is constitutive for the Westphalian system, must
not be confused with international governance, which is a much more
recent development. Second, it is still true that, since the early nineteenth century – many see the Congress of Vienna after the Napoleonic
Wars as the starting point – international institutions have assisted states
in the attainment of governance goals. What is new about more recent
developments is not only the sheer amount of governance with governments but also the types and objects of regulation. Earlier international
institutions regulated the interactions between states, be it in the field of
security (for instance, alliance or arms treaties) or in the economy (reduction of tariffs). The current rise of international institutions is mainly
to assist states in regulating societal actors. Regarding the governance
goal of reducing external and internal threats to the security of human
beings and their environment, most international environmental regimes
exemplify this development. In addition, new issues are taken up. In the
field of economy, the development of the General Agreement on Tariffs
and Trade (GATT) regime is a case in point. The early GATT removed
government intervention at the borders – that is, tariffs on manufactured

goods. Over time, this increased the importance of non-tariff barriers, thus inducing demands for a new type of market-making regulations that focused on behind-the-border issues. The Tokyo Round of negotiations (1973–1979) began to deal with non-tariff barriers such as anti-dumping, government subsidies, government procurement, and customs and licensing procedures. The results of the Uruguay Round (1986–1994) are a major step forward in this direction (see Kahler 1995).[30] International institutions have thus changed their character. They aim increasingly at regulating not only the actions of state actors but also those of societal actors. Furthermore, they rely increasingly not only on negative regulations (i.e. regulations that prohibit states from taking certain measures) but also on positive regulations (i.e. regulations that require states to take certain measures).[31] The extent and the objects of international governance no longer match the notion of the sovereign state in a national constellation.

Supranational governance

Supranational governance even more clearly contradicts the notion of a sovereign state in the national constellation. Supranational institutions develop rules that are considered superior to national law and involve servants that possess autonomy from national governments.[32] The demand for supranational governance rises to the extent that the density and scope of international governance grows. With international governance covering more and more issue areas, overlapping and colliding jurisdictions of international regulations with other international or national regulations become more likely. Supranational bodies are a logical response to resolve these collisions. Moreover, the more international regimes address behind-the-border issues, which are especially difficult to monitor and have significant impacts on societal actors, the more the question of credibility of commitments arises. A logical way to increase the credibility of commitments is to develop supranational bodies that monitor regulations and resolve conflicts (see Moravcsik 1998: 73–77).

The best-known supranational institutions that meet these expectations can be found in the European Union (EU): these are the European Commission, the European Parliament, and the European Court of Justice (ECJ).[33] The direct effect associated with the supremacy of European law over national law and the direct enforcing effect of ECJ case law through the Preliminary-Ruling Procedure of Article 177 EC guarantees European law undoubted validity in all member states. Hence, Community provisions are an inseparable part of the body of law valid for EU citizens (Weiler 1993). Other elements of the EU polity also contain elements of supranationality. In 1996, for instance, in the multi-level system of the EU there were 409 committees active in the implementation of general Council decisions and which, in fact, enjoy extensive interpretative freedom in their work (see Falke 1996; Wessels 1998). The committee members are mainly experts and representatives of concerned interest groups, as well as national civil servants selected by their governments. However, the quality and adequacy of these committees' decisions usually meet with approval (see Eichener 1996) and can even be interpreted as an element of "deliberative supranationalism" (Joerges and Neyer 1997). Given that the EU is the most supranational institution, it is quite significant that the total number of EU directives, regulations, and decisions increased from 36 in 1961 to 347 in 1970 and 627 in 1980. While the number of EU rules has remained quite constant since then, with a temporary peak of almost 800 in 1986, it is noteworthy that the relative weight of EU legislation has clearly increased in comparison to national legislation in Germany, France, and Great Britain. The yearly national legislative output has remained more or less constant since the 1960s (Beisheim et al. 1999: 328–330).

Beyond Europe, supranational institutions are still rare. However, even here there have been some notable recent developments. First of all, the World Trade Organization (WTO) brought in new monitoring and dispute-settlement procedures to deal more effectively with behind-the-border issues. The Dispute Settlement Body and the Appellate Body seem to evolve towards a supranational institution, at least in relation to the "Agreement on the Application of Sanitary and Phytosanitary Measures,"[34] and thus to some extent resemble the supranational role of the European Court (Godt 1998). Moreover, the Rome Statute of the International Criminal Court of 1998, which seeks to establish a court of justice as permanent institution, also indicates a move in the direction of supranationality. This court "shall have the power to exercise its jurisdiction over persons for the most serious crimes of international concern (...)."[35] Finally, in as much as infringements of rights can be brought directly before independent bodies by individuals, as in the case of the "Civil Covenant," the "Race-Discrimination Convention," and the "Convention against Torture" (see Liese 1998), one may also speak of an element of supranationality. Given these very recent developments and the effects these agreements may have on other issue areas,[36] it is fair to conclude that the extent to which institutions with supranational elements have emerged in global politics transcends the expectations of even only ten years ago.

Governance without government

Although the role of *governance without government* has increased over the last two decades, it is arguably still less significant than government with many governments. To be sure, the number of transnational organizations has grown significantly over the last decades.[37] However, some of these organizations are standard-setting associations that work as part of a larger international institution established by intergovernmental agreement, while others are part of an issue-area specific policy network with national governments still in the position to accept or veto agreements. As Thomas Risse-Kappen (1995: 30) puts it: "The more regulated the interstate relationship by cooperative international institutions in the particular issue area, the more are transnational activities expected to flourish." Nevertheless, in some issue areas the roles of transnational regimes, organizations, and networks are remarkable. To the extent to which governance without government gains autonomy from states and governance with governments even becomes dependent on transnational relations, the deviation from the notion of state sovereignty in the national constellation becomes evident. These developments indicate both transnationalization and privatization.

- The *lex mercatoria* is a good example of such a development.[38] It is an established *transnational regime* for the arbitration of cross-border business disputes with the aim of bypassing national courts (see e.g. Cutler 1999). Although its roots are pre-modern, the *lex mercatoria* seems to have grown in importance in recent years. In some cases, parties to the business transaction deliberately prefer to settle disputes on the basis of the *lex mercatoria* instead of the nation-state-based system of "choice of law" (Dasser 1991). Moreover, national courts regularly back arbitration panels that use *lex mercatoria* norms, because the party rejecting arbitration awards loses most often in national courts. There are other important transnational regimes as, for instance, the development of some of the technical standards related to the Internet such as the Transmission Control Protocol/Internet Protocol (TCP/IP) protocol. The Internet Engineering Task Force (IETF), a sub-organization of the Internet Society (ISOC), developed the TCP/IP protocol. This issue network is open to all users and being on the mailing list constitutes membership. Decisions are made on the basis of discourses in different forums, which are regulated by a number of procedural rules. Balloting takes place by a strongly qualified majority and after the new standard has demonstrated its effectiveness in practice. The decisions are then made public via the mailing lists (see e.g. Hofmann 1998).
- One may further distinguish two types of *transnational organizations*. Some transnational organizations provide the organizational and infrastructural support for transnational regimes. The International Chamber of Commerce and the ISOC are examples of about 600 such organizations (Shanks, Jacobsen, and Kaplan 1996: 596). Other transnational organizations aim to influence governmental policies by addressing

transnational public opinion. Greenpeace and Amnesty International are only the best-known of this species. In this way, non-governmental organizations (NGOs) exert some control on governments from outside the country.[39]

- Transnational organizations interact with each other and create *networks* that can be seen as the constituents for international and transnational policies. Against this background it comes as no surprise that, in more recent analyses, particular attention is paid to these transnational networks. Their role seems to be especially salient within the field of international environmental politics. After the admission of transnational NGOs to international negotiations, the latter received an impetus which distinguished them from conventional intergovernmental negotiations, while at the same time giving so-called epistemic communities a more prominent status (Adler and Haas 1992; Princen and Finger 1994). It is owing to these epistemic communities that, as opposed to simple bargaining, deliberative elements are at less of a disadvantage than is commonly the case, and that particular interests are balanced by public or diffuse interests (see Gehring 1995).[40] In this sense one may speak of the emergence of transnational sectoral publics and "sectoral demoi" (Abromeit and Schmidt 1998).

This brief examination of the development of different types of institutions for governance beyond the nation-state – be they transnational, international, or even supranational – shows that, parallel to the growth of societal denationalization, governance beyond the nation-state has increased. In particular, the shape of more recent international, transnational, and supranational institutions is hardly compatible with the traditional notion of state sovereignty in the national constellation. Governments and other political organizations do not merely sit back and watch denationalization and the decline in the effectiveness of unilateral policies. They respond to the challenges by setting up new institutions, and this should not be neglected in the analysis and understanding of postnational governance. The national constellation – that is, the convergence of resources, recognition, and the realization of governance goals in one political organization (the nation-state) – seems to be in a process of transformation into a postnational constellation. The nation-state is no longer the only site of authority and the normativity that accompanies it.

This transformation process itself can be separated into different stages. The first stage can be regarded most plausibly as a more or less *unintended, indirect outcome* of political responses following (perceived) functional demands. The permanent deepening of some international regimes, so that they now deal with positive interventions into the society and with behind-the-border issues, is part of this first stage. The same seems to be true of the need for credible commitments in designing these more ambitious regimes and the development of supranational bodies to deal with collisions between different regulations.[41] The second stage of the transformation is much more *reflective*. When society and political actors begin to comprehend the change, they begin to include issues of transboundary identity and transboundary ethics in their considerations. Pressures to improve the life conditions for people of other nationality and race that live in other countries thousands of miles away, as well as the debate about European identity and democracy, are first signs of this reflective stage in the transformation process.

The new architecture

The state as the most important political system in the national constellation has been characterized by the coincidence of the dimensions of political systems in *one* political organization – that is, the nation-state. The monopoly of force and the ability to collect taxes, the authority to recognize states as such, and the capability to design policies that show a certain degree of public-interest orientation, could all be found at the level of the nation-state. The challenges of, and responses to, denationalization seem, however, to transform this national constellation.

Attainment of governance goals

Nation-states have increasing difficulties in designing unilateral policies that are of use in attaining the governance goals of security, legal certainty, legitimacy, and social welfare. The incongruence of political and social spaces leads systematically to challenges to the effectiveness of national policies (pp. 59–62). Governments and other political groups react to these unintended consequences of social change that were partially encouraged by national policies. The primary response is the formation of intergovernmental institutions that help to readjust political and social spaces and thus to regain the effectiveness of policies, either by directly regulating cross-border activities or, more often, by coordinating national decisions to a large extent. Hence, systems of interest mediation (i.e. the institutions which transform interests into political demands) that are restricted to the nation-state lose importance, especially since political actors such as national executives, who play at both levels, can use their privileged position for manipulation. A secondary response for more powerful interest groups therefore is to participate directly at the level of international institutions, which happens increasingly, as indicated by the rise of transnational organizations and transnational networks. In this sense, the formulation of policies for most of the issue areas affected by the challenges of denationalization has been transferred to levels beyond the nation-state. At these levels, state agents are the most important actors but not the sole ones. Transnationally organized interest groups and non-governmental actors do play a role in agenda-setting and, to a lesser extent, in actual negotiations.[42] The family of international organizations that makes up the United Nations system is probably the most important forum for the formulation of policies serving the four governance goals at the global level.

As mentioned earlier, the rise of international institutions is not the only response to societal denationalization. One can also observe outright resistance to societal denationalization, as exemplified by some of the extreme right-wing parties in Western Europe. Moreover, the revival of regionalist movements can be also seen as a response to the problems and challenges that are posed by societal denationalization to the effectiveness of nation-states. Regionalist movements such as those in Scotland, Quebec, and Catalonia increasingly justify their preference for (more) independence by the need to make their interests and points of view in international forums and by the related obsolescence of nation-states (Zürn and Lange 1999). To the extent that those movements aim at very open and non-exclusive political organizations that are constitutionally bound to political institutions beyond the nation-state, these movements are more than just cases of political fragmentation. They may then also be interpreted as cases of a new sovereignty and as movements towards a postnational constellation.

Resources

The changes in the dimension of goal attainment should, however, by no means be regarded as indications of the end of the nation-state. First, the developments described apply only to denationalized issue areas, while others still follow the logic of the national constellation. Second, and more importantly, it is hard to see how governance goals can be achieved without the nation-state, even in strongly denationalized issue areas. To put it in terms of functional theories, the increasing inability of an institution to fulfil a function can be seen as an indicator of its impending extinction only if there are rival institutions that can be expected to fulfil that function more efficiently (Spruyt 1994). For instance, the elimination of the problems relating to global financial markets, organized crime, or global environmental risks is hardly conceivable without nation-states. In particular, for the implementation of policies the nation-state seems, owing to the control of resources (based on its legal monopoly of force and its capacity to raise taxes), to be indispensable. Even with respect to this dimension some notable changes have taken place. The high degree of cooperation between governmental agencies and the rise of transgovernmental networks indicates that many governments see their counterparts in other countries less as competitors in a hostile environment than as allies in the search for effective policy instruments and efficient administration.

Recognition

The most complicated and important changes seem to take place with regard to recognition. External recognition as a sovereign state, once attained, was, in principle, valid for eternity. States disappeared only for internal developments or for brute force that circumvented the principle of sovereignty. Nowadays, the recognition of a state increasingly seems to depend upon its respect of human rights and fundamental freedoms that can be claimed by individuals at the European Court of Human Rights and, in a more circumscribed fashion, before UN human-rights bodies. The pertinent pressure on states like Cuba and China has increased. In extreme cases, the violation of human rights can even be regarded as a justification for intervention – the war in Kosovo may be seen as a case in point. Moreover, the growing use of international observers at national elections indicates a trend towards making critical elections into global events (Rosenau 1997: 259), and the concept of "good governance" is now also used for evaluations of national policies through international institutions such as the World Bank (1997). In the light of these developments, it seems that the recognition of a state as such tends now to be less a one-shot constitutive act and increasingly the result of a *permanent legitimacy monitoring*. Thomas M. Franck (1992: 50) pointed out a few years ago: "We are witnessing a sea change in international law, as a result of which the legitimacy of each government someday will be measured definitely by international rules and processes" (see also Friedman 1996).

Moreover, the *subject* performing this monitoring function is today not only the international society of states but increasingly also an *emergent transnational society*, as well as supranational bodies that act with some autonomy from national governments (see pp. 66–67). Supranational bodies judge on the basis of reason whether deviant state behaviour is defensible. Transnational society, then, in outrageous or in repetitive cases, may question the legitimacy of a nation-state. Along these lines, UN Secretary-General Kofi Annan also adopted the perspective that states must serve peoples. "If they fail to do so and permit serious human rights abuses," he said, "they open themselves to justified intervention by the international community in the form of the UN itself."[43] In this scenario, however, actions of the United Nations depend on an empowerment by the society of states *and* the transnational society. Taking this notion further, the authority that assigns sovereignty – that is, the exclusive right to set or adopt the rules for a given territory – seems to change: it is not any more only states but also transnational groups that are essential in recognizing nation-states as legitimate. What seem to be in the process of changing in world politics are thus both the criteria for recognition and the subject with the authority to recognize a state.

How is it possible to talk about institutions that assign states rights, as long as states maintain their superiority in resources? Is it not the capacity for the enforcement of norms and rules that is decisive? Speculating further by extrapolating current trends, good reasons can be advanced for the position that the traditional linkage of governance to a sanction-endowed, superordinate central body derives more from our (backward-looking) nation-state-marked tradition of thought than from a forward-looking analysis of postnational political systems. To begin with, law-like rules have a compliance-pull of their own. It is therefore possible to envisage beyond the nation-state a community of law (*Rechtsgemeinschaft*) without a community of enforcement (*Zwangsgemeinschaft*), to use this early characterization of the EU by Walter Hallstein.[44] Moreover, "good governance" can often increase compliance with regulations without resort to enforcement at all. Non-compliance by nation-states is rarely the result of deliberate cheating. Quite often, compliance can be induced by a number of institutional features short of enforcement (see Chayes and Chayes 1995). In fact, the stress on the connection between compulsion and the facticity[45] of the norms is almost always combined with a preference for hierarchical enforcement. It does not take into account the possibility of horizontal, reciprocal compulsion deriving from social interdependence. To be sure, the civilizing effect of a monopoly of force cannot be overestimated. In governance beyond the nation-state, the decentralized sanctioning bodies, which act in the name of transnational society and supranational bodies – the democratic welfare states – are, however, qualitatively different agents from the force-wielders of medieval society. Nation-states in the OECD world are internally civilized and do not necessarily require an external "Leviathan." In the postnational constellation, then, the question arises whether enforcement necessarily needs to be hierarchical. The EU experience over the last decade has made it clear that governance with significant rule compliance is, in certain circumstances, possible even without a force-equipped, hierarchically superior agent. In this sense, in a denationalized world it may be not only policy formation that will be horizontalized but also its control and enforcement. In other words, the horizontalization of governance can be accompanied by a horizontalization of enforcement (Zürn and Wolf 1999).

About the future of governance

Multilevel systems of governance will be constituted by the interplay of different levels and organizations, with each level and organization unable to work unilaterally. Governance in the postnational constellation will be the result of complex arrangements of governing institutions with and without national governments. In this postnational constellation, nation-states will not relinquish their resources such as the monopoly of force or the privilege to collect taxes in a given territory. Nevertheless, although the nation-state will play a significant role in multilevel systems of governance, it will no longer be the paramount political institution, but one among others. Not only will policy formulation in most denationalized issue areas be transferred from the nation-state to loci beyond the nation-state but also legitimacy will no longer be conferred by nation-states (externally) and national societies (internally). To a greater extent than ever before, transnational society and supranational institutions will play a decisive role in the recognition of nation-states. The concrete mode of politics within such a polity can still vary to a large extent, as it does among and within nation-states.[46] In any case, political systems themselves will become functionally differentiated in the postnational constellation and it is likely that the convergence of the dimensions of political systems in one political organization will come to an end.

Is this good news? Will governance by multilevel systems of governance deliver the goods? Will the provision of security, legal certainty, channels of participation, and social welfare be comparable to the standards set by the national welfare state? One has to be sceptical about that. As in any political system, multilevel systems also embody rule and authority and thus may in normative terms turn out to be more questionable than appears at first sight. First of all, the above sketch of a postnational constellation is based on an extrapolation of current trends. Whereas multilevel systems of governance may be functional, the transition from the "national equilibrium" to the "postnational equilibrium" may be fraught with problems and disadvantages with no guarantee that a new and workable equilibrium will even be reached. More importantly, the postnational constellation, even when fully developed, may be deficient when it comes to the attainment of governance goals.

It is the postnational *relationship* between nation-states, multinational economic actors, and (national and transnational) civil society that will determine the degree to which governance goals can be realized. Therefore, the configuration of interests among, and the relative capabilities of, these actors will set a constraining framework for political outcomes in the postnational constellation. These outcomes will also depend on new ideas and specific institutional designs, which, in turn, may modify the constraints. When thinking about the attainment of governance goals through multilevel systems of governance in the postnational constellation, it seems advisable to start with a rough analysis of interests and power.

Multinational enterprises and civil society coincide to some extent in their interests when it comes to security and legal certainty. In transnational economic spaces the economic interests in waging war are negligible. Most multinational enterprises are also interested in low crime rates – that is, internal security. Given these interests, the opportunities of political classes or specific national governments to benefit from wars or from crime are minimal. In addition, economic actors have a strong interest in the provision of regulations that ensure legal certainty in the market-place and thus increase economic efficiency. Although multinational enterprises have no intrinsic economic motives in the rule of law including human rights in general, they also usually have no economic incentives against it, especially since property rights and non-discrimination as economic fundamentals are embedded in the rule of law.[47] Moreover, when it comes to the transnational rule of law, transnational society (with respect to human rights and democratic elections) and supranational institutions (with respect to non-discrimination in the economic sphere) are already in a good position to defend it. Hence, political classes and national governments can gain little and lose a lot when they use their resources to circumvent the rule of law. Therefore, one may hypothesize that *the attainment of the governance goals of security and the rule of law in the postnational constellation will be at least as successful as in the national constellation.* A reduced incidence of wars among denationalized countries, the improvement of human-rights records in the OECD world, and the rise of the strongest international institutions in the field of economic legal certainty can serve as at least fragmentary evidence in support of this proposition.[48]

The attainment of the governance goals of effective participation channels and social welfare will be much more difficult in the postnational constellation. This second proposition is based on the argument that transnational public interests lack the social prerequisites for effective organization to achieve these goals and that the influence in international institutions is thus distorted in favour of state agents (political classes) and economic interests. It is, therefore, less surprising that state agents do not show signs of serious resistance against the movement towards postnational systems of governance than it would appear by merely looking at economic globalization and the pressures to reduce state expenditures. Although economic actors traditionally have little intrinsic interest in welfare policies, and state agents traditionally had little interest in democratic participation and control, these governance goals became legitimate standards of appropriate ways of policy-making in the last century of the national constellation. This may again change in the postnational constellation. The dependence of political systems on the provision of all governance goals varies according to the extent to which public interests are constitutionally embedded. Free elections, discursive will-formation, party systems that favour parties representing a broad range of interests, and majority decisions are mechanisms through which the political participation of broad segments of the public and the pursuit and enactment of welfare policies became possible. Only through these mechanisms has it been possible to strengthen a broadened public-interest orientation of nation-states in the nineteenth and twentieth centuries. These mechanisms not only are lacking beyond the nation-state – the level where most policies are formulated in multilevel systems of governance – they are, in addition, dependent on sociocultural prerequisites such as the "we-feeling" as a political community. Whereas it seems to me to be premature categorically to rule out transnational political communities, it can safely be stated that they do not yet exist to their full extent.[49] Against this background it can be expected that multilevel systems will be less majoritarian, less territorially organized, and less controlled by public interests than has been possible in the national constellation. Moreover, redistributive and strongly interventionist policies will be more scarce; policies will rely heavily on market-compatible instruments and on private agencies.[50]

There are many questions and issues relating to these expectations and trends. Is it really possibly to conceive a postnational polity that lacks a compliance-enforcing centre? Do the expectations about the future attainment of governance goals really hold when more careful and methodologically sound studies are carried out? If so, do these trends reflect structural deficits of multilevel systems of governance or the problems of transformation? What can be done about it? Being sceptical about structural explanations and believing in the importance of social reflectivity, I tend to believe that civil society and public interests will, in the long run, find ways to bind postnational governance more closely back to the attainment of governance goals. If so, one of the most important tasks will certainly be to study in what ways, and to what extent, new ideas and intelligent institutional designs can be developed that help to avoid the deficient attainment of governance goals in the postnational constellation.

Notes

1. This project was initiated by an invitation from Richard Appelbaum, Bill Felstiner, and Volkmar Gessner (2000) to develop an argument about the globalization of law. This article represents a significant extension and revision of the first-fruit of the project. The invitation to work at the Centre of Advanced Studies at the Norwegian Academy of Sciences offered a unique opportunity to pursue this project further in an intellectually stimulating environment that has protected me from the usual distractions. For this rare opportunity, I very much want to thank Arild Underdal and the other colleagues at the Centre. In addition, my thanks go to all participants in this project of the United Nations University who provided me with helpful comments at a meeting in Paris, and to Bernhard Zangl. Volker Rittberger, in addition, provided extremely helpful comments and recommendations for revising the manuscript. Last but not least, many thanks to Vicki May for brushing up my English.

2. See for instance contributions to Holm and Sørensen (1995), Krasner (1999), Litfin (1997), contributions to Lyons and Mastanduno (1995), Rosenau (1997), Sørensen (1999), and Thomson (1995).

3. See for instance Sassen (1998), Hirsch (1995), and Held et al. (1999).

4. The argument of this contribution builds on the typology of states introduced by Sørensen (1998), who distinguishes between pre-Westphalian, Westphalian, and post-Westphalian states. Most of this contribution discusses the transformation of West-phalian to post-Westphalian states without questioning that, in many parts of the world, pre-Westphalian states may be still dominant.

5. Krasner (1993) is, therefore, clearly right when he emphasizes that it is a major over-simplification to see the Peace of Westphalia as a turning point in history. Sovereignty has been contested for many centuries, before and since 1648, and has never prevailed in a pure form. It thus seems premature to conclude from some observations about deviations from the principle of sovereignty that sovereignty is in decline.

6. The distinction between internal and external "recognition" must not be confused with the one between internal and external "sovereignty" (see e.g. Rittberger 1995; Reinicke 1998). Whereas internal/external recognition refers to different "recognizing subjects," the more traditional distinction refers to internal authority versus independence from external resources, as already implied in Morgenthau's definition (Morgenthau 1967).

7. See Suchmann (1995: 574) for a similar definition relating to organizations in general.

8. Resolution 1514 (XV), 14.12.60.

9. Jackson (1990) coined the term "quasi-states" for these organizations. See also Knieper (1991) and especially Sørensen (1997) on this issue.

10. Historical state theory refers to the "minimum activities of the state," which include warfare, state-building, the protection of individuals, and the collection of taxes (Tilly 1990: chap. 4). Economic theory of the state regards internal and external protection and the provision of public goods as the central "duties of the state" (Smith 1776; cf. also North 1981). Legal theory discusses the "duties (functions) for regulating human coexistence in the relevant state" and identifies peace, liberty, social security, social integration, and cooperation as these duties (Horn 1996: 22–25). Sociological theory established the classic distinction between civil (guaranteed individual liberties), political (participation in political power), and social (minimum social security) subjective rights – that is, legitimate demands on the state (Marshall 1992). In a more recent contribution, Anthony Giddens (1994: 246) discusses the reduction of force and violence, the challenging of arbitrary claims to power, the establishment of compensation for environmental damage, and the struggle against poverty as fundamental political orientations. In political theory, Seyla Benhabib (1996: 67) identifies legitimacy, economic

welfare, and a collective identity as the "public goods" that must be provided in modern societies. Modern political economy identifies the political regulation of the market, the provision of a public infrastructure, and sociopolitical adjustments as the "main functions" of the state within the "socio-economic sphere" (cf. Cerny 1996: 124–130; Majone 1996: 54).

11. I use the term "governance goals" for two reasons. First, it should not hastily be concluded that the attainment of these goals depends purely on the existence of a state. If we are to consider the concept of governance beyond the nation-state, then we must analyse the above objectives separately from the state. In this respect, terms such as "state functions," "state aims," "state objectives," etc. are unsatisfactory. Second, it is important to avoid teleological characterizations of the state or of governance (Kaufmann 1994: 17) without falling back on the argument that desirable and necessary state activities are historically and culturally contingent. The term "governance goals" is, I think, a better expression of the desirable middle position than, say, purpose or function (which sound like a teleological characterization) or activities (which sound completely contingent).

12. He puts forward a challenging argument according to which the rise of international institutions can be adequately interpreted as a new form of "Staatsräson" – through which states gain autonomy from society – instead of an attempt to achieve societally desirable governance goals (Wolf 2000).

13. This aspect is especially emphasized by Moravcsik's conceptualization (Moravcsik 1998) of the state in explaining European integration.

14. Organization theory emphasizes that purposes are constitutional to organizations. Bogdandy (1999: 23) makes that argument in a similar context.

15. To be sure, the term "de-bordering" is used in quite different ways. Whereas some use it in the sense of "despatialization" [especially Brock and Albert (1995), Albert (1996), and Brock (1998)], Kohler-Koch (1998) uses it in a way that, to a large extent, resembles the notion of denationalization.

16. This figure counts only the most important coastal provinces of China as "threshold countries," but not the whole of China. If China as a whole were included, its share in world trade would increase marginally but its population ratio would increase by 15 per cent. See Reinicke (1998: 39–51) for additional economic indicators showing the OECD focus of the transnational economy.

17. Instead of the distinction between societal and political denationalization, one could also use the terms "denationalization" (indicating societal processes) and "destateization" (indicating political processes). The specific feature of the nation-state has been, however, that all the three dimensions of (so to speak) statehood converged at the national level. In this sense, the defining feature of the current changes is denationalization, less destateization.

18. In a research project funded by the German Research Association, we developed 72 indicators to determine the extent of societal denationalization in different issue areas and different, large OECD countries (see Beisheim et al. 1999). The findings reported in this paragraph draw from it. For a similar undertaking with similar results, see Held et al. (1999).

19. To be sure, at least for environmental regulations this fear seems to be unsubstantiated (see Héritier, Knill, and Mingers 1996; Vogel 1995; Jänicke 1998). While there indeed seems to be a parallel drop in corporate taxes in most OECD countries, the question whether there is a downward convergence of national regulations with respect to social policies is most contested (see e.g. Garrett 1998).

20. This specific version of the principle of congruence is discussed in Held (1995: 16).

21. Rosenau (1992: 5). See also Kohler-Koch (1993), Mayer, Rittberger, and Zürn (1993), and Young (1994).

22. See Young (1978) for arguments why a world state is neither possible nor desirable.
23. See Marks et al. (1996) and Jachtenfuchs and Kohler-Koch (1996).
24. See Krasner (1983: 3). See Rittberger (1993), and Levy, Young, and Zürn (1995), for further elaborations on the definition of international regimes.
25. The distinction between international regimes and international networks is similar to the one drawn by Mayntz (1996), between networks for the management of ad hoc problems and institutions for the regulation of recurring problems.
26. The formal term is International Governmental Organizations (IGOs), as opposed to Transnational Non-Governmental Organizations (NGOs). The latter consist of any kind of professional association, such as the International Political Science Association, and also of profit-seeking NGOs – that is, multinational enterprises.
27. Emanations include those organizations that have other IGOs' names in their titles, have been created by a provision in another IGO's charter, or are a joint or internal IGO committee or an international centre or institute. See Shanks, Jacobson, and Kaplan (1996: 597). For a good treatment of the development of international organizations, see Rittberger and Zangl (1995).
28. See Zacher with Sutton (1996) and Beisheim et al. (1999: 341). In this field it is hard to assess the precise amount of regulatory output in the most recent period, since a de facto decline of ITU importance relative to other regulating agencies has taken place (see Genschel 1995).
29. See Keohane and Nye (1971) for a seminal volume that introduced, among other things, the notion of transgovernmental relations. More recently, Robert Cox's work (Cox 1992: 30) has emphasized the importance of "transnational networks that link policy-making from country to country."
30. See also Hirschi, Serdült, and Widmer (1999: 43), who demonstrate quantitatively the expansion of issue areas in which Switzerland has signed international treaties and has thus made them part of their foreign policy.
31. See Corbey (1995) and Scharpf (1996) for recent contributions using this distinction.
32. Moravcsik (1998: 67) distinguishes between "pooled sovereignty," when governments agree to decide future matters by voting procedures other than unanimity, and "delegated sovereignty," when supranational actors are permitted to take certain autonomous decisions, without an intervening interstate vote or unilateral veto. On the basis of this distinction between two subtypes of supranationality, even some intergovernmental institutions contain supranational components.
33. See Bogdandy (1999) and Neyer (1999) for a beneficial use of the term "supranational governance."
34. Victor, David G. 1999. "Risk Management and the World Trading System: Regulating International Trade Distortions of National Sanitary and Phytosanitary Policies." Unpublished paper, New York.
35. Article 1; see Internet: ⟨http://www.un.org/law/icc/index.htm⟩.
36. Sassen (1998: 20–22), for instance, points out that domestic courts severely restrained policies to control immigration, and thus the right of the nation-state to control its border, since they would violate international agreements.
37. See the data of the Union of International Associations (UIA).
38. Its character as a generically transnational regime is reflected in the legal debate on the extent to which this law can be regarded as autonomous from state law (see De Ly 2001).
39. To be sure, the evidence on the amount and the sources of their influence is not yet definitive. See Beck (1997: 121–128) for an interesting case study of the Brent Spar case.
40. The best conceptualization of the arguing–bargaining distinction is still Elster (1992, 1998).

41. See, especially, Burley and Mattli (1993) and Alter (1998) for convincing accounts of how the ECJ was not the outcome of intergovernmental design.
42. Parts of the literature on transnational NGOs focus on their role in the formulation and implementation of international policies. See the review by Zürn (1998b: 642–648).
43. *Financial Times*, "People first", 22 September 1999: 13.
44. See the discussion of these concepts in Bogdandy (1999: 53).
45. Facticity = "the social facts (in other words: laws) defining the "free choice" within which the individual may determine his actions." Translation used in Habermas. See http://www.csudh.edu/dearhabermas/lwhndbk01.htm#facticity.
46. See Helen Wallace, "European Policies and Polities." Paper prepared for DGXII workshop on Governance and Citizenship, 8–9 September 1999, for a very useful distinction of five modes of policy development in the EU, based on the one hand on the relative importance of major actors and on the other on the kind of policy in question.
47. To be sure, individual firms do have an interest in violating human rights as long as it provides them with a comparative advantage, as is amply demonstrated by the working conditions in factories of multinationals outside the OECD world and even in sweatshops within some of the OECD countries. Multinational corporations, however, usually have few objections to market-braking – i.e. redistributive (on this term see Streeck 1995) – *regulations* as long as they apply to all and do not lead to comparative disadvantages.
48. See Zangl and Zürn (1999) for an argument along these lines and also for further references.
49. See Zürn (2000) for an argument along these lines and for further references.
50. Note that these hypotheses are based on grounds that differ from those that are built on the notion of a race-to-the-bottom of regulatory standards. Whereas the latter argue against the background of a national constellation (competition between sovereign nation-states), the hypotheses put forward here are formulated against the background of a postnational constellation. Whereas the national constellation-based explanations have difficulty explaining why it is possible to employ regulatory policies with remarkable distributional consequences in the environmental field, but it is not possible when it comes to social policies, an explanation based on the notion of a postnational constellation may be more successful.

REFERENCES

Abromeit, Heidrun and Thomas Schmidt. 1998. "Grenzprobleme der Demokratie." In: *Regieren in entgrenzten Räumen, (PVS-Sonderheft 29)*, ed. Beate Kohler-Koch. Opladen: Westdeutscher Verlag, 293–320.

Adler, Emanuel and Peter M. Haas. 1992. "Conclusion: Epistemic Communities, World Order, and the Creation of a Reflective Research Program." *International Organization* 46(1): 367–390.

Albert, Matthias. 1996. *Fallen der (Welt)-Ordnung. Internationale Beziehungen und ihre Theorien zwischen Moderne und Postmoderne*. Opladen: Leske & Budrich.

Alter, Karen J. 1998. "Who Are the 'Masters of the Treaty'? European Governments and the ECJ." *International Organization* 52(1): 121–147.

Anderson, Benedict. 1991. *Imagined Communities. Reflections on the Origin and Spread of Nationalism*, 2nd edn. London: Verso.

Appelbaum, Richard, William Felstiner and Volkmar Gessner, eds. 2000. *The Legal Culture of Global Business Transactions*. Oxford: Hart Publishers.

Beck, Ulrich. 1997. *Was ist Globalisierung?* Frankfurt/M: Suhrkamp.

Beisheim, Marianne, Sabine Dreher, Gregor Walter, Bernhard Zangl, and Michael Zürn. 1999. *Im Zeitalter der Globalisierung? Thesen und Daten zur gesellschaftlichen und politischen Denationalisierung*. Baden-Baden: Nomos.

Benhabib, Seyla. 1996. "Toward a Deliberative Model of Democratic Legitimacy." In: *Democracy and Difference. Contesting the Boundaries of the Political*, ed. Seyla Benhabib. Princeton, NJ: Princeton University Press, 67–94.

Böckenförde, Ernst. 1969. "Entstehung und Wandel des Rechtsstaatbegriffs." In: *Festschrift für Adolf Arndt*, ed. Horst Ehmke. Frankfurt/M: Europäische Verlagsanstalt, 53–76.

Bogdandy, Armin von. 1999. *Supranationaler Föderalismus als Wirklichkeit und Idee einer Herrschaftsform. Zur Gestalt der Europäischen Union nach Amsterdam*. Baden-Baden: Nomos.

Braudel, Fernand. 1992. *The Wheels of Commerce. Vol. 2: Civilization and Capitalism 15th–18th Century*. Berkeley, CA: California University Press.

Brock, Lothar. 1998. "Die Grenzen der Demokratie. Selbstbestimmung im Kontext des globalen Strukturwandels." In: *Regieren in entgrenzten Räumen (PVS-Sonderheft 29)*, ed. Beate Kohler-Koch. Opladen: Westdeutscher Verlag.

Brock, Lothar and Matthias Albert. 1995. "Entgrenzung der Staatenwelt. Zur Analyse weltgesellschaftlicher Entwicklungstendenzen." *Zeitschrift für Internationale Beziehungen* 2(2): 259–285.

Bruder, Wolfgang and Nicolai Dose. 1992. "Öffentliche Verwaltung." In: *Lexikon der Politik. Vol. 3: Die westlichen Länder*, ed. Manfred Schmidt. München: Beck, 274–283.

Bull, Hedley. 1977. *The Anarchical Society: A Study of Order in World Politics*. London: Macmillan.

Burley, Anne-Marie and Walter Mattli. 1993. "Europe Before the Court: A Political Theory of Legal Integration." *International Organization* 47(1): 41–76.

Cerny, Philip G. 1996. "What Next for the State?" In: *Globalization: Theory and Practice*, eds Eleonore Kofman and Gillian Youngs. London: Pinter, 123–137.

Chayes, Abram and Antonia Handler Chayes. 1995. *The New Sovereignty: Compliance With International Regulatory Agreements*. Cambridge, MA: Harvard University Press.

Corbey, Dorette. 1995. "Dialectical Functionalism: Stagnation as a Booster of European Integration." *International Organization* 49(2): 253–284.

Cox, Robert W. 1992. "Global Perestroika." In: *Socialist Register 1992*, ed. Ralph Miliband and Leo Panitch. London: Merlin Press, 26–43.

Cutler, Claire A. 1999. "Locating 'Authority' in the Global Political Economy." *International Studies Quarterly* 43(1): 59–81.

Dasser, Felix. 1991. "Lex Mercatoria: Werkzeug der Praktiker oder Spielzeug der Lehre?" *Schweizerische Zeitschrift für internationales und europäisches Recht* 3/91, 299–323.

De Ly, Filip. 2001. "Lex Mercatoria: Globalization and International Self-Regulation." In: *The Legal Culture of Global Business Transactions*, eds

Richard Appelbaum, William Felstiner, and Volkmar Gessner. Oxford: Hart Publishers, in press.

Deutsch, Karl W. 1969. *Nationalism and its Alternatives*. New York: The Free Press.

Eichener, Volker. 1996. "Die Rückwirkungen der europäischen Integration auf nationale Politikmuster." In: *Europäische Integration*, eds Markus Jachtenfuchs and Beate Kohler-Koch. Opladen: Leske & Budrich, 249–280.

Elias, Norbert. 1976. *Über den Prozeß der Zivilisation. Soziogenetische und psychogenetische Untersuchungen*. Frankfurt/M: Suhrkamp.

Elster, Jon. 1992. "Arguing and Bargaining in the Federal Convention and the Assemblée Constituante." In: *Rationality and Institutions. Essays in Honour of Knut Midgaard*, eds Raino Malnes and Arild Underdal. Oslo: Universitetsforlaget, 13–50.

Elster, Jon, Ed. 1998. *Deliberative Democracy*. Cambridge: Cambridge University Press.

Falke, Josef. 1996. "Comitology and Other Committees: A Preliminary Empirical Assessment." In: *Shaping European Law and Policy: The Role of Committees and Comitology in the Political Process*, eds. Robin H. Pedler and Guenther F. Schaefer. Maastricht: EIPA, 117–165.

Franck, Thomas M. 1992. "The Emerging Right to Democratic Governance." *American Journal of International Law* 86(1): 46–91.

Frieden, Jeffry A. and Ronald Rogowski. 1996. "The Impact of the International Economy on National Policies: An Analytical Overview." In: *Internationalization and Domestic Politics*, eds Robert O. Keohane and Helen V. Milner. Cambridge: Cambridge University Press, 25–47.

Friedman, Lawrence. 1996. "Borders: On the Emerging Sociology of International Law." *Stanford Journal of International Law* 32: 65–90.

Garrett, Geoffrey. 1998. *Partisan Politics in the Global Economy*. Cambridge: Cambridge University Press.

Gehring, Thomas. 1995. "Regieren im internationalen System. Verhandlungen, Normen und internationale Regime." *Politische Vierteljahresschrift* 36(2): 197–219.

Gellner, Ernest. 1991. *Nations and Nationalism*, 3rd edn. Ithaca, NY: Cornell University Press.

Genschel, Philipp. 1995. *Standards in der Informationstechnik. Institutionaller Wandel in der internationalen Standardisierung*. Frankfurt/M: Campus.

Giddens, Anthony. 1985. *The National State and Violence*. Berkeley, CA: University of California Press.

Giddens, Anthony. 1994. *Beyond Left and Right. The Future of Radical Politics*. Cambridge: Polity Press.

Godt, Christine. 1998. Der Bericht des Appellate Body der WTO zum EG-Einfuhrverbot von Hormonfleisch. Risikoregulierung im Weltmarkt. *Europäisches Wirtschafts- und Steuerrecht* 9(6): 202–209.

Grimm, Dieter. 1994. Staatsaufgaben – eine Bilanz. In: *Staatsaufgaben*, ed. Dieter Grimm. Baden-Baden: Nomos, 771–785.

Held, David. 1995. *Democracy and the Global Order. From the Modern State to Cosmopolitan Governance*. Cambridge: Polity Press.

Held, David, Anthony McGrew, David Goldblatt, and Jonathan Perraton. 1999. *Global Transformations: Politics, Economics and Culture.* Cambridge: Polity Press.

Helleiner, Eric. 1994. *States and the Reemergence of Global Finance. From Bretton Woods to the 1990s.* Ithaca, NY: Cornell University Press.

Héritier, Adrienne, Christoph Knill, and Susanne Mingers. 1996. *Ringing the Changes in Europe. Regulatory Competition and Redefinition of the State? Britain, France, Germany.* Berlin: Walter de Gruyter.

Hirsch, Joachim. 1995. *Der nationale Wettbewerbsstaat. Staat, Demokratie und Politik im globalen Kapitalismus.* Berlin: Edition ID-Archiv.

Hirschi, Christian, Uwe Serdült, and Thomas Widmer. 1999. "Schweizerische Außenpolitik im Wandel." *Schweizerische Zeitschrift für Politikwissenschaft* 5(1): 31–56.

Hirst, Paul and Grahame Thompson. 1996. *Globalization in Question. The International Economy and the Possibilities of Governance.* Cambridge: Cambridge University Press.

Hobsbawm, Eric J. 1992. *Nations and Nationalism since 1780. Programme, Myth, Reality,* 2nd edn. Cambridge: Cambridge University Press.

Hofmann, Jeanette. 1998. "Am Herzen der Dinge – Regierungsmacht im Internet." In: *Internet und Demokratie,* eds Wienand Gellner and Fritz von Korff. Baden-Baden: Nomos, 55–77.

Holm, Hans-Henrik and Georg Sørensen, eds. 1995. *Whose World Order? Uneven Globalization and the End of the Cold War.* Boulder, CO: Westview Press.

Horn, Norbert. 1996. *Einführung in die Rechtswissenschaft und Rechtsphilosophie.* Heidelberg: Müller.

Jachtenfuchs, Markus and Beate Kohler-Koch. 1996. "Regieren im dynamischen Mehrebenensystem." In: *Europäische Integration,* eds Markus Jachtenfuchs and Beate Kohler-Koch. Opladen: Leske & Budrich, 15–44.

Jackson, Robert H. 1990. *Quasi-States: Sovereignty, International Relations, and the Third World.* Cambridge: Cambridge University Press.

Jänicke, Martin. 1998. "Umweltpolitik: Global am Ende oder am Ende global?" In: *Perspektiven der Weltgesellschaft,* ed. Ulrich Beck. Frankfurt/M: Suhrkamp, 322–344.

Joerges, Christian and Jürgen Neyer. 1997. "Transforming Strategic Interaction Into Deliberative Problem-Solving: European Comitology in the Foodstuffs Sector." *Journal of European Public Policy* 4(4): 609–625.

Kahler, Mile. 1995. *International Institutions and the Political Economy of Integration.* Washington DC: The Brookings Institution.

Kaufmann, Franz-Xaver. 1994. "Diskurse über Staatsaufgaben." In: *Staatsaufgaben,* ed. Dieter Grimm. Baden-Baden: Nomos, 14–41.

Keohane, Robert. 1993. "Sovereignty, Interdependence and International Institutions." In: *Ideas and Ideals. Essays on Politics in Honor of Stanley Hoffmann,* eds Linda B. Miller and Michael Joseph Smith. Boulder, CO: Westview Press, 91–107.

Keohane, Robert O. and Joseph S. Nye, Jr, eds. 1971. *Transnational Relations and World Politics.* Cambridge, MA: Harvard University Press.

Knieper, Rolf. 1991. *Nationale Souveränität: Versuch über Ende und Anfang einer Weltordnung.* Frankfurt/M: Fischer.

Kohler-Koch, Beate. 1993. "Die Welt regieren ohne Weltregierung." In: *Regieren im 21. Jahrhundert. Zwischen Globalisierung und Regionalisierung. Festgabe für Hans-Hermann Hartwich zum 65. Geburtstag,* eds Carl Böhret and Göttrik Wewer. Opladen: Leske & Budrich, 109–141.

Kohler-Koch, Beate, ed. 1998. *Regieren in entgrenzten Räumen (PVS-Sonderheft 29).* Opladen: Westdeutscher Verlag.

Krasner, Stephen D. 1983. "Structural Causes and Regime Consequences: Regimes as Intervening Variables." In: *International Regimes,* ed. Stephen D. Krasner. Ithaca: Cornell University Press, 1–21.

Krasner, Stephen. 1999. *Sovereignty. Organized Hypocrisy.* Princeton, NJ: Princeton University Press.

Leibfried, Stephan and Paul Pierson. 1995. "Semi-Sovereign Welfare States: Social Policy in a Multi-Tiered Europe." In: *European Social Policy: Between Fragmentation and Integration,* eds Stephan Leibfried and Paul Pierson. Washington, DC: Brookings Institution, 43–77.

Levy, Marc A., Oran R. Young, and Michael Zürn. 1995. "The Study of International Regimes." *European Journal of International Relations* 1(3): 267–330.

Liese, Andrea. 1998. "Menschenrechsschutz durch Nichtregierungsorganisationen." *Aus Politik und Zeitgeschichte* B46–47: 36–42.

Lindblom, Charles E. 1977. *Politics and Markets: The World's Political–Economic Systems.* New York: Basic Books.

Litfin, Karen. 1997. "Sovereignty in World Ecopolitics." *Mershon International Studies Review* 41(2): 167–204.

Lyons, Gene M. and Michael Mastanduno, eds. 1995. *Beyond Westphalia? State Sovereignty and International Intervention.* Baltimore: Johns Hopkins University Press.

Majone, Giandomenico, ed. 1996. *Regulating Europe.* London: Routledge.

Marks, Gary, Fritz W. Scharpf, Philippe C. Schmitter, and Wolfgang Streeck, eds. 1996. *Governance in the European Union.* London: Sage.

Marshall, Thomas H. 1992. *Citizenship and Social Class.* London: Pluto Press.

Mayer, Peter, Volker Rittberger, and Michael Zürn. 1993. "Regime Theory. State of the Art and Perspectives." In: *Regime Theory and International Relations,* ed. Volker Rittberger, with the assistance of Peter Mayer. Oxford: Clarendon Press, 391–430.

Mayntz, Renate. 1996. "Politische Steuerung: Aufstieg, Niedergang und Transformation einer Theorie." In: *Politische Theorien in der Ära der Transformation (PVS-Sonderheft 26),* eds Klaus von Beyme and Claus Offe. Opladen: Westdeutscher Verlag, 148–168.

Moravcsik, Andrew. 1998. *Choice for Europe. Social Purpose and State Power from Messina to Maastricht.* Ithaca, NY: Cornell University Press.

Morgenthau, Hans. 1967. *Politics among Nations. The Struggle for Power and Peace,* 4th edn. New York: Alfred Knopf.

Nettl, J. P. 1968. "The State as a Conceptual Variable." *World Politics* 20(4): 559–592.

Neyer, Jürgen. 1999. "Legitimes Recht oberhalb des demokratischen Rechts-staates? Supranationalität als Herausforderung für die Politikwissenschaft." *Politische Vierteljahresschrift* 40(3): 390–414.

North, Douglass C. 1981. *Structure and Change in Economic History*. New York: Norton.

Offe, Claus. 1973. *Strukturprobleme des kapitalistischen Staates: Aufsätze zur politischen Soziologie*. Frankfurt/M: Suhrkamp.

Offe, Claus. 1975. *Berufsbildungsreform. Eine Fallstudie über Reformpolitik*. Frankfurt/M: Suhrkamp.

Princen, Thomas and Mathias Finger. 1994. *Environmental NGOs in World Politics. Linking the Local and the Global*. London: Routledge.

Reinicke, Wolfgang H. 1998. *Global Public Policy. Governing without Government?* Washington, DC: Brookings Institution.

Reus-Smit, Christian. 1997. "The Constitutional Structure of International Society and the Nature of Fundamental Institutions." *International Organization* 51(4): 555–589.

Risse-Kappen, Thomas. 1995. "Bringing Transnational Relations Back In: Introduction." In: *Bringing Transnational Relations Back In: Non-State Actors, Domestic Structures and International Institutions*, ed. Thomas Risse-Kappen. Cambridge: Cambridge University Press, 3–33.

Rittberger, Volker. 1993. "Research on International Regimes in Germany: The Adaptive Internalization of an American Social Science Concept." In: *Regime Theory and International Relations*, eds Volker Rittberger with the assistance of Peter Mayer. Oxford: Clarendon Press, 3–22.

Rittberger, Volker. 1995. "The Future of Sovereignty – Rethinking a Key Concept of International Relations." Paper prepared for UNU 20th Anniversary Symposium on the United Nations System in the 21st century, Tokyo, 21–22 November 1995.

Rittberger, Volker, with Peter Mayer, eds. 1993. *Regime Theory and International Relations*. Oxford: Clarendon Press.

Rittberger, Volker and Bernhard Zangl. 1995. *Internationale Organisationen: Politik und Geschichte*, 2nd edn. Opladen: Leske & Budrich.

Rosenau, James N. 1992. "Governance, Order, and Change in World Politics." In: *Governance without Government. Order and Change in World Politics*, eds James N. Rosenau and Ernst-Otto Czempiel. Cambridge, MA: Lexington Press, 1–29.

Rosenau, James N. 1997. *Along the Domestic–Foreign Frontier. Exploring Governance in a Turbulent World*. Cambridge: Cambridge University Press.

Sassen, Saskia. 1998. *Globalization and its Discontents*. New York: Free Press.

Scharpf, Fritz W. 1996. "Politische Optionen im vollendeten Binnenmarkt." In: *Europäische Integration*, eds Markus Jachtenfuchs and Beate Kohler-Koch. Opladen: Leske & Budrich, 109–140.

Schmalz-Bruns, Rainer. 1998. "Grenzerfahrungen und Grenzüberschreitungen: Demokratie im integrierten Europa." In: *Regieren in entgrenzten Räumen (PVS-Sonderheft 29)*, ed. Beate Kohler-Koch. Opladen: Westdeutscher Verlag, 369–380.

Shanks, Cheryl, Harold K. Jacobson, and Jeffrey H. Kaplan. 1996. "Inertia and Change in the Constellation of International Governmental Organizations, 1981–1992." *International Organization* 50(4): 593–629.

Slaughter, Ann-Marie. 1997. "The Real New World Order." *Foreign Affairs* 76(5): 183–197.

Smith, Adam. 1776. *Inquiry into the Nature and the Causes of the Wealth of Nations*. London: W. Strahan & T. Cadell.

Sørensen, Georg. 1997. "An Analysis of Contemporary Statehood. Consequences for Conflict and Cooperation." *Review of International Studies* 23(3): 253–269.

Sørensen, Georg. 1998. "States are not 'Like Units'. Types of States and Forms of Anarchy in the Present International System." *Journal of Political Philosophy* 6(1): 79–98.

Sørensen, Georg. 1999. "Sovereignty at the Millennium – Change and Continuity in a Fundamental Institution." *Political Studies* 47(3): 590–604.

Spruyt, Hendrik. 1994. *The Sovereign State and its Competitors. The Analysis of Systems Change*. Princeton, NJ.: Princeton University Press.

Streeck, *German Capitalism: Does It Exist? Can It Survive?* Köln: Max Planck Institut für Gesellschaftsforschung. 1995. Wolfgang.

Suchmann, Marc C. 1995. "Managing Legitimacy: Strategic and Institutional Approaches." *Academy of Management Review* 20(3): 571–610.

Thomson, Janice E. 1994. *Mercenaries, Pirates, and Sovereigns. State-Building and Extraterritorial Violence in Early Modern Europe*. Princeton, NJ: Princeton University Press.

Thomson, Janice E. 1995. "State Sovereignty and International Relations. Bridging the Gap Between Theory and Empirical Research." *International Studies Quarterly* 39(2): 213–233.

Tilly, Charles. 1985. "War Making and State Making as Organized Crime." In: *Bringing the State Back In*, eds Peter B. Evans, Dietrich Rueschemeyer, and Theda Skocpol. Cambridge: Cambridge University Press, 169–191.

Tilly, Charles. 1990. *Coercion, Capital and European States*, AD 990–1990. Oxford: Blackwell.

Vogel, David. 1995. *Trading up. Consumer and Environmental Regulation in a Global Economy*. Cambridge, MA: Harvard University Press.

Weiler, Joseph H. H. 1993. "Journey to an Unknown Destination: A Retrospective and Prospective of the European Court of Justice in the Arena of Political Integration." *Journal of Common Market Studies* 31(4): 417–446.

Wesel, Uwe. 1997. *Geschichte des Rechts. Von den Frühformen bis zum Vertrag von Maastricht*. München: Beck.

Wessels, Wolfgang. 1998. "Comitology: Fusion in Action. Politico-administrative Trends in the EU System." *Journal of European Public Policy* 5(2): 209–234.

Wolf, Klaus Dieter. 2000. *Die neue Staatsräson – Zwischenstaatliche Kooperation als Demokratieproblem in der Weltgesellschaft*. Baden-Baden: Nomos.

World Bank. 1997. *World Development Report 1997*. Washington, DC: World Bank.

Young, Oran R. 1978. "Anarchy and Social Choice. Reflections on the International Polity." *World Politics* 31(2): 241–263.

Young, Oran R. 1994. *International Governance. Protecting the Environment in a Stateless Society*. Ithaca, NY: Cornell University Press.

Zacher, Mark W., with Brent A. Sutton 1996. *Governing Global Networks. International Regimes for Transportation and Communication*. Cambridge: Cambridge University Press.

Zangl, Bernhard and Michael Zürn. 1999. "The Effects of Denationalisation on Security in the OECD World." *Global Society* 13(2): 139–161.

Zürn, Michael. 1998a. *Regieren jenseits des Nationalstaates. Denationalisierung und Globalisierung als Chance*. Frankfurt/M: Suhrkamp.

Zürn, Michael. 1998b. "The Rise of International Environmental Politics: A Review of Current Research." *World Politics* 50(4): 617–649.

Zürn, Michael. 2000. "Democracy beyond the Nation State." *European Journal of International Relations* 6(2): 183–221.

Zürn, Michael and Niels Lange. 1999. "Regionalism in the Age of Globalization." InIIS-Working Paper, 16/99, Bremen.

Zürn, Michael and Dieter Wolf. 1999. "European Law and International Regimes: The Features of Law Beyond the Nation State." *European Law Journal* 5(3): 272–292.

3

Security-community building for better global governance

Sorpong Peou

Introduction

This chapter attempts to shed light on another dimension of global governance by analysing why states build effective regional international organizations or regional security communities, the existence of which may ultimately help strengthen the UN system with the aim of promoting world peace. The approach taken here differs from that found in the mainstream literature (Adler and Barnett 1998; Weiss 1998; Alagappa and Inoguchi 1999), which tends to focus on one region and often fails to produce generalizations or to generate a coherent perspective on the subject matter (which has been a central aim of social science). A number of studies looking at specific countries or regions have offered rich insights into the problems of, and prospects for, future international governance at the regional level, but they do not tell us a great deal about why some regions are better at building communities whose members develop dependable expectations for peaceful change. This study is more ambitious than the existing literature in that it surveys regional security communities around the world and proposes that a comparative analysis of patterns of peace and security in the world's major regions (the Americas, Europe, Eurasia, Asia, Africa, and the Arab region) may shed more light on why some are more stable or peaceful than others. Still, such variation is meaningless unless we can systematically identify key determinants to help explain why states in some regions are more able than others to create and maintain security communities.

The chapter is divided into three main sections. The next section (pp. 89–98) describes some of the great challenges to the efforts of the United Nations to promote global governance; it then argues that security-community building is a better way to global governance; finally, it develops four criteria for judging success and failure in such endeavours. Although (1) rich experience in conflict management and (2) small size of membership are important criteria for security-community building, it is shared (3) democratic values/performance and (4) political leadership that matter most. The section on pages 98–108 proves that success in security-community building in North America and Europe – mainly by the North Atlantic Treaty Organization (NATO), the EU, and the Organization for Security and Cooperation in Europe (OSCE), whereby the latter's geographic range is much broader – owes much to the fact that states in these regions have met most of the four criteria, especially democratic performance and political leadership. The section on pages 108–119 explains why states in the various non-Western or less-developed regions have proved themselves far less competent than their Western counterparts in regional community-building efforts – by the Organization of American States (OAS), the Association of South-East Asian Nations (ASEAN), the Gulf Cooperation Council (GCC), the Commonwealth of Independent States (CIS), and the OAU (Organization of African Unity) – mainly because they have met fewer criteria, particularly those of democratic performance and political leadership.

The UN for global governance? A case for security-community building

The extent to which the United Nations can help promote international security and world peace is a matter of debate. Evidence indicates that the world organization still faces many great challenges. Most important, insecurity is growing especially in non-Western, or developing, regions; meanwhile, the United Nations' ability to maintain or restore peace has been reduced. That results from the fact that the United Nations (as shall be seen) possesses only a limited institutional and logistical capacity to undertake major peace operations around the world. By helping to build effective regional organizations and security communities, however, the United Nations has a better chance of achieving its goals.

Conflicts and prospects for regional security

Much of the world remains inflicted by poverty, repressive violence, and war. Prior to the end of the Second World War, most of the non-Western or developing states had suffered at the hands of Western and Japanese colonialism and imperialism. After independence, they bore much of the world's burden, measured by the number of armed conflicts, human- and democratic-rights abuses, poverty levels, and environmental scarcity (defined in terms of environmental degradation, population growth, and unequal distribution of resources) (Homer-Dixon 1998). During the cold war, armed conflicts within and between states broke out in all non-Western regions – Latin America, Asia, and Africa. Between 1945 and 1989, the number of wars worldwide grew to well over a hundred. Of the 58 instances of war listed in Kalevi J. Holsti's extensive work, 56 (the exceptions being the Turkish invasion of Cyprus and the Korean War) "took place in areas constituent of the Third World." Strikingly, he points out, "[this] is an incidence of more than one war per year, approximately forty times the incidence of war within the industrial world" (Holsti 1991: 304–305).

The end of the cold war has witnessed growing numbers of conflicts in the various non-Western regions, and most of them have been intrastate. Even during the cold war, every internal war broke out in regions outside Western regions. In the 1945–1989 period, more than 125 wars broke out within non-Western states. Between 1989 and 1992 there were 82 armed conflicts in the world, of which only three were between states (United Nations Development Programme 1994: 47). In 1993–1994, only two additional interstate conflicts broke out, but nine more intrastate conflicts erupted. Thus, during the 1989–1994 period, 96 armed conflicts broke out, of which only 5 were between two states. Peter Wallensteen and Margareta Sollenberg have therefore declared "the end of international war" (Wallensteen and Sollenberg 1995).

Liberal scholars argue that the number of armed conflicts between and within states could be reduced by the spread of democracy around the world. Although this may be true, Western-type democracy continues to face numerous challenges. At a first glance, some progress has been made towards democracy, although it is still limited. The number of democracies around the world has increased dramatically, but it is not particularly meaningful, because the quality, or maturity, of democracy is also important. Here, the empirical findings are not very positive. "Mature democracies" outside the West are still far too few. Fareed Zakaria argues that the number of illiberal democracies (or neo-authoritarian states) has increased. As he puts it: "From Peru to the Palestinian Authority, from Sierra Leone to Slovakia, from Pakistan to the Philippines, we see the rise of a disturbing phenomenon in international life – illiberal democracy" (Zakaria 1997: 22). Democracy, defined as a free and fair electoral process, is "flourishing"; however, constitutional liberalism; the rule of law; the separation of powers; and the protection of the basic liberties of speech, assembly, religion, and property, are not. The future of global governance based on liberal democracy remains precarious.

Nevertheless, there is still hope for long-term stability and peace in non-Western regions, partly because not all of them have experienced the same degree of war and repressive violence. Between 1945 and 1996, Latin America (with 17 wars) was more peaceful than the Middle East (25), which was more stable than Africa (27) and Asia (29) (Harada and Tanako 1999: 333, 345). In recent years, some regions have become more stable. During the cold war, East Asia experienced seven full-scale inter-state wars and has not seen one since the 1990s.

Even more encouraging for the future development in these regions is the fact that achieving regional stability and peace is not a total impossibility. Western regions have by far been the most successful in building stable security communities. It is now almost inconceivable today that states in either North America or most of Europe would wage war against each other. These regions had not always been peaceful, of course: prior to the American Civil War, for instance, the United States and Canada remained hostile to each other, often on the brink of war (and crossing it in the war of 1812). Between 1839 and 1842, they almost fought again, over defining the border between Maine and New Brunswick. After the end of the American Civil War, their hostile bilateral relations were transformed into peaceful ones. They have yet to turn themselves into a supranational entity similar to the EU, but they have enjoyed stable, peaceful relations. Western Europe has also become one of the world's most stable regions, although it was not always so. During the fifteenth century, the Spanish crown drove out the Jews. In the sixteenth century, the French did the same to the Huguenots. During the seventeenth and eighteenth centuries, the British crown induced Protestant dissenters to migrate to the American colonies. Then came the nineteenth century's "ethnic cleansing," which occurred throughout Eastern Europe when Bulgarians, Greeks, Jews, Turks, Hungarians, Serbs, and Macedonians were put to flight. During the last 500 years of the second millennium, Europe was the world's primary generator of war. One of the bloodiest wars in European history, the "Thirty Years War," occurred there in the first half of the seventeenth century (Holsti 1991: 28–29). As recently as the first half of the twentieth century, two bloody world wars broke out in Europe and claimed some 50 million lives. Europe again became the main focus of world attention during the cold war between the United

States and the Soviet Union. However, the prospects for war among Western European states never re-emerged: Europe enjoyed what came to be known as the "long peace" (Gaddis 1987).

The end of the cold war in the early 1990s has, to date, largely refuted the neo-realist argument that "we will soon miss the cold war" (because Europe would no longer stay peaceful in the absence of a common threat from the Soviet Union) (Mearsheimer 1990). Even some realist-inclined scholars have now found a new faith in the fact that war among Western states is very unlikely. Samuel Huntington asserts that "[military] conflict among Western states is unthinkable" (Huntington 1993: 39). Robert Jervis, another realist, also sees in Western Europe "the triumph of interests over passions" and views Western Europeans as less inclined to believe that "war is ... good, or even ... honorable" (Jervis 1991/1992: 52).

The limits of United Nations peace operations

If the United Nations is to help promote peace and stable global governance systems, it must be able to take action to promote peaceful change toward liberal democracy by engaging in preventive diplomacy, peace-making, peace-keeping, peace enforcement, and peace building in war-torn and authoritarian states. Preventive diplomacy is the attempt to resolve disputes before they escalate into violent clashes. Peacemaking refers to all forms of diplomatic action intended to manage or resolve conflict prior to or after the outbreak of hostilities. Peace-keeping is an operation involving UN military personnel from member states separating adversaries with the hope of restoring peace on the basis of three principles – consent, impartiality, and the limited use of force for self-defence. Peace enforcement involves military action or intervention of UN-mandated armed forces of member states when peacemaking or peace-keeping efforts have failed. Peace building is a post-conflict international effort with a goal broader than peace-keeping in that the international community works to promote national governance in the following areas: creating or strengthening national institutions, monitoring elections, promoting human rights, providing for reintegration and rehabilitation programmes, and creating conditions for resumed development.[1]

The entire UN system has undoubtedly contributed to the process of peace building in the developing world. The UN Economic and Social Council (ECOSOC), for instance, has done much to meet the rising demands of developing countries in the various regions of the world. Regional economic (or economic and social) commissions have been set up for Europe, Asia and the Pacific, Latin America and the Caribbean,

Western Asia, and Africa. The Economic Commission for Europe helped to rebuild Western Europe from the devastation of the Second World War. The Economic Commission for Asia and the Far East (later renamed the Economic Commission for Asia and the Pacific) has done much to promote economic development and regional free trade. The Economic Commission for Latin America and the Caribbean is known for its contribution to the establishment of the Inter-American Development Bank, the Latin American Free Trade Association, the Central American Common Market, and other cooperative projects.

Nevertheless, it would be fair to say that these regional commissions have had a limited impact on regional peace and stability. Their operational effectiveness often depends on the socio-economic and political conditions of each region. The Economic Commission for Africa and the Economic and Social Commission for Western Asia have not done as well as the commissions in the other regions. In Africa, the commission's operations have encountered numerous obstacles (thus limiting its effectiveness), including "the abject poverty of many of its peoples and political rivalries among its members, many of which have ineffective and authoritarian governments" (Ziring, Riggs, and Plano 2000: 452). More can be said about the commission in Western Asia, where the war between Israel and Lebanon and the latter's internal strife forced the commission to move its headquarters from Lebanon to Baghdad. Its headquarters remained in Baghdad, but "the development activities of the commission have yet to materialize." Moreover, the unsuccessful attempt to establish a Middle East Commission resulted from "the lack of regional harmony" (Ziring, Riggs, and Plano 2000: 452).

Unfortunately, the growing insecurity of non-Western regions coincides with the weakening ability of the United Nations to maintain or restore regional stability and peace. One indicator of the growing weakness of the United Nations is the declining number of its international peace-keeping operations since the mid-1990s. Previously, there was an extraordinary growth in peace-keeping operations in the early 1990s: whereas the United Nations undertook only 15 peace-keeping operations between 1945 and 1989, the Security Council authorized 18 such peace-keeping operations between 1989 and 1994, which peaked in 1993 (with a total deployment of some 80,000 Blue Helmets, compared with fewer than 10,000 in 1987). During the second half of the 1990s, however, the United Nations started to wane in global influence: in 1998, only 14,000 peace-keepers were deployed, although the number went up again to 27,000 in 2000.

The small number of UN personnel and peace-keepers has failed to meet the need to promote global governance. The decline of UN peace activities seems correlated to the fact that the United Nations no longer possesses the institutional and logistic capacity necessary to undertake major peace operations. In the mid-1990s, the United Nations had an overall Secretariat staff of around 12,000 (including those in the Secretariat in New York City and those based in Geneva, Nairobi, and Vienna). In 1997, the United Nations was expected to cut its staff to 9,000 employees, who would serve a world population of six billion. Even the UN peace-keeping staff at UN headquarters in New York remains tiny, with 32 military officers overseeing 27,000 troops deployed in 14 peace missions around the world and with only nine police specialists supervising 8,600 police officers. The (UN-commissioned) Brahimi Report makes a critical assessment of UN peace operations with searing honesty: it acknowledges that "the United Nations has [over the last decade] repeatedly failed to [save succeeding generations from the scourge of war]." It adds that "it can do no better today."[2] UN Secretary-General Kofi Annan has now admitted that the world organization has a "credibility crisis": "Too many vulnerable communities in too many regions of the world now hesitate to look to the United Nations to assist them in their hour of need" (*International Herald Tribune*, 9–10 September 2000: 1).

Increasing financial shortages have limited the capacity of the United Nations to undertake peace operations. Top UN bureaucrats have long realized that the future of their organization is at stake. Former UN Undersecretary-General for Peace-keeping Marrack Goulding, for instance, argues that the United Nations "is now facing a danger analogous to that faced by the League of Nations at its very inception." He spoke of the "loss of the confidence and support of the richest and most powerful country in the world [the US]" (Goulding 1999: 62).[3] Goulding considers lack of money to be "the greatest threat to the United Nations' capacity to perform" (Goulding 1999: 62). At the peak of UN peace-keeping, unpaid dues for the regular budget and peace-keeping operations amounted to $2 billion; the United Nations' cash reserves ($380 million) were not much higher than its monthly expenditures ($310 million). The United Nations' annual regular budget from 1994 to 1997 was only $1.3 billion, only 3.4 per cent of New York City's budget ($38 billion) for the 1998 fiscal year (Mendez 1997: 284). It should also be worth noting that the UN regular budget further decreased from a mere $1.3 billion (1997) to $1.19 billion (1998), nearly $1 billion less than the annual cost of Tokyo's Fire Department.

This does not mean that the United Nations has given up on its efforts to enhance world peace. Faced with growing challenges, the United Nations has, in recent years, sought to do more with less. The United Nations became more willing to entrust matters of international peace and security to regional organizations, simply because it no longer appeared up to the task of doing it on its own. Former UN Secretary-General Boutros Boutros-Ghali recommended that regional organizations assume a more active role in conflict management, and current UN Secretary-General Kofi Annan has encouraged them to do so, provided that they receive a mandate from the Security Council. He sought to intensify co-operation between the global and regional organizations, particularly in the area of conflict prevention, stressing the virtue of comparative advantage and cooperation based on the principles of complementarity and "subsidiarity" (or what is generally known as "subcontracting") (Griffin 1999a). Complementarity means that various actors do not work at cross purposes, but support each other in peace missions; subsidiarity allows policy-making to take place at the lowest appropriate level (Griffin 1999b). Andy Knight further describes the subsidiarity model as a sharing of tasks between the United Nations and regional institutions, whereby the former should perform a task necessary for the smooth running of governance if the latter should shy away from it (Knight 1996). This form of regionalism must be seen in the larger context of universalism in that the UN Security Council remains the pillar of international peace and security.

However, arguments against the regionalization of peacemaking, peace-keeping, and peace building are numerous. First, the growth of regional organizations raises the question of "democratic deficit," as national leaders make decisions without consulting their citizens. Second, critics see the process of entrusting matters of international peace and security to regional organizations as ignoring the fact that their knowledge of regional problems may not be readily translated into effective action. During the cold war, regional organizations fared no better than the United Nations (Holsti 1989: 117). Moreover, their motives for intervention may not be altruistic: they may have agendas based on their interests and therefore fail to act with impartiality, a condition necessary for effective peace-keeping (Smith and Weiss 1998: 228). Third, the Security Council's motives behind such burden-sharing arrangements are also questionable. Some critics feel that the "Council's growing penchant for formally subcontracting or informally delegating the promotion of international peace and security is not always appropriate or well-intentioned" (Berman 1998: 2) and that the United States' desire to save money and the lives of its own citizens "primarily accounts for the trend" (Berman 1998: 3). The subsidiarity model may also promote regional leadership in that dominant states in the different regions of the world will seek to intervene in the affairs of other states. This may encourage more of the external interventions that occurred during the cold-war period, which often exacerbated and internationalized domestic conflicts. Fourth, the United Nations has not defined a specific division of labour between the two types of institutions. This is partly attributed to the UN Charter, which does not prescribe what the two types of organizations should do and how they should cooperate (Griffin 1999b: 21). Fifth, the vision also ignores the fact that regional institutions are generally less capable than the United Nations.

Although these criticisms present real challenges to the "regionalization" efforts of the United Nations, they should not overshadow the fact that regional security communities still have a lot of potential to lay the groundwork for promoting global governance.

Global governance and security communities: Some criteria

For analytical purposes, it is worth defining global governance. According to the Commission on Global Governance, "governance is not synonymous with government." Global governance is neither world government nor global federalism. The idea of world government runs contrary to that of global governance in the sense that the former would render the world "less democratic, more accommodating to power, more hospitable to hegemonic ambition, and more enforcing the roles of states and governments rather than the rights of people" (Commission on Global Governance 1995: xvi). According to James Rosenau, "while [both] refer to purposive behavior, to goal-oriented activities, to systems of rule ... government suggests activities that are backed by formal authority, by police powers to insure the implementation of duly constituted principles." But "governance refers to activities by shared goals that may or may not derive from legal and formally prescribed responsibilities and that do not necessarily rely on police powers to overcome defiance and attain compliance." It "is a system of rule that works only if it is accepted by the majority" (Rosenau 1992: 4). Although governance is linked to order, it is defined in terms of legitimacy rather than coercive power and is more people-oriented. In the context of global governance, there is a marked conceptual shift from the concept of state sovereignty to that of popular sovereignty in that the new world order would better reflect the UN Charter's aspiration: "We the Peoples of the United Nations."

Security-community building is a project that can help the United Nations in promoting global governance. Security communities should be treated as part of global governance, which stands between a utopian world (one without strife) and the Hobbesian world (in which a constant possibility of interstate war exists). Michael Barnett and Emanuel Adler capture this point well in their assertion that "[security] communities ... do not portray an ideal world of international security." Rather, they add, such regional communities "show that international security changes with time, and such changes are a result of mixtures of anarchy and hierarchy, coercion and communication" (Barnett and Adler 1998: 438).

Security communities are generally defined as ones whose members develop dependable expectations for peaceful change. Evidence suggests the existence of such communities when their members "renounce military violence" and have "deeply entrenched habits of the peaceful resolution of conflicts." Their governance structure, aimed at overcoming defection and attaining compliance, thus relies less on police powers and more on shared goals and inter-subjective meanings (Adler and Barnett 1998: 35). This does not mean that coercive power will soon become irrelevant or unnecessary; even in stable liberal democracies, this form of power remains as important as ever. As is discussed later, liberal-democratic political leadership serves as a key basis for successful security-community building.

In this chapter, "success" in regional community building is defined on two different levels. On one level, a group of states within a particular region can claim success in such endeavours only when they no longer expect to go to war against each other. Thus, the peaceful process of regional cooperation or integration is considered "success." On the second level, success can also be defined in terms of a regional organization's ability to restore peace and promote dependable expectations for peaceful change with or among non-member states outside its own region.

The question is how non-Western regions can build stable security communities, such as those in the Western regions. This study rejects cultural determinism, goes beyond the sociological perspective that gives attention only to socialization among all types of élite groups but disregards the role of ideology,[4] and develops a type of constructivism that takes into account some liberal and realist insights.

Criterion 1: Experience in conflict management

Experience in conflict management/resolution is essential to success in community building. The more experienced the member states of a regional organization are in managing/resolving conflict, the more likely it is that they will succeed in community building.

Criterion 2: Membership size

Members of an organization seeking to build a community must be small in size. As Kenneth Waltz puts it, "for the sake of stability ... smaller is better ... [and] two is best of all" (Waltz 1979: 161). The seminal work by Mancur Olson on the logic of collective action helps to explain the collective goods problem (Olson 1965). A regional organization with a large number of members is less likely to surmount coordination problems. Member states tend to adopt decision-making procedures based on the principle of consensus, which makes it hard for them to arrive at decisions effectively.

Criterion 3: Democratic performance

Community building is easier if member states of a regional organization have become liberal democracies or, at least, have a very high degree of respect for human rights (Doyle 1986, 1996; Maoz and Russett 1993). Democracies are less likely to revert to authoritarianism largely if they are generally wealthy and their populations enjoy equitable distributions of wealth and incomes. According to Adam Przeworski and others, democracy in a country with an annual income per capita of less than $1,000 lasts on average only about 8.5 years; it lasts 16 years in one with income between $1,000 and $2,000, 33 years between $2,000 and $4,000, and 100 years where the income is between $4,000 and $6,000 (Przeworski, Alvarez, and Cheibub 1996).

Criterion 4: Political leadership

Ultimately, regional security communities must have a regional political foundation. That is, the member states must have among themselves a democratic leader,[5] who also possesses adequate material capabilities (military and economic) for effective democratic intervention. This does not mean that, when a regional democratic leader exists, there will be a stable security community. Unless that leader is committed to democratic intervention, a security community will not emerge or grow stable (or mature) (Meernik 1996).[6] Democratic leadership helps to build security communities.

This study's hypothesis is that the larger the number of the above criteria a group of states is able to fulfil, the more successful its community-building efforts are likely to be.

North America and Western Europe: Meeting most criteria for security-community building

The extent to which international organizations in different regions have succeeded in promoting national and regional governance is not easy to determine. It appears, however, that there is clear variation in regional stability and peace. Grouped together for comparative analysis, the North American region, the EU, NATO, and the OSCE show varying degrees of success, with the last one being the least successful regional organization. The varying successes enjoyed by the EU, NATO, and the

OSCE during and after the cold war can be assessed at two levels: these are (1) dependable expectations of peaceful change among the member states and (2) their efforts to promote such expectations outside their organizational boundaries. The latter is put to the test in the handling of the armed conflicts in the Balkans. As is shown later, the OSCE has proved less successful than the EU and NATO on level one (among their own members).

The North American community

North America has been known as one of the most stable security communities in the world. Initially made up of Canada and the United States, the community has now expanded to include Mexico. Canada and the United States have a growing number of transactions and a high degree of interdependence, but have not established formal organizations for political cooperation. In 1988 they also created a two-nation free trade area. They also have a long tradition of military cooperation. As Kalevi J. Holsti puts it, "there is little question that Canada and the United States constitute a pluralistic security community." The two neighbouring states have experienced problems that impinge upon their national interests; however, "there is little likelihood of conflict leading to violence." Government officials and bureaucrats from both sides "seldom go beyond the use of warnings, protests, and occasional nonviolent threats" (Holsti 1988: 439). Sean Shore also argues that the two states "constitute a striking example of a pluralistic security community," based on the assurance that they would settle their disputes through peaceful means (Shore 1998: 333).

In recent years, Mexico has also developed positive relations with both Canada and the United States. Together, the three states created a North American Free Trade Agreement (NAFTA), which entered into force in 1994. None of them is prepared for war against the others. This is not to suggest that they no longer have disputes among themselves; NAFTA has been a principal source of tension among them. New problems, such as opposition to American and Canadian losses of jobs to Mexico and the tide of illegal migrants, have in fact created anti-free trade sentiment in both Canada and the United States. However, there is no evidence that they are militarily hostile to each other.

The European Union

Ole Wæver characterizes Western Europe as a "classic" security community. Although the EU itself is not usually viewed as a security organization, "integration itself has far greater security importance" (Wæver 1998: 100). The process of regional integration through membership enlargement and deeper relations among EU members still continues.

At their summit in December 1999, the 15 EU leaders agreed to throw the regional door open to new applicants from outside Western Europe. Negotiations with six states – Poland, Hungary, the Czech Republic, Estonia, Slovenia, and Cyprus – continue. Six other states – Bulgaria, Romania, Latvia, Lithuania, Slovakia, and Malta – have been accepted as formal candidates. Turkey was promised acceptance as a future candidate, although with conditions and without any clear time-frame. Greece and Turkey – two rivals which have devoted financial and organizational resources to the possibility of war with each other – have now agreed to accept each other.

The EU continues to mature as a security community. With the single market in 1992 completing the Common Market programme launched with the Treaty of Rome in 1957, a single currency, and a single central bank, the EU has now entered a much deeper phase of regional integration. At their summit late in 1999, the 15 EU leaders made their joint decision, which ushered in a new Europe. A foundation for their common defence strategy was laid when they agreed to establish the capacity to field joint military forces up to 60,000 and political and military structures to direct them. Although the force will not function before 2003, "it is already being hailed by some Europeans as the vanguard of an entirely unified military, in the same way the EU member states have uniform policies in fields ranging from farm subsidies to rail transport" (*Japan Times*, 9 December 1999: 21).

The EU, however, has not yet become much more successful in restoring peace with or among non-members – for example, such as putting an end to ethnic conflict in the Balkans. A European Commission staff member acknowledges a "glaring discrepancy between the economic and political influence of the EU," especially *vis-à-vis* its ineffectiveness associated with the Yugoslavian disintegration (Rhodes 1998: 19). This does not mean that the EU has not been useful as an instrument for peace building. The EU Stability Pact for south-eastern Europe has been aimed at luring fragile states in the Balkans in the way that the EU has lured central European states. After the NATO attacks on Yugoslavia in 1999, the EU has also been active in providing financial support for the peace-building process.

The North Atlantic Treaty Organization

NATO has been transformed in the last ten years into a better security community involved in peace-keeping, promoting ethnic coexistence, and providing a secure environment for democratic elections. Within the context of NATO, the member states from North America to Western Europe have become known as a "transatlantic security community," in which "[no] country ... expects to go to war with any other" (Ruggie 1998: 229).

NATO came in when the EU and the OSCE failed to put out the ethnic flames in the Balkans. This is not to say that NATO enjoyed complete success, but it has done much better than hard-nosed political realists had foreseen. Since 1991, it has undertaken a new task – out-of-area peace operations. In 1992, NATO agreed to consider enforcing the UN Security Council's decisions and those of the OSCE on a case-by-case basis. NATO began monitoring the UN embargo against the warring parties in the Balkan war in July 1992. The following year saw NATO enforcing a no-fly zone in Bosnia. In 1994, NATO pledged to defend Sarajevo with air strikes. That same year, when NATO used force for the first time in Bosnia, it was in support of the UN mission there. In February, NATO fired its first shots "in anger." This came after NATO had warned warring parties to remove heavy weapons from an exclusion zone around Sarajevo. NATO's first-ever combat began in August 1995, when the United States and Britain launched joint air strikes against the Serbs in the Bosnian battlefield (Leurdijk 1996).

NATO's much-publicized air strikes on Serbia (beginning on 24 March 1999 and lasting 11 weeks until 4 June) testified to the fact that the organization was more willing and more able to intervene in ethnic conflict outside its original mandate. In the end, NATO prevailed. The government in Belgrade allowed NATO and the UN to keep the peace in Kosovo and agreed to let the Albanian refugees return to their homes. Whether the unprecedented NATO combat mission is "a perfect failure" or a "success" is a matter of debate for the months and years to come (Mandelbaum 1999; Steinberg 1999). At best, the NATO mission has produced an incomplete peace; it is hoped that the successes will outweigh the failures.

The Organization for Security and Cooperation in Europe

Although former American diplomat James Goodby predicted that the OSCE would outstrip old and tired security bodies such as NATO and the Western European Union (WEU, by now a military wing of the EU, originally created in 1948 for collective self-defence; Goodby 1993), NATO still plays the dominant role in the security field. There are limits to what the OSCE can accomplish (Lucas 1996). It is the least effective, when compared with the EU and NATO, in terms of transforming itself into a true security community in which all of its members have developed dependable expectations of peaceful change, but it has made a useful contribution to security. It has in recent years been active in a "soft-security" role in the Balkans, in the CIS, and in the Baltic States, with several peace missions trying to resolve conflicts. Its performance in fields of its specific competence – such as early warning, early action, and early prevention – has been characterized as positive. Its successes include the role it has played in the implementation of the Dayton peace agreement in Bosnia–Herzegovina, its numerous attempts at getting Albania's warring parties to settle their differences peacefully, and its investigations of the conditions of Russian minorities in such states as Estonia, Latvia, and Lithuania.

What the OSCE has achieved can be judged as less than a moderate success, but not a complete failure. Although the OSCE mandate includes conflict prevention and resolution, it has not performed this role to the satisfaction of its proponents. Accordingly, Emanuel Adler considers the OSCE to be a "security community-building institution" only. He does not feel that "the entire OSCE will ultimately succeed in establishing a pluralistic security community in the OSCE region" (Adler 1998: 122). In his view, "[while] OSCE conflict-prevention and crisis-management practices have made some difference in a few areas ... the OSCE was almost powerless to stop conflicts after they erupted" (Adler 1998: 130).

Explanation of the varying degrees of success of regional organizations[7]

Criterion 1: Experience in security management

Within the North American community, Canada and the United States have accumulated much experience in conflict management. The two states did have several military crises, which spurred them to prepare for war. By the mid-1870s the United States had stopped spending on fortifications along the Canadian border. Canada took similar steps. According to Sean M. Shore, "[between] 1871 and 1876 ... Canada ... cut defense spending by two-thirds, and allowed its fortifications to lapse" (Shore 1998: 343). The two neighbours have since not taken steps to promote regional integration as members of the EU have done, but much of their collaboration and coordination occur at different government levels. According to K. J. Holsti, Canadian and American bureaucrats "at all levels and from all departments communicate and meet to negotiate proposals, elicit responses, hammer out details, and draft treaties or establish the frameworks that will guide national policies or coordinated ventures." Moreover, "the vast majority of problems that impinge upon interests of both states are handled in this manner" (Holsti 1988: 439).

The varying degrees of success experienced by the EU, NATO, and the OSCE can also be explained in terms of their different abilities in meeting criterion 1. Among the three regional organizations, the EU is (although it was founded after NATO) no doubt the most experienced in conflict management among its members. Before the integration process began after the Second World War, European states had experienced centuries of war. In that time, European states had accumulated experience of conflict management and institution building (the Concert of Europe during the first half of the nineteenth century being a good example). These "lessons learned" have proved helpful for building new and more effective institutions after the Second World War.

In comparison to the EU, NATO as a transatlantic organization is less experienced in conflict management because it has been a collective defence alliance directed at a third party whose containment during the cold war was pursued by military means. Formed after the Second World War with the aim of deterring Soviet incursion in Europe, NATO has grown into the world's mightiest military alliance. Within 50 years its membership has demonstrated its effectiveness. No other military alliance in the world can compare with it. NATO members have been involved in numerous meetings for consultation. However, the organization has also experienced problems of its own, including France's withdrawal from military integration in NATO in 1966–1967 and serious conflict among some of its members, such as that of Greece and Turkey over Cyprus. According to John Ruggie, "the EU is better equipped than NATO to deal with many of the non-military tasks the United States, in particular, has sought to place on NATO's shoulders *vis-à-vis* Central and Eastern Europe" (Ruggie 1998: 232).

In contrast to EU and NATO, the OSCE as an organization has accumulated a more limited experience in conflict management/resolution although most of its members have gained considerable experience in arms control and confidence building. OSCE emerged as a process only in 1975, known as the Conference on Security and Cooperation in Europe (CSCE). At the time when Yugoslavia collapsed, the organization did not even have any collective tools which could be used "to diffuse substate conflict through mediation or through promoting confidence-building exercises among conflicting groups." It was not until 1992 that the member states created several new security mechanisms, including a High Commissioner on National Minorities and "missions of long duration" (Flynn and Farrell 1999: 506).

Criterion 2: Membership size

If a smaller number of states within a particular region indeed creates a better quality of regional security, then North America fits that criterion. The community initially consisted of only two states (Canada and the

United States) and now has only three members, including Mexico. If the
EU is more successful than NATO and OSCE in terms of integration
among its members, it may be partly because of its smaller size so far.
The EU membership was initially small (starting with only six members,
when France and Germany gave birth to the European Coal and Steel
Community, together with Italy, Belgium, the Netherlands, and Luxem-
burg). Nowadays, the EU has 15 member states and thus remains smaller
than NATO (19 members) and the OSCE (55 members). The EU remains divided mainly between the original six who want closer political
integration and a minority (led by Britain) who have long wanted nothing more than a free trade arrangement. According to Roy Denman, a
former representative of the European Commission in Washington, "the
gap between the two camps shows no sign of closing. Opposition in Britain to any closer involvement with Europe is rising steadily" (*International Herald Tribune*, 26 April 2000: 8). No wonder the recent EU decision to consider 12 new applicants for admission into its fold has raised
concerns about its future. At the Helsinki summit in June 1999, Luxem-
burg Prime Minister Jean-Claude Juncker was among the sceptics who
asked how far Europe could go. Recently, both Valéry Giscard d'Estaing
(former President of France) and Helmut Schmidt (former Chancellor of
West Germany) also warned that "[already] with 15 member states, EU
institutions are not functioning well." They added their concern, saying
"[haste] to enlarge the Union can lead to a sequence of severe crises in
the first decade of the new century" (*International Herald Tribune*, 11
April 2000: 8).

By comparison, NATO and the OSCE have more members than the
EU. The rather large number of members has posed a challenge to collective action. The fact that each member can veto a proposed military
action is one explanation for the hesitant NATO intervention in Kosovo.
The member states disagreed, for instance, on whether to launch a land
attack on Serbia. Thus, deciding on the intervention in Kosovo, according to US Admiral Leighton W. Smith, who commanded NATO forces
in Bosnia in 1996, "... was Viet Nam 19 times. This lowest common-
denominator approach is no way to fight a war." Washington had to
shift "from trying to defeat Mr Milosevic to preserving the cohesion of
NATO" (*International Herald Tribune*, 21 April 2000: 6).

If OSCE has been generally less successful than the EU and NATO
in terms of achieving cooperation among member states and of coordinating their common activities, it is partly because the OSCE has fallen
short of meeting criterion 2. Its membership size has always been much
larger than that of the other two organizations. The number of the found-
ing members was 35, comprising Canada, the United States, and every
European state (including the Soviet Union) except Albania. Following the collapse of the Soviet Union and Yugoslavia, however, the mem-

bership quickly jumped to 55. With such a large membership and operating on the basis of consensus-minus-one, the OSCE has often been indecisive with regard to taking security-related action because of the threat of veto. According to Gregory Flynn and Henry Farrell, "there is ample evidence that states small and large were not shy about using this power" (Flynn and Farrell 1999: 513). Although the group adopted the consensus-minus-one rule in January 1992 (allowing the Council of Ministers to take action against any participating state deemed guilty of gross human rights violations), it is far from clear that this rule has worked well. For example, the organization used the rule to suspend Yugoslavia in the Spring of 1992, but "in the face of the violence that accompanied the collapse of Yugoslavia, the CSCE was powerless" (Flynn and Farrell 1999: 520).

In general, members of the three Western institutions have also proved to be more capable of working together to achieve certain common purposes and coordination. Interventions in Bosnia–Herzegovina and Kosovo, for instance, were not the work of NATO alone: the OSCE and the EU collaborated with NATO, which has promoted the concept of "interlocking institutions." In Barry Hughes' words, "[no] single organization is likely to organize the future security environment of Europe" (Hughes 1995: 237).

Criterion 3: Democratic values and performance

More importantly, almost all members of Western security communities have met this criterion. Most are mature liberal democracies with developed economies. Although peaceful relations between the United States and Canada need to be explained in terms of small size (two neighbours), the two states are among the world's most mature democracies. Sean Shore adopted a constructivist approach to help shed light on this security community (Shore 1998). One of the critical points he makes is that this community emerged during the 1870s, after the American Civil War. Although the "German question" and the Soviet threat induced states in Western Europe to cooperate, the reason for cooperation between the United States and Canada was not because they faced any such common threat; in fact, it was not until after the First World War broke out that the two neighbours shared a perception of a common threat. Although the stable peace in North America could not be replicated somewhere else, as Shore argues, it is more appropriate to explain this security community by considering the fact that Canada came to be perceived by the Americans as a liberal democracy. Prior to that period they considered Canada's parliamentary system to be antidemocratic and tyrannical.

After Mexico had adopted a policy of economic liberalization and become more democratic, its leaders took steps to promote better relations with Canada and the United States. It was President Carlos Salina of the Institutional Revolutionary Party (PRI, which has dominated the country since the late 1920s), who won the approval of NAFTA. During the second half of the 1990s, the PRI began to lose its grip on power. The elections of July 2000 finally put an end to 71 years of one-party rule and allowed a peaceful democratic transition of power. The newly elected leadership is committed to fighting against corruption, working for accountability of public officials, promoting the rule of law and security for all citizens, and accelerating economic growth. Current President Vicente Fox also pledged to engage his country's partners in NAFTA (*International Herald Tribune*, 26–27 August 2000: 6).

Western European states have also become mature democracies after centuries of violent state building. All EU members are democratic states and have sought to promote human rights. The EU carries on this tradition. Clearly, in seeking to enlarge their union, the existing members have undertaken a democratic project. Such applicants as Turkey (which fails to meet the EU's democratic and human-rights standards) have failed to gain full admission to the union. Stephen Van Evera argues that "key pre-conditions for democracy ... are now far more widespread in Europe than they were eighty years ago" (Van Evera 1990/1991: 26). These European democracies are also stable or mature, partly because they are wealthier than their predecessors. Their populations have benefited from more equitable distributions of wealth and incomes, thus making them less subject to the evils of militarism and hyper-nationalism.

The fact that the OSCE has been less successful than the EU and NATO in terms of cooperation among member states and humanitarian intervention also can be explained by the fact that its members do not fully share and practise liberal democracy. Although OSCE members were committed to working with the United Nations and pledged to promote human rights, several of them remain unstable democracies. Russia and other Eastern European members are fragile or illiberal democracies still with the potential to revert to authoritarianism. According to the 1995 US President's Report on OSCE activities, 15 of the 23 former Communist OSCE members received good marks on democracy, 14 in the rule of law, and 13 in human rights. The report also states, however, that "there is ample proof of the continuing existence of old, undemocratic attitudes and habits which reflect the great difficulty in changing deeply rooted totalitarian behavior and show that many countries have a long way to go" (Adler 1998: 131).

Criterion 4: Political leadership

Most importantly, the role of political leadership has been essential to the building and maintaining of Western security communities. Shared democratic values between Canada and the United States did not play the most decisive role in shaping the North American security community. Sean Shore fails to explain that Canada was the weaker state which could not expect to fight a successful war with the United States. Prior to confederation in 1867, "Canada was not even a unified state" (Shore 1998: 335). It also "disarmed after 1867" (Shore 1998: 333). More noteworthy is the fact that the development of this community came at a time when Britain had already decided to "quit the day-to-day defense of the continent in 1871, and left the task to the new [Canadian] government" (Shore 1998: 342). As the lesser power, Canada clearly posed little military threat to the United States and definitely could not entertain any idea of resisting the United States or of maintaining hostile relations with the latter. Being a NATO member, Canada has also been locked into this US-led military alliance. The "democratic peace" between the two nations must thus take the reality of US preponderance of power into account. Also noteworthy is the argument put forward by Sean Shore, who believes that "American preponderance ... facilitated a certain kind of trust, one that would have been more difficult to come by had Canada been more powerful" (Shore 1998: 344).

American leadership has also played an extremely important role in the development of democratic security communities in the West. The post-Second World War democratic-order project by the United States, for instance, resulted in the establishment of international institutions among Western democracies and Japan. The United States succeeded not only in turning Germany and Japan into liberal democracies but also in reintegrating them into the community of strong industrial economies (Nakamura 1998).

Why other Western democracies joined the United States is a matter of debate. However, as Michael Doyle acknowledges, American military leadership has helped to dampen the prospects of Western Europe and Japan re-emerging as independent military powers. In his view, the liberal peace could have been imperilled if Western Europe and Japan had established substantial forces independent of the United States (Doyle 1996: 28).

Within Western Europe itself, France and Germany have provided firm leadership in the process of regional integration. Robert Gilpin makes a very persuasive argument that the EU rests on a political foundation. European treaties, such as the Treaty of Paris and the Treaty of Rome, contain political objectives; thus, the desire to rid Europe of the French–German rivalry became the driving force for regional integration. The drive for European unification also arose from European leaders' realization that their continent was losing influence in world affairs. Gilpin views the "French–German alliance" as central to the ambition to create Euroland (Gilpin 2000). If the EU were to succeed in building a European army, it would be mainly because France and Germany took the lead. It was they who also set up Eurocorps in the 1990s.

However, the EU's unsuccessful intervention efforts in the former Yugoslavia can be explained by the fact that, before Kosovo, it was still unable to forge an effective common defence and foreign policy. The WEU, the military defence mechanism in the region, still lacks the institutional and logistical capacity to undertake peace-enforcement operations, as some EU member states (such as the United Kingdom) had remained committed to NATO. One analyst describes the WEU as "an organization in limbo and on hold" (Vierucci 1995: 308). Although the Kosovo crisis has led the EU to develop a new vision for the region by taking new steps to strengthen what is now called the "European Security and Defense Identity," the EU still remains an economically driven supranational organization. NATO's military power, however, compensated for the EU inability to terminate ethnic conflicts in the Balkans.

Recent NATO successes in humanitarian intervention, however modest, had much to do with the fact that the member states were led by powerful, mature democracies, such as the United States, Britain, and France. NATO was fortunate to have them lead the air campaign against Serbia. The United States provided 70 per cent of NATO's military capacity. Although its members had not always been willing to follow its lead, they resisted the Americans only so far, and did not risk the cohesion of the organization.

The OSCE, however, not only lacks resources but also faces the absence of a powerful democratic leader. President George Bush and Secretary of State James Baker referred to the CSCE as part of their vision for a "Europe whole and free." Its successes resulted from its members' shared values and norms as well as from the constructive role played by the great powers, most of whom are liberal democracies (Baker 1993). However, within the OSCE, neither the United States nor Russia is the dominant leader: besides not being a liberal democratic leader, Russia has been on the decline as a great power; neither can the United States be considered a power commanding obedience from the large number of states belonging to the OSCE.

Non-Western regions: Meeting few criteria for community building

On the basis of the four criteria of success in regional security community building, this chapter shows that regional organizations in the non-Western world have proved themselves far less effective than their

Western counterparts. A look at each of the well-known regional organizations bears this out. They include the OAS, the ASEAN, the GCC, the CIS, the OAU, the Southern African Development Community (SADC), and the Economic Community of Western African States (ECOWAS). This section compares the varying degrees of operational effectiveness in these regional organizations and assesses the performance of each in its security-community building efforts.

A survey of non-Western regional security communities

Whether Latin America has already created a security community is unclear. In the last decade, however, positive changes have taken place – from rivalry to institutionalized security and economic cooperation, especially in the form of Mercosur (the Southern Common Market) established in 1991 and with a common external tariff in 1995. According to Andrew Hurrell, even the enduring rivalry between two regional powers – Brazil and Argentina – was replaced by *rapprochement* at the end of the 1980s. This dramatic shift involved confidence-building measures and arms-control agreements. Shifts in military posture toward defensive orientation and a decline in military spending have also contributed to an avoidance of the balance-of-power rhetoric evident in the 1960s and 1970s (Hurrell 1998: 231).

This appears to coincide with the fact that the OAS has, over time, become more effective in its efforts to promote peace, to stabilize the region, and to strengthen human rights and democratic institutions. During the 1980s, the OAS could do little to help such war-torn countries as Nicaragua (where the organization was "conspicuous in its absence") and El Salvador (MacFarlane and Weiss 1994: 288). In 1989, its mediation efforts in Panama ended in failure and finally led to US intervention. The OAS intervention in Peru in 1992 was seen as endorsing undemocratic practices (Baranyi 1995). Nevertheless, some, such as Joaquín Tacsan, talk of "a renewed optimism toward the OAS" during the 1990s (Tacsan 1998: 91). In 1993, it helped to end the crisis in Guatemala. It also enjoyed a somewhat positive experience in Haiti, where it played a leading role in the deployment of a mission to the country to promote democracy and human rights. By and large, the OAS's performance in peace-building activity is less than impressive.

Admiral Dennis Blair, commander of the US forces in the Pacific, recently argued that "security communities are the way ahead for Asia" (*International Herald Tribune*, 21 April 2000: 6). However, more must be done to achieve this goal. The few existing regional organizations in Asia have been less effective than their counterparts in the West or even Latin and Central America. The Asia-Pacific Economic Cooperation (APEC),

ASEAN, and the ASEAN Regional Forum have come under criticism for failing to resolve the Asian economic crisis. Michael Finnegan has even acknowledged that "constructivist predictions of a security community for Northeast Asia are obviously some way from coming to pass" (Finnegan 1998: 7). Asia's best-known regional grouping, ASEAN, remains underinstitutionalized: it has a secretariat, formal and informal summits of heads of states, annual meetings of foreign ministers, and so on. However, it does not have such common institutions as an ASEAN Council, a Council of Ministers, an ASEAN Commission, an ASEAN Parliament, or an ASEAN Court of Justice. Since the end of the cold war, bilateral tensions have even been on the rise among ASEAN members (Ganesan 1999). Although ASEAN has a foundation for a security community, it has yet to develop further. Although the likelihood of interstate military confrontation has lessened, ASEAN has not reached the level of integration where its members agree on a common definition of external threat, a common defence and foreign policy with unfortified borders (Acharya 1998). Neither has ASEAN been largely responsible for promoting peace in member states such as Indonesia (the East Timor crisis) and in non-member states such as Cambodia.

A security community has yet to emerge in the Arab world. The GCC (with six members – Oman, Bahrain, the United Arab Emirates, Kuwait, Qatar, and Saudi Arabia) came into existence in 1981 when leaders signed the GCC Charter. The members have failed to transform themselves into a community with dependable expectations for peaceful change. Michael Barnett and F. Gregory Gause III argue that the GCC is a poor candidate for a security community in the foreseeable future because its member states still imagine the possibility of using force to settle their differences. After Iraq's invasion of one of its members (Kuwait) in August 1990, the GCC stood behind Kuwait from the outset. The member states cooperated under a single command, but they maintained their national organization and officers; the Gulf War did not lead to a stronger sense of regionalism among them. As Barnett and Gause point out, "perhaps the single result of the Gulf War was not the promotion of regionalism but rather the retreat to [unbridled] statism" (Barnett and Gause III 1998: 181). Qatar and Bahrain still pose a threat to each other in territorial disputes. As recently as 1992, Saudi Arabia and Qatar clashed over their border.

In the former Soviet Union, the CIS's security-related performance has also been less impressive than that of the OAS or ASEAN. Granted observer status at the United Nations as a regional organization as defined in Chapter VIII of the UN Charter, the CIS has undertaken peacekeeping operations in several of the new states torn by ethnic conflict. According to Ambassador Vladimir Zemskii (Secretary-General of the

Collective Security Council in the CIS), "[old] seats of conflicts remain and new ones are emerging on the perimeter of the member states borders on the regional level." Furthermore, the use of force based on ideological and military confrontation has been renounced, but military-bloc relapses have not been barred or averted. The region has not been freed from such menaces as the proliferation of weapons of mass destruction, international terrorism, illegal arms trafficking, aggressive nationalism, and ethnic and religious extremism (Zemskii 1999: 102). The CIS has sought to end civil wars between two minorities (the Ossetians and the Abkhaz) in the Republic of Georgia. Along with the OSCE, the CIS has tried to "make a considerable contribution to ensuring that there is no accidental resumption of hostilities" and thus "has allowed a degree of normalization in Georgia"; however, there was little movement toward a settlement of the dispute in South Ossetia (MacFarlane 1998: 121, 122), neither was there much progress towards a political settlement allowing the return of refugees and the restoration of Georgian jurisdiction in Abkhazia. The hostilities remain unresolved.

In Africa, (sub)regional organizations have also met with fewer successes. The major regional organizations have poor records. The OAU has a history of failure: it chose not to intervene in several conflicts, such as the Nigerian civil war in 1966. When the OAU decided to intervene in Chad between 1980 and 1982, its operation failed. It initially declined the request of the United Nations to intervene in Rwanda, on the grounds that the latter could do better. Although it finally sent military observer missions to Rwanda in the early 1990s and managed to send in 6,000 troops, it failed to prevent the large-scale massacre that occurred there in 1994. Troop deployment was delayed for almost five months. In early 2000, some 16 million people (half of them were in Ethiopia) in 16 states in East Africa still faced starvation. The OAU also failed to prevent or terminate the war between Ethiopia and Eritrea, which has sapped the strength of their impoverished economies. However, this is not the only war in Africa. The civil war in the Democratic Republic of the Congo involved about 10,000 troops from Zimbabwe, Angola, and Namibia supporting Congolese President Laurent Kabila's armed forces against rebels backed by Uganda and Rwanda. US Secretary of State Madelaine Albright even described the war as "Africa's first world war."

Other subregional organizations in Africa have not fared better. The ECOWAS in Liberia (a mission known as the ECOWAS Monitoring Group or ECOMOG) managed to create a political environment conducive to substantially free and fair elections (held on 19 July 1997). Nevertheless, this came at a very high price: during the course of a seven-year intervention, the security situation deteriorated considerably. At the time of ECOMOG's arrival, the civil war had already produced 5,000 deaths and 250,000 refugees. The next seven years, however, witnessed a dramatic rise of casualties – some 150,000 deaths and 700,000 refugees. According to Eric Berman, "[not] only did ECOMOG exacerbate the Liberian civil war, it also undermined regional peace and security" in that it "contributed to the civil war in neighboring Sierra Leone" (Berman 1998: 9). In his view, "Liberians and the region would have been better off without ECOMOG" (Berman 1998: 8). The newest of Africa's seven major subregional organizations, the Southern African Development ment Community (SADC) – formed in 1992 and whose security and defence commitments can be seen through the 1994 establishment of the Inter-State Defense and Security Committee (or ISDSC) – has not performed effectively. These African institutions have had some positive impact on the region. In 1994, for instance, SADC managed to bring pressure to bear on Lesotho when the military intervened to overthrow a recently elected civilian government. In the mid-1990s, the SADC and the OAU helped to prevent the genocide in Rwanda from spreading into Burundi. The ECOWAS also improved its record when it launched its ECOMOG operation in Sierra Leone at the beginning of February 1998 and ousted the Armed Forces Revolutionary Council/Revolutionary United Front (AFRC/RUF) junta. Unfortunately, these success stories are far too few and may not have a lasting effect.

The OAS as the most successful non-Western security community

In comparative terms, as is described later, the OAS's security-community building efforts have borne more fruit than those of most of the non-Western organizations. The earlier failures of the OAS can be easily explained in terms of its inability to meet most, if not all, of the aforementioned four criteria. These include limited experience in conflict management (criterion 1),[8] large membership size (32 states in the late 1980s; criterion 2), lack of commitment to democratic institutions (criterion 3),[9] and a general unwillingness of member states to endorse American political leadership (criterion 4).[10]

The relative successes of the OAS in recent years seem correlated to its growing ability to meet more of the four criteria. Its relatively successful interventions in member states, such as Guatemala in 1993, reveal that, with more experience in conflict management and democratic intervention, this old organization (formed as the International Union of American Republics in 1890) could better meet criterion 1.

More and more states in the region have also adopted similar policies, based on economic and political liberalism (meeting more of criterion 3). They have gradually implemented liberal market policies. South America's principal rivals – Brazil and Argentina – have become more co-operative after a shift toward market liberalism and the process of democratization has taken root. Every country in the region except Cuba has had democratic elections. In 1977, 14 of the 20 Latin American states were under military rule. In 1997, the number of countries believed to have made their way to democracy was 19. According to Peter Hakim, "[nowhere] in Latin America today is democratic rule threatened by military takeover, as it has been through most of the region's history" (Hakim 1999/2000: 113). Brazilian President Henrique Cardoso, once a leading dependency theorist, converted to economic liberalism. He also calls for "a bolstering of international democratic solidarity among states," as they face "threats of praetorian coups, bigotry, and all kinds of intolerance" (Cardoso 2000: 40). This came at a time after the OAS had come to favour democracy and human rights as liberal norms. In the Santiago commitment of June 1991, for instance, the OAS member states declared their intention to "internationalize issues of domestic governance" and stated that "democracy and human rights are essential to regional identity." In December 1994, the Summit of the Americas further adopted a Declaration of Principles reaffirming the OAS commitment to the active pursuit and defence of democratic institutions in the hemisphere. However, the small number of mature democracies in the region still plagues the OAS. The year 2000 saw worrisome democratic setbacks. The *Washington Post* now bemoans "democracy's decay in Latin America" (*Japan Times*, 6 June 2000: 16). Others also fear a "return of Latin America's strongmen" (*Japan Times*, 5 June 2000: 10).

Fortunately, the OAS region has not openly challenged the leadership of the United States (criterion 4). Unlike the period during the cold war when the unilateral actions of the United States offended OAS members, the last decade has seen better cooperation between them. The adoption of the liberal market model by most Latin American states "has removed many sources of friction that have traditionally set the United States in opposition to Latin America" (Eguizábal 1998: 361). In recent years, the United States has also seemed more determined to uphold human rights and democratic institutions. Mexico, for its part, had been sceptical about using multilateralism to impose such liberal values on states in the region. At the Santiago meeting in June 1991, Mexico successfully opposed a resolution proposing the automatic expulsion from the OAS of any member state whose democratic system was abolished by a *coup d'état*. In 1992, it resisted the attempt to remove the Fujimori government of Peru from the OAS, contending that such a measure would not help to restore democracy. Although Mexico continued to challenge the idea of democratic imposition, its leaders have made a subtle change and softened their stance. In 1993, for instance, the Mexican government supported the OAS's diplomatic role during the constitutional crisis in Guatemala (Gonzalez and Haggard 1998: 316–317).

Had the United States not intervened militarily in Haiti, the ousted President Aristide would not have been restored to power in 1994. Prior to the US intervention (backed by 20,000 US troops), the UN Security Council had instituted an embargo and frozen funds against the military leadership in Haiti; almost all Latin American countries, as well as France and the United States, violated the embargo, however. The attempt to restore President Aristide to power was eventually successful, mainly because the United States was both willing to take unilateral action (with the blessing of the OAS) and able to accomplish the mission by military means.

Reasons for lack of success in other non-Western regions

Regional organizations in Asia, such as ASEAN (Asia's oldest), appear to be less successful than the OAS in security-community-building efforts. The grouping has met few key criteria. ASEAN is a relatively young organization; although it is only 10 years younger than the EU, its members have not accumulated experience in security matters (criterion 1). During their first ten years together, ASEAN states made few efforts to promote regional cooperation; this came to be known as a "getting-to-know-each-other" period. As discussed later, extraregional powers have done more in helping resolve major security problems in the region.

Although there were only 5 ASEAN members in 1967, this number has since grown to 10, now with a strong possibility of increasing to 11 when newly independent East Timor decides to join the fold (thus meeting less of criterion 2). Regional coordination has been another of ASEAN's problems. Although it is known to be second only to the EU in terms of its success in promoting cooperation among member states, ASEAN has yet to become a defence community capable of conducting joint military operations. The Vietnamese occupation of Cambodia exposed the group's lack of military capabilities and coordination. ASEAN has so far failed to undertake peacemaking, peace-keeping, and peace building operations in its own region. Its members did not even coordinate the national forces they contributed to the UN Transitional Authority in Cambodia (UNTAC) from 1991 to 1993 (Peou 1998). The ASEAN members continue to disagree on what to do with the principle of non-interference in the domestic affairs of states and that of consensus-based decision-making. Adherence to decision-by-consensus has meant that collective action still proves elusive: they did not even agree on the need to intervene in East Timor (formerly part of Indonesia).

Moreover, ASEAN has met less of criterion 3. Amitav Acharya is partly correct in stressing that a community project in ASEAN has been undertaken without liberalism and in questioning whether liberalism is a necessary condition for security communities (Acharya 1998). His argument overlooks two factors. Economic liberalism has become a common ideology shared to varying degrees by the ten members (Solingen 1999), including communist Viet Nam and the military in Myanmar. It is worth recalling that the new ASEAN members joined the group after the heads of ASEAN states at the Singapore Summit 1992 agreed to establish the ASEAN Free Trade Area (AFTA) by the year 2008. Now with ten members, ASEAN may have become a two-tier institution, divided along economic and ideological lines between the rich and poor as well as between democratic and autocratic members.

If ASEAN has yet to become a security community, it only proves that, without democratic norms fully shared by the members, the possibility that they may be transformed into such a community is limited. Only two of the ten ASEAN member states, Thailand and the Philippines, can be considered to be newly emerging democracies, but they are still ridden with unresolved economic problems. Cambodia and Indonesia have made precarious transitions to democracy, because they remain among the poorest states in the region; the rest are either semi-democracies or full-blown authoritarian states. ASEAN also has two stable illiberal democracies with strong economies: these are Singapore and Malaysia. Three of its members still maintain near-totalitarian rule. The Communist Party in Laos dominates every aspect of political and social life. Viet Nam's system is also similar to that of China, based on Leninism. Myanmar has been ruled by a group of generals who have refused to transfer power to the winner of the election of 1990. The recent economic crises have reduced the progress of most of these countries. If current trends continue, the number of poor people in East Asia is likely to jump from only 40 million to more than 100 million in 2002.

Most importantly, ASEAN has been unable to meet criterion 4: it has never had a competent regional democratic leader. This is not to suggest that ASEAN never had a leader; from the beginning, Indonesia provided de facto leadership. In fact, one leading Asian scholar argues that it was the initiator of ASEAN creation (Anwar 1994). However, since Indonesia became mired in economic and financial crises, ASEAN has been adrift. No one within the group seems willing or able to provide effective democratic leadership. Indonesia, still in transition toward democracy, remains overwhelmingly self-absorbed. Neither democratic Thailand nor the democratic Philippines has played this role. One leading Thai scholar has admitted that "Thailand has been burned on various fronts [when it tried to take a leadership position]" (*Asiaweek*, 1 September 2000: 46).

Wealthy Singapore was both unwilling and unable to take the lead during the Asian economic crisis; Malaysia has turned inward; other autocracies objected to any form of intervention in the domestic affairs of states.

However, the absence of a regional democratic leader in the ASEAN region has been compensated by extraregional democratic states, such as Australia, France, and the United States. During the 10-year Vietnamese occupation of Cambodia, the latter enjoyed enormous diplomatic support from the West. The moderate successes of conflict management in the ASEAN region have resulted largely from the work of democratic powers outside the region. The absence of democratic leadership in South-East Asia has constrained its role in conflict management. The UN intervention in Cambodia from 1991 to 1993 stemmed from the new unity of the five Permanent Members (P-5) of the UN Security Council and their active support (Peou 1997, 2000). Between 1991 and 1999, foreign powers (most of which were liberal democracies) spent more than $4 billion on Cambodia. The United Nations has also been actively involved in East Timor. Australia (a mature liberal democracy not in South-East Asia) sent its forces into East Timor with the active support of the P-5 of the UN Security Council. Community-building efforts in East Asia have not taken place in the total absence of a democratic leader. In South-East Asia, no state has ever seriously ignored the need to keep the United States' military presence in the region. ASEAN states have sought to keep the United States in the region by offering naval access agreements.

Much more can be said about less-successful regional organizations in the Arab region. The GCC has not emerged as a security community: its members have failed to meet several key criteria. Although there are few members (only six, thus meeting criterion 2), they have resisted the idea of turning themselves into a security organization. One major problem is that the GCC is younger and less experienced than ASEAN (it was established in the 1980s in response to the Iran–Iraq war). The member states are all oil-rich, Islamic, and share several common historical features (which helped bring them together); these member states remain a club of staunch autocracies (failing criterion 3). They "all are monarchies developed out of tribal political structures, differentiating them from their larger republican neighbors (Iraq, Iran, and Yemen)" (Barnett and Gause 1998: 166–167). Despite its efforts to get into the GCC, North Yemen was turned down, simply because of its republican character.

Another main obstacle to Arab regionalism is that there is no democratic leader capable of leading the region or the council (failing criterion 4). Saudi Arabia is said to be "the logical candidate to be a core state"; however, "to other GCC states it looks less like a core state in a potential security community than it does a hegemon in classical realism" (Barnett and Gause 1998: 191). Saudi Arabia is not a regional democratic leader and is also believed to have even worked against democratizing trends in Kuwait, thus causing other GCC members to distrust it and to regard its potential leadership in the context of power alone.

It is also not difficult to discern why the CIS has been less impressive than ASEAN. The CIS has also failed to meet criterion 1: formed as recently as 1991, the CIS remains a very young organization and still lacks experience in conflict management. It comprises a large number (12) of member states, which are Armenia, Azerbaijan, Belarus, Georgia, Kazakhstan, Kyrgyztan, Moldova, Russia, Tajikstan, Turkmenistan, Ukraine, and Uzbekistan, and thus meets less of criterion 2. Moreover, CIS member states have been unable to act in concert: although they signed the Collective Security Treaty in 1992, the CIS lacks institutional cohesion (Zemskii 1999). The CIS has weakened to the point where one Russian scholar called it "a paper organization."[11] As former communist states, the CIS members still struggle painfully with democratic values. Russia has become more of an illiberal democracy (thus failing criterion 3) (*International Herald Tribune*, 26 June 2000: 8).

The CIS region is fortunate inasmuch as Russia has been both willing and able to play some leadership role in helping to manage civil wars in the region. CIS peace-keeping forces have been predominantly composed of Russian troops and commanded by Russian officers, without whom peace-keeping would not have been possible. Unfortunately, Russia is not a capable regional democratic leader (failing criterion 4). Since the Soviet Union collapsed in 1991, Russia has taken the lead in regional peace-keeping only with the aim of promoting its own strategic interests (MacFarlane 1998). Moscow has been widely perceived as having even encouraged some of the regional conflicts, having done little to promote international norms, and having made little effort to help the adversaries in the CIS reach political compromise. As a leading contributor to peace-keeping in the CIS region, Russia has apparently become less effective. According to Dov Lynch, Russia has shifted from picking sides and meddling with military force to the realization that conflicts in the region have become "costly and dangerous" (Lynch 2000). As an emerging illiberal democracy, Russia has helped dictators to stay in power. Like China, it has routinely defended both Iraq and Serbia in the UN Security Council (*International Herald Tribune*, 26 June 2000: 8).

If Africa appears to be the unlikeliest potential candidate for security-community building, it is mainly because regional organizations in Africa, such as the OAU and ECOWAS, have also met few of the requirements for promoting effective peace-keeping and peace building. Formed in 1963, the OAU is older than ASEAN but younger than the EU. The OAU seems unable to meet criterion 1 (experience in conflict management/ resolution). Before the 1980 OAU intervention in Chad, for instance, the organization had no experience in humanitarian actions.

Moreover, the OAU membership size is very large. The original membership was 30 and has grown to include about 50 states by the early 1990s, almost as large as the OSCE (thus not effectively meeting criterion 2). The OAU has not been up to the task of coordinating military activities. Its role in Chad was hampered by lack of "an institutional and legal structure for an armed intervention" (May and Massey 1998: 51).

Africa has definitely failed to meet criteria 3 and 4. Few states, if any, can be considered mature liberal democracies. The absence of capable democratic leaders in subregions also poses another major problem to any community-building efforts. When a regional leader is willing to play a leadership role, it does not prove to be effective. Nigeria played the role of a regional leader (which made interventions in Chad on behalf of the OAU possible) and took the lead in the Liberian peace operation (contributing 80 per cent of the multinational force, when ECOMOG's strength finally reached 12,000 during "Operation Octopus" in October 1992). Without Nigeria (and, to a lesser extent, Ghana, with the second-largest number of troops), no intervention would have been possible. Because of their relatively small armies, other members were reluctant to contribute their troops: Senegal pulled out its troops immediately after nine were massacred by the National Patriotic Front of Liberia. The troops from East African states also left Liberia after having realized that they were exposed to too much danger.

Nigeria has not been a capable democratic leader. Although the current government was democratically elected, it is unclear whether the democratic process will grow stronger. Although the country claimed to have spent $10 billion in the last ten years on peace-keeping, it is also unclear whether the claim is accurate or if the country would have that kind of money to spend on peace-keeping in the future. Nigeria itself had previously experienced political crises at home (for example, its civil war, which started in 1966, was probably the most extensive in the region at the time) and has since continued to struggle with limited resources (Adibe 1998). The country has a legacy of nearly 16 years of military dictatorship. Although it is potentially one of Africa's wealthiest countries, the economy has been in a shambles. The late military dictator Sami Abacha and his cronies are alleged to have stolen as much as $6 billion in official funds from the country over his five-year reign. The country now bears a heavy debt burden of more than $30 billion.

Unlike ASEAN, Africa has not received as much attention as it should have from leading members of the United Nations. To be fair, the region has seen several UN peace missions in the last ten years, but they came in either too late or not well equipped to deal with the crises. During the OAU intervention in Chad, for instance, the United Nations not only failed to authorize the interventions but also "appeared unwilling to approve an unprecedented subvention for an operation not under UN control." Neither did the Western states or members of the Council offer any support for funding (May and Massey 1998: 59).[12] Nothing is closer to the truth than the failure of the United Nations to prevent the slaughter of more than half a million civilians in Rwanda. In April 2000, the Security Council accepted responsibility for having failed to stop the massacres and vowed to do more to prevent such atrocities – a vow remaining to be fulfilled. Although the Council has now tried to put the peace process in the Congo back on track by authorizing a 5,500-member peace-keeping force, its commitments remain far less than desirable.

Conclusions

This study has pointed to variation in regional peace and stability. North America and Western Europe have become the most stable regional security communities in the world, whereas regions in the non-Western world have not experienced the same levels of stability and peace. In terms of security-community-building potential among non-Western regions, Latin and Central America have generally become more peaceful and stable than Asia, which has become slightly more stable and peaceful than the GCC and the CIS areas, which in turn have achieved greater stability than Africa.

Variation in regional stability and peace depends on the number of criteria for success in community building that the member states of each region have attained over the years. Table 3.1 shows that North America, the EU, and NATO as security communities have met the most criteria, followed by the OSCE, OAS, ASEAN, GCC, CIS, and African organizations.

Among the four criteria identified in this study, democratic values/ performance within a regional organization (criterion 3) and the presence of democratic leadership (criterion 4) are most fundamental to security-community building. Although experience in conflict management (criterion 1) matters, it is, in itself, not the best answer to regional instability. Membership size (criterion 2) is much more important to regional community building, but not the most decisive one: neither ASEAN nor the GCC has developed into a stable security community, despite the fact that each has a small number of members compared with the other regional organizations. Where there is only an attempt to build a regional security community whose members do not share democratic

Table 3.1 Comparison of the community-building criteria of regional organizations

Criteria	Region[a] Western				Non-Western				
	NA	EU	NATO	OSCE	OAS	ASEAN	GCC	CIS	OAU[b]
Experience in conflict management	XXX[c]	XXX	XX(X)	XX	XX	XX	X	X	X
Membership size	XXX	XX	XX	X	X	XX	XX	XX	X
Democratic values/ performance	XXX	XXX	XXX	XX	XX	X	X	X	X
Democratic leadership	XXX	XXX	XXX	XX	XX	X	X	X	X
Total no. of Xs[d]	12	11	10	7	7	6	5	5	4

a. NA, North America; EU, European Union; NATO, North Atlantic Treaty Organization; OSCE, Organization for Security and Cooperation in Europe; OAS, Organization of American States; ASEAN, Association of South-East Asian Nations; GCC, Gulf Cooperation Council; CIS, Commonwealth of Independent States; OAU, Organization of African Unity.
b. This includes other African subregional organizations, such as the Southern African Development Community (SADC) and the Economic Community of Western African States (ECOWAS).
c. XXX = very strong; XX = strong; X = weak.
d. The more Xs for a region, the better the quality of security community the region is likely to experience.

values, the prospect for success is slimmer (criterion 3). Non-Western regions have not fully met criterion 4.

Where there are democracies without a capable democratic leader, nascent security communities will not prosper. Not surprisingly, only North America and Western Europe have fulfilled this criterion. The question of leadership has now been recognized by UN Secretary-General Kofi Annan, who made it clear that "unless the Security Council is restored to its pre-eminent position as the sole source of legitimacy on the use of force, we are on a dangerous path to anarchy" (*International Herald Tribune*, 22 November 1999: 10). This implies a need for effective leadership and (more importantly) one to be provided by stable liberal democracies. To help promote global governance, the Council will need to have more permanent members that are liberal democracies, to ensure more effective collective action.

To promote global governance through security-community building, the United Nations and stable liberal democracies in the Western regions may have to think creatively about how to help transform powerful regional states – such as China (in Asia), Russia (in the CIS region), and Nigeria (in Africa) – into stable democracies. (This is not to promote liberal imperialism or excessive military intervention by powerful liberal democracies.) Until that happens, however, leading Western democracies need to engage and/or restrain potentially aggressive non-democratic states and should stay closely involved by doing more to encourage the growth of small non-Western organizations.

Notes

1. See "An Agenda for Peace, Preventive Diplomacy, Peacemaking and Peace Building. Report of the Secretary-General pursuant to the statement adopted by the Summit Meeting of the Security Council on 31 January 1992." UN Document, A/47/277-S/24111, 17 June 1992, para. 21. "The Causes of Conflict and the Promotion of Durable Peace and Sustainable Development in Africa. Report of the Secretary-General to the United Nations Security Council." UN Document A/52/871-S/1998/318, 16 April 1998, para. 63.
2. "Report of the Panel on United Nations Peace Operations." UN Document A/55/305, S/2000/809, 17 August 2000, p. viii.
3. As of 15 June 1999, 24 member states were in arrears under the terms of Article 19 of the UN Charter, which states that any member with arrears equal to two years of assessments will automatically lose its vote in the UN General Assembly. The USA still owed the United Nations over $1.3 billion.
4. Some scholars, such as Amitav Acharya, adopt a sociological perspective in their contention that security communities can also be built on a non-liberal foundation. This point is discussed later in the chapter.
5. The role of political leadership is acknowledged in this study. Not all realists believe that states always balance against power. Stephen Walt argues that states balance against threats and "bandwagon" with any power that does not threaten them (Walt 1995). Randall Schweller argues that states bandwagon with powerful states when they are opportunistic as well as when they are threatened (Schweller 1995). Even Kantian internationalists such as Michael Doyle recognize the importance of power distribution and leadership. According to Doyle, "independent and more substantial European and Japanese military forces pose problems for liberal cooperation" (Doyle 1996: 28). Constructivist thinking is not free from power considerations, either. Alexander Wendt, for instance, accepts that the impact of great powers remains fundamental in international politics: "[I]t is the great powers, the states with the greatest national means, that may have the hardest time learning this lesson," whereas "small powers do not have the luxury of relying on national means and may therefore learn faster that collective recognition is a cornerstone of security" (Wendt 1995: 153). In their book *Security Communities*, Emanuel Adler and Michael Barnett also argue that "the study of security communities offers a blend of *idealism* ... and *realism*" (Adler and Barnett 1998: 14) (italics original). More importantly, constructivists are pro-status quo in the sense that their understanding of peaceful change does not rest on a vision based on the idea of

equalizing power asymmetries among the member states of a particular security community. Mutual trust and collective identity do not negate the fact that some of their members are more powerful. In this context, trust- and identity-building processes are not independent from power relations. As Adler and Barnett put it: "[P]ower can be a magnet; a community formed around a group of strong powers creates the expectations that weaker states will be able to enjoy the security and potentially other benefits that are associated with that community." In other words, "those powerful states who belong to the core of strength do not create security *per se*; rather, because of their positive images of security or material progress that are associated with powerful and successful states, security communities develop around them" (Adler and Barnett 1998: 40). They further contend that "the development of a security community is not antagonistic to the language of power; indeed, it is *dependent on* it" (Adler and Barnett 1998: 52) (italics added).

6. James Meernik (1996), for instance, found that if the US President declares democracy as a goal of the intervention and if the US government is opposed to the targeted regime, democracy is likely to be promoted.

7. Cf. Table 3.1.

8. According to Neil MacFarlane and Thomas Weiss, its "main experience was as an American surrogate in 1968 for the so-called peacekeeping operation in the Dominican Republic." Neil MacFarlane and Thomas Weiss, "The United Nations, Regional Organization and Human Security: Building Theory in Central America," (MacFarlane and Weiss 1994: 289).

9. In the early 1980s, the OAS General Assembly refused to comment on human rights abuses in Chile and Argentina. Later, the OAS condemned General Manuel Noriega and his regime for "grave events and abuses" and urged him to transfer power "with complete respect for the sovereign will of the Panamanian people." However, most members were not committed to the defence of human rights and democratic institutions. As described later, it was not until June 1991 that they began to accept human and democratic rights as liberal norms to guide their action.

10. This was the case for Panama, where the OAS Permanent Council condemned the US invasion in 1989.

11. Professor Sergei M. Plekhanov of York University, Toronto; personal discussion, 30 July 1999.

12. Generally, (sub)regional institutions in Africa do not enjoy high degrees of international legitimacy or credibility. They often act or intervene in other countries without authorization from the Security Council. This was also the case with the Great Lakes region, where the military involvement of Angola, Rwanda, and Zimbabwe in the Democratic Republic of Congo's domestic conflict received no active responses from the Security Council.

REFERENCES

Acharya, Amitav. 1998. "Collective Identity and Conflict Management in Southeast Asia." In: *Security Communities*, eds Emanuel Adler and Michael Barnett. Cambridge: Cambridge University Press.

Adibe, Clement E. 1998. "The Liberian Conflict and the ECOWAS–UN Partnership." In: *Beyond UN Subcontracting: Task-sharing with Regional Security Arrangements and Service Providing NGOs*, ed. Thomas Weiss. New York: St Martin's Press.

Adler, Emanuel. 1998. "Seeds of Peaceful Change: the OSCE's Security Community-building Model." In: *Security Communities*, eds Emanuel Adler and Michael Barnett. Cambridge: Cambridge University Press.

Adler, Emanuel and Michael Barnett. 1998. "Security Communities in Theoretical Perspective." In: *Security Communities*, eds Emanuel Adler and Michael Barnett. Cambridge: Cambridge University Press.

Alagappa, Muthiah and Takashi Inoguchi, eds. 1999. *International Security Management and the United Nations*. Tokyo: United Nations University Press.

Anwar, Dewi Fortuna. 1994. *Indonesia in ASEAN: Foreign Policy and Regionalism*. Singapore: Institute of Southeast Asian Studies.

Baker, James. 1993. "A New Europe, A New Atlanticism: Architecture for a New Era." Washington, DC: United States Department of State, Bureau of Public Affairs, No. 12, 299–322.

Baranyi, Stephen. 1995. "Peace Missions and Subsidiarity in the Americas: Conflict Management in the Western Hemisphere." *International Journal* 50(2): 343–369.

Barnett, Michael and Emanuel Adler. 1998. "Studying Security Communities in Theory, Comparison, and History." In: *Security Communities*, eds Emanuel Adler and Michael Barnett. Cambridge: Cambridge University Press.

Barnett, Michael and F. Gregory Gause III. 1998. "Caravans in Opposite Directions: Society, State, and the Development of Community in the Gulf Cooperation Council." In: *Security Communities*, eds Emanuel Adler and Michael Barnett. Cambridge: Cambridge University Press.

Berman, Eric. 1998. "The Security Council's Increasing Reliance on Burden-Sharing: Collaboration or Abrogation?" *International Peacekeeping* 4(1): 1–21.

Cardoso, Fernando Henrique. 2000. "Naming a New Era: An Age of Citizenship." *Foreign Policy* 119 (Summer), 40–42.

Commission on Global Governance. 1995. *Our Global Neighborhood*. New York: Oxford University Press.

Doyle, Michael. 1986. "Liberalism and World Politics." *American Political Science Review* 80(4): 1151–1169.

Doyle, Michael. 1996. "Kant, Liberal Legacies, and Foreign Affairs." In: *Debating the Democratic Peace*, eds Michael Brown, Sean M. Lynn-Jones, and Steven E. Miller. Cambridge, MA: MIT Press.

Eguizábal, Christina. 1998. "Regional Arrangements, the United Nations, and Security in Latin America." In: *Security Communities*, eds Emanuel Adler and Michael Barnett. Cambridge: Cambridge University Press.

Finnegan, Michael J. 1998. *Constructing Cooperation: Toward Multilateral Security Cooperation in Northeast Asia. Paper No. 18*. Toronto, Canada: CANCAPS.

Flynn, Gregory and Henry Farrell. 1999. "Piecing Together the Democratic Peace: The CSCE, Norms, and the 'Construction of Security' in Post-Cold War Europe." *International Organization* 53(3): 505–535.

Gaddis, John Lewis. 1987. *The Long Peace: Inquiries into the History of the Cold War*. New York: Oxford University Press.

Ganesan, N. 1999. *Bilateral Tensions in Post-Cold War ASEAN*. Singapore: Institute of Southeast Asian Studies.

Gilpin, Robert. 2000. *The Challenge of Global Capitalism: The World Economy in the 21st century*. Princeton, NJ: Princeton University Press.

Goodby, James E. 1993. "Collective Security in Europe After the Cold War." *Journal of International Affairs* 46(2): 299–322.

Gonzalez, Guadalupe and Stephen Haggard. 1998. "The United States and Mexico: a Pluralistic Security Community?" In: *Security Communities*, eds Emanuel Adler and Michael Barnett. Cambridge: Cambridge University Press.

Goulding, Marrack. 1999. "Globalization and the United Nations: New Opportunities, New Demands." *International Relations* 14(4): 55–62.

Griffin, Michèle. 1999a. "Blue Helmet Blues: Assessing the Trend Towards 'Subcontracting' UN Peace Operations." *Security Dialogue* 30(1): 43–60.

Griffin, Michèle. 1999b. "Retrenchment, Reform and Regionalization: Trends in UN Peace Support Operations." *International Peacekeeping* 6(1): 1–31.

Hakim, Peter. 1999/2000. "Is Latin America Doomed to Failure?" *Foreign Policy* 117 (Winter 1999–2000), 104–119.

Harada, Shiro and Akihiko Tanako. 1999. "Regional Arrangements, the United Nations, and Security in Asia." In: *International Security Management and the United Nations*, eds Muthiah Alagappa and Takashi Inoguchi. Tokyo: United Nations University Press.

Holsti, Kalevi J. 1988. *International Politics: A Framework for Analysis*, 5th edn. Englewood Cliffs, NJ: Prentice-Hall.

Holsti, Kalevi J. 1989. "Paths to Peace? Theories of Conflict Resolution and Realities of International Politics." In: *International Conflict Resolution*, ed. Ramesh Thakur. Boulder, CO: Westview Press.

Holsti, Kalevi J. 1991. *Peace and War: Armed Conflicts and International Order 1648–1989*. Cambridge: Cambridge University Press.

Homer-Dixon, Thomas F. 1998. "Environmental Scarcities and Violent Conflict." In: *Theories of War and Peace*, eds Michael Brown, Owen R. Cote, Sean Lynn-Jones, and Steven M. Miller. Cambridge, MA: MIT Press.

Hughes, Barry B. 1995. "Evolving Patterns of European Integration and Governance: Implications for Theories of World Politics." In: *Controversies in International Relations Theory: Realism and the Neoliberal Challenge*, ed. Charles W. Kegley, Jr. New York: St Martin's Press.

Huntington, Samuel. 1993. "The Clash of Civilizations." *Foreign Affairs* 72(3): 22–49.

Hurrell, Andrew. 1998. "An Emerging Security Community in South America?" In: *Security Communities*, eds Emanuel Adler and Michael Barnett. Cambridge: Cambridge University Press.

Jervis, Robert. 1991/1992. "The Future of World Politics: Will It Resemble the Past?" *International Security* 16(3): 39–73.

Knight, Andy. 1996. "Toward a Subsidiarity Model for Peacemaking and Preventive Diplomacy: Making Chapter VIII of the UN Charter Operational." *Third World Quarterly* 17(1): 31–52.

Leurdijk, Dick A. 1996. *The United Nations and NATO in Former Yugoslavia, 1991–1996 Limits to Diplomacy and War*. The Hague: The Netherlands Atlantic Commission.

Lucas, Michael R. 1996. "The OSEC Code of Conduct and its Relevance in Contemporary Europe." *Aussenpolitik* [English edn] 47(3): 223–235.

Lynch, Dov. 2000. *Russian Peacekeeping Strategies in the CIS: The Cases of Moldova, Georgia, and Tajikistan*. New York: St Martin's Press.

MacFarlane, S. Neil. 1998. "On the Front Lives in the Near Abroad: The CIS and the OSCE in Georgia's Civil Wars." In: *Beyond UN Subcontracting: Tasksharing with Regional Security Arrangements and Service Providing NGOs*, ed. Thomas Weiss. New York: St Martin's Press.

MacFarlane, S. Neil and Thomas G. Weiss. 1994. "The United Nations, Regional Organizations and Human Security: Building Theory in Central America." *Third World Quarterly* 15(2): 277–295.

Mandelbaum, Michael. 1999. "A Perfect Failure." *Foreign Affairs* 78(5): 2–8.

Maoz, Zeev and Bruce Russett. 1993. "Normative Structural Causes of Democratic Peace, 1946–1986." *American Political Science Review* 87(3): 624–638.

May, Roy and Simon Massey. 1998. "The OAU Interventions in Chad: Mission Impossible or Mission Evaded?" *International Peacekeeping* 15(1): 46–65.

Mearsheimer, John J. 1990. "Back to the Future: Instability in Europe after the Cold War." *International Security* 15(1): 5–56.

Meernik, James. 1996. "United States Military Intervention and the Promotion of Democracy." *Journal of Peace Research* 33(4): 391–402.

Mendez, Ruben P. 1997. "Financing the United Nations and the International Public Sector: Problems and Reform." *Global Governance* 3(3): 283–310.

Nakamura, Masanori. 1998. "Democratization, Peace, and Economic Development in Occupied Japan, 1945–1952." In: *Democracy in East Asia*, eds Larry Diamond and Marc F. Plattner. Baltimore: Johns Hopkins University Press.

Olson, Mancur. 1965. *The Logic of Collective Action*. Cambridge, MA: Harvard University Press.

Peou, Sorpong. 1997. *Conflict Neutralization in the Cambodia War: from Battlefield to Ballot-Box*. New York: Oxford University Press.

Peou, Sorpong. 1998. "The Subsidiarity Model of Global Governance in the UN–ASEAN Context." *Global Governance* 4(4): 439–459.

Peou, Sorpong. 2000. *Foreign Intervention and Regime Change in Cambodia: Towards Democracy?* New York: St Martin's Press/Singapore: Institute of Southeast Asian Studies.

Przeworski, Adam, Michael Alvarez, and José Antonio Cheibub. 1996. "What Makes Democracies Endure?" *Journal of Democracy* 7(1): 39–55.

Rhodes, Carolyn, ed. 1998. *The European Union in the World Community*. Boulder, CO: Lynne Rienner.

Rosenau, James. 1992. "Governance, Order, and Change in World Politics." In: *Governance Without Government: Order and Change in World Politics*, eds James Rosenau and Ernst-Otto Czempiel. Cambridge: Cambridge University Press.

Ruggie, John G. 1998. *Constructing the World Polity*. New York: Routledge.

Schweller, Randall. 1995. "Bandwagoning for Profit: Bringing in the State Back In." In: *The Perils of Anarchy: Contemporary Realism and International Anarchy*, eds Michael Brown, Sean Lynn-Jones, and Steve Miller. Cambridge, MA: MIT Press.

Shore, Sean M. 1998. "No Fences Make Good Neighbors: The Development of the Canadian–US Security Community, 1871–1940." In: *Security Communities*, eds Emanuel Adler and Michael Barnett. Cambridge: Cambridge University Press.

Smith, Edwin M. and Thomas G. Weiss. 1998. "UN Task-Sharing: Toward or

Away from Global Governance." In: *Beyond UN Subcontracting: Task-sharing with Regional Security Arrangements and Service Providing NGOs*, ed. Thomas G. Weiss. New York: St Martin's Press.

Solingen, Etel. 1999. "ASEAN, Quo Vadis? Domestic Coalitions and Regional Cooperation." *Contemporary Southeast Asia* 21(1): 30–53.

Steinberg, James B. 1999. "A Perfect Polemic: Blind to Reality on Kosovo." *Foreign Affairs* 78(6): 128–133.

Tacsan, Joauín. 1998. "Searching for OAS/UN Task-Sharing Opportunities in Central America and Haiti." In: *Beyond UN Subcontracting: Task-sharing with Regional Security Arrangements and Service Providing NGOs*, ed. Thomas Weiss. New York: St Martin's Press.

United Nations Development Programme. 1994. *Human Development Report 1994.* New York: United Nations.

Van Evera, Stephen. 1990/1991. "Primed for Peace: Europe After the Cold War." *International Security* 15(3): 7–57.

Vierucci, Luisa. 1995. "The Role of the Western European Union (WEU) in the Maintenance of International Peace and Security." *International Peacekeeping* 2(3): 309–329.

Wæver, Ole. 1998. "Insecurity, Security, and Asecurity in the Western European non-war Community." In: *Security Communities*, eds Emanuel Adler and Michael Barnett. Cambridge: Cambridge University Press.

Wallensteen, Peter and Margareta Sollenberg. 1995. "The End of International War: Armed Conflict 1989–95." *Journal of Peace Research* 33(3): 353–370.

Walt, Stephen. 1995. "Alliance Formation and the Balance of World Power." In: *The Perils of Anarchy: Contemporary Realism and International Anarchy*, eds Michael Brown, Sean Lynn-Jones, and Steve Miller. Cambridge, MA: MIT Press.

Waltz, Kenneth. 1979. *Theory of International Politics*. Reading, MA: Addison-Wesley.

Weiss, Thomas G., ed. 1998. *Beyond UN Subcontracting: Task-sharing with Regional Security Arrangements and Service Providing NGOs*. New York, NY: St Martin's Press.

Wendt, Alexander. 1995. "Anarchy Is What States Make of It: The Social Construction of Power Politics." In: *International Theory: Critical Investigations*, ed. James Der Derian. New York: New York University Press.

Zakaria, Fareed. 1997. "The Rise of Illiberal Democracy." *Foreign Affairs* 76(6): 22–43.

Zemskii, Vladimir. 1999. "Collective Security in the CIS." *International Affairs* 45(1): 97–104.

Ziring, Lawrence, Robert Riggs, and Jack Plano. 2000. *The United Nations: International Organization and World Politics*. Fort Worth, TX: Harcourt College Publishers.

4

Economic globalization and global governance: Towards a post-Washington Consensus?[1]

Richard Higgott

Introduction

At first glance, a chapter focusing on the relationship between market forces and governance seems like an exercise in confusion, if not contradiction. For many observers, "the market" implies the opposite of "governance." This at least has been the credo of the "free" market during its intellectual-cum-ideological hegemony of the last two decades. Yet even at the height of a neo-liberal understanding of economic globalization that characterized the post-cold-war world of the first half of the 1990s, such a stark polarization was always misleading. Markets, as Karl Polanyi (1994) told us a long time ago, have always been socially constructed.

Only since the rapid expansion and deregulation of the global financial markets over the last decade, driven by advances in technology and communication, which saw daily financial flows grow from something like $200 million per day in the mid-1980s to $1.5 trillion per day in the late 1990s (Beddoes 1999: 16), have we begun to assume that market power has totally escaped the jurisdiction of state authority.[2] Furthermore, only since the financial crises of 1997 have influential policy makers (as opposed to largely uninfluential scholarly analysts of a "market-sceptical" persuasion) begun to think that this might be functionally problematic and in need of serious political (as opposed to economic) attention. The early twenty-first century is a period of intellectual rethinking about the relationship between the market and the state.

A major dynamic of this rethinking is to be found in the relationship between the imperative to preserve the openness and continued liberalization of markets and provide for stable governance of the international economy to ensure this continued openness while at the same time mitigating the worst excesses and inequality-generating activities of markets under conditions of globalization. For, in the wake of the post-1997–1999 "globalization backlash" it is recognized, even in some of the most market-zealous circles, that without some governance of its worst excesses, market liberalization under conditions of globalization might contain within it the seeds of its own downfall.

Globalization is the most overused and underspecified concept in the lexicon of the social and policy sciences since the end of the cold war. Its many meanings – be they economic, political, cultural, sociological, or anthropological – cannot be reviewed in this chapter.[3] However, the brief of this chapter is to examine the relationship between "market forces and global governance," so a simple definition must prevail. Globalization is thus defined as the tendency towards international economic integration, liberalization, and financial deregulation beyond the sovereignty of the territorial state. Again in equally simple terms, governance is seen as those arrangements – across a spectrum from weak to strong in influence – that various actors attempt to put in place to advance, manage, retard, control, regulate, or mitigate market globalization.

This chapter looks at the dynamics of this relationship between the market and the theory and practice of governance beyond the territorial state under conditions of globalization in three contexts: (1) the ideological contest to define the nature of this relationship – especially the struggle between liberalization and demands for some international re-regulation of the liberalization processes that developed after the currency crises from July 1997; (2) the increasing interplay of intergovernmental actors and powerful states with some governmental and non-state actors (the weaker states and the stronger non-governmental organizations [NGOs]); and (3) a recognition that the core of the coming struggle over the continued pace of liberalization is the political struggles about the distribution of global wealth, not merely technical economic struggles about how best to produce that wealth.

We are witnessing an emerging contest in the domain of international economic governance between "winners" and "losers" under conditions of globalization. The transnationalization of market forces, notwithstanding its ability to increase aggregate wealth, is widely thought to exacerbate inequality. In so doing, it is reducing the capacity of international organizations, in particular those of the UN system, to generate acceptable institutional processes of extraterritorial governance that might mitigate this growing inequality and accompanying political resentment. Globalization not only is perceived to be enlarging the gap between rich and poor, it is also increasing the political tensions between states that have international political influence and states that do not.

The institutions of international economic governance as currently constituted (G-7, the Bretton Woods institutions, the World Trade Organization [WTO]) represent the interests of the powerful, not the poorer states. Those global norms and rules that underwrote the institutional architecture of the last decade of the twentieth century (the Washington Consensus [WC][4]), and attempts to reform these norms and rules in the domains of trade, investment, labour standards, the environment, transparency, capacity building and, yes, "governance" (what I call here attempts to develop a post-Washington Consensus [PWC]) are still driven by "northern agendas." The less powerful states remain "rule takers" within international economic institutions. However, a process of political contest and transition is under way (or so it is argued in this chapter). It is too early to know the outcome of this process, but it may be that either the rules on offer will lack legitimacy and/or not be enforced by the poorer states or (as is also possible) the states concerned may lack the necessary governmental effectiveness to enforce them, should they wish to do so.

Either way, these processes have negative implications for a consensus-based evolution of global governance norms. The "top down" global governance agenda of the late 1990s is driven by an understanding of governance as *effectiveness and efficiency*, not by one of democracy, accountability, and justice. Rather than these reforms creating a new array of global public goods of a reformist nature (their avowed goal), the possibility is that they might generate new forms of resistance. Without a normative and practical commitment to stem the globalization of inequity, international politics may be on the verge of a call for a New International Economic Order of the kind that stalemated North–South economic relations in the 1970s.

In the second section of this chapter (pp. 130–134), some relevant aspects of the evolution of contemporary globalization and their relevance for an understanding of its relationship to governance questions are set out. It asks why, despite its success as a generator of aggregate wealth, has international economic liberalization's triumph not been total? The third section (pp. 134–144) looks at the issue of "global governance." While recognizing the problematic and contested nature of the term, it argues that, in the move from a WC to a PWC, there is an international institutional exercise in train to see in what ways the collective provision of global public goods (the Washington policy community is not yet ready for the concept of "global governance"!) might be advanced in order to stem the worst excesses of globalization. The fourth section (pp. 144–

147) offers some pointers towards the emerging reform agenda on offer at this historical juncture. The chapter's Conclusion (pp. 148–152) is, however, pessimistic. Success is unlikely, given the limited nature of the exercise and its unlikely acceptance in the developing world.

The "triumph" of market globalization

Early understandings of globalization, especially economic ones, were primarily "process" or "flow" definitions – identifying the increasing mobility of factors such as capital, labour, information, and technology brought about by liberalization, privatization, and deregulation. These activities are not historically "new" (Polyani 1994); rather, it is their volume, scope, depth, speed, and clustering that is unprecedented. Market reform and the retreat of the state may have occurred in previous historical eras, but not in combination with a rapid growth of foreign direct investments (FDI) and of multilateral institutions and the spread of a single ideology. This definition also assumes that globalization leads to convergence, through market pressures that emphasize "best practices" (Williamson 1996: 278). While there is evidence to demonstrate recent major change in the international economy, especially in the deregulation of global capital markets, the degree of convergence of macroeconomic policy around a single neo-liberal model is overstated.[5]

Early definitions also demonstrated an optimistic, progressive, modernist teleology of a (now clichéd) borderless world in which the nation-state becomes irrelevant[6] and in which globalization becomes a "normalizing discourse" of power conditioning the policy responses of governments to the perception, if not always the reality, of global market integration. Nowhere was this better exemplified than in analyses that see a revolution taking place not only in relations between the state and the economy but also within civil society. In its most bullish form, proponents of this view contend that:

[N]ew technology will lead to big productivity increases that will cause high economic growth – actually, waves of technology will continue to roll out through the early part of the 21st century ... and a new ethos of openness ... will transform our world into the beginnings of a global civilisation, a new civilisation of civilisations, that will blossom through the coming century. (Schwarz and Leyden 1997: 116)

This view is influential amongst representatives of the "networked economy"; that is, those members of the international managerial and policy élite, vertically linked into the global economy in a flexible fashion, who travel easily between the corporate worlds of New York and the major European financial hubs and their counterparts in the foreign and finance ministries of the major countries of the Organization for Economic Co-operation and Development (OECD) and the international financial institutions. As this chapter argues, they were the key players in the construction of Williamson's "Washington Consensus."[7] It is a technological–economistic definition, but it is bereft of any sense of the limits of liberalization or any serious political theory that might lead to a realization of the problematic nature of the teleology espoused. Prior to the economic downturns of 1997 it demonstrated little appreciation of any of the downsides of globalization or, indeed, the countervailing pressures it called forth; it was a triumphalist view of globalization (see Zuckerman 1998: 18–31).

In short, the neo-liberal approach to globalization seemed everywhere predominant. The secular case for liberalization and open markets as generators of wealth had been won at both evidentiary and intellectual levels. Between 1950 and 1996 the volume of world output rose 6-fold, world merchandise trade expanded 16-fold, output of manufactures grew 9-fold, and trade in manufactures grew 31-fold (*Financial Times*, May 18 1998: 4). Open trade benefited consumers, and protection dulled incentives for innovation. The commitment to liberalization spread geographically from Europe and North America to other parts of the world, notably East Asia and the other parts of the Americas and, since the end of the cold war, to East and Central Europe and even China (albeit in the context of China's two-systems logic). Experiments with protectionism and import substitution had been progressively abandoned by those states that had pursued them in the past. The empirical record on the alleviation of human suffering in the late twentieth century, notwithstanding remaining human hardship, was, according to Richard Cooper, "... unambiguously positive ... the fraction of the world's population living in poverty has gone way down" (Hoagland 1999: 8).

So, with such a track record for success, why has market liberalization's victory not been final? The answer is political and theoretical. At a political level, globalizers are not winning all the arguments. With two billion people living on less than US$2 a day, and as many without access to clean water, the benefits of liberalization are not unambiguous. Further, there is a strong and growing body of non-state actors (NGOs and Global Social Movements [GSMs]) increasingly capable of articulating the case against globalization. The information revolution may ensure that the rich get richer, and do so faster, but it also connects the dispossessed in a more articulate fashion than in the past. The nature of the global political dialogue on globalization changed at the end of the century, especially after the "Battle of Seattle" of November 1999.

The poor and the dispossessed are unlikely to remain passive actors in the face of what they see as growing inequalities wrought by liberalization.

At the theoretical level, the strength of liberal economics is also a weakness. Far from being the "dismal science" when it examines globalization, economics appears to be an excessively optimistic science. Its concentration on the goal of openness and growth at the expense of non-economic factors has led to a parsimony of theorizing in economics that no other social science can match. This theoretical parsimony has parallels in practice, the effect of which is to minimize the salience of other aspects of the policy process and make it especially analytically unresponsive to combative politics that constitute the downside of economic liberalization. In this regard, the ability of economic theory to understand how to create wealth is surpassed only by its limited moral sense and an inability to understand social relations. Rapid increases in aggregate global wealth and production have been accompanied by a corresponding political and social *naïveté* as to the effects of these processes on the civil polities of developed and developing societies alike (Higgott 1999: 23–26). Further, initial post-Asian crisis Western hubris has given way, at a practical political level, to a feeling that 1997–1999 represented "... a historic setback to the advance of Western style capitalism" (Bluestein 1998: 13).

In short, the window of opportunity closed and the first backlash against globalization began. At the very least, the closing years of the twentieth century saw US and International Monetary Fund (IMF) dreams of ever more open capital markets put on the back burner, replaced by fears that the anti-globalization sentiments, already strong in many "emerging markets" and growing in the USA, could spread to other OECD countries. In effect, the closing years of the second millennium hosted the first post-cold-war "crisis of globalization." Economic analysis alone was ill-equipped to deal with this crisis. Such a view gained currency, not simply amongst third world economic nationalists and radical academic critiques of the neo-liberal agenda[8] but also within the mainstream of the economic community and the international policy community.[9]

If the urge for free markets and lean government created asymmetries in the relationship between the global economy and the national state that undermined John Ruggie's "embedded liberal compromise" (Ruggie 1995), then these changes have come gradually to be resisted. More groups now recognize that, when pursued in combination, free markets and the reduction of compensatory domestic welfare generate radical responses by the dispossessed.[10] The standard neo-classical economic response – that globalization enhances aggregate welfare overall – might well be correct, but irrelevant. The internationalization of trade and finance ceases to be simply sound economic theory; it also becomes contentious political practice. Globalization is thought to have negative redistributive consequences that disturb prevailing social structures. Increasingly articulate NGOs voice objections to the side-effects of liberalization. This is not the simple protectionist view of many narrow-interest groups; rather, in contexts where communities attach value to means as well as ends, these groups exhibit genuine concerns about the socially disintegrative effects of liberalization.

As is now recognized within international economic institutions and even corporate boardrooms, securing domestic political support for the continued liberalization of the global economy requires more than just the assertion of its economic virtue. If the benefits of the rapid economic growth of the last several decades are not to be jeopardized, then how social cohesion is maintained in the face of liberalization will represent a major question for governments and international institutions in the twenty-first century. Embedded liberalism is probably more important to political stability and economic prosperity in the contemporary period than it has ever been (Garrett 1998), but can it be maintained or revivified? More importantly, can it be globalized? Economic theory has always demonstrated a myopia to the stabilizing political and social processes of the civil polities of developed societies.

Its views of the state were also simple. From a neo-classical economic perspective, government – especially the welfare state in the post-Second World War era – is inefficient. Thus, beyond the provision of basic public goods – the rule of law and external security – the dismantling of the public economy would come, sooner or later, in an era of globalization. As the next section shows, the debate in the 1990s focused on the question of good governance, largely with a limited neo-classical economic and neo-liberal political "night watchman" view of the state. Moreover, there is still now only a reluctant willingness in the international economic policy community to recognize the manner in which markets are sociopolitical constructions, that their functioning depends on their legitimacy and support within civil society, and that the welfare state might be important for the stability of an open international economy.

This myopia has been unfortunate, to say the least. Much modern economic analysis has ignored the degree to which domestic compensation – Ruggie's embedded liberal compromise – has been an important factor in enhancing international openness. It mitigated the tensions inherent in the relationship between capitalism as a system of economic production and exchange, on the one hand, and democracy as a process of legitimation of this system, on the other. The problem with the neo-liberal agenda, especially prior to the 1997 economic crises, was that economic liberalization became an end in itself. Little consideration was given to its effect on prevailing values and norms within societies and polities.

Managing globalization: Governance without politics?

The preceding discussion of the dynamics of global economic liberalization supports three explanations as to why the issue of governance has become so important in the international policy community. First, and bluntly, a move to flag up "governance issues" allows the international financial institutions to dig themselves out of the intellectual corner into which their adherence to unfettered free market ideals had forced them. The financial crises since 1997 have provided a way out of the "economism" that had dominated policy-making throughout the 1980s and 1990s.[11]

Second, if governance is about the conditions for ordered rule and collective action, it differs little from government in terms of output. The crucial differences become those of process, structure, style, and actors. In the recent public-policy literature, governance refers to "... the development of governing styles in which boundaries between and within public and private sectors have become blurred" (Stoker 1999). But this definition fails also to note how globalization has blurred the domestic–international divide as both material fact and the development of systems of emerging international norms and regimes (both public and private) that represent the elements of a framework of "governance without government" under globalization.[12]

Third, given the impact of globalization, "governance" becomes an essential term not only for understanding transnational processes that require institutional responses but also for identifying those non-traditional actors (third and voluntary sector non-state actors such as NGOs, GSMs, and networks) that participate in the governance of a globalized economy beyond the traditional confines of government. Thus the concept of "global governance" becomes a mobilizing agent for broadening and deepening policy understanding beyond the traditional international activities of states.

It is in this evolving theoretical context that the WC, which governed international economic thinking throughout the 1980s and 1990s, became a moving feast as the major financial institutions, at odds with each other over the appropriate policy responses to the 1997 financial crises, sought a new approach – paradigm even – the contours of which are now emerging. The original well-known buzzwords of the WC were liberalization, deregulation, and privatization. To these, the PWC has added civil society, social capital, capacity building, governance, transparency, a new international economic architecture, institution building, and safety nets.

These themes had, of course, been emerging in the World Bank for some time,[13] where Joseph Stiglitz, its then chief economist, helped to move the Bank beyond the initial consensus (Stiglitz 1998, 1999). From the time of the Asian crisis, even the IMF and the World Trade Organization (WTO) have begun to take these issues more seriously (cf. Scholte, O'Brien, and Williams 1998). Add to the PWC the United Nations Development Programme (UNDP) initiatives on "governance" and "global public goods"[14] and the United Nations' "global compact"[15] with the private sector to promote human rights and raise labour and environmental standards and we have, as we enter the next millennium, a new rhetoric of globalism to accompany globalization as process. That the "global compact" reads like an attempt to globalize embedded liberalism is hardly surprising: the intellectual architect of this agenda was John Ruggie in his capacity as Chief Adviser for Strategic Planning to UN Secretary General Kofi Annan (1997–2001).

The details of the PWC, especially its emphasis on governance, civil society, and safety nets, cannot, and need not, be spelt out here, save to note that it is an understanding of governance underwritten by (a) a managerialist ideology of effectiveness and efficiency of governmental institutions and (b) an understanding of civil society based on the mobilization and management of social capital rather than one of representation and accountability. In the context of the PWC, civil society is not, in contrast to Robert Cox's recent reformulation, a site of resistance (Cox 1999). However, the PWC understanding of governance does represent a departure from the narrowly economistic and technocratic decision-making models of the WC. The PWC does not reject the WC emphasis on open markets: rather, the PWC is an attempt to embed institutionally, and even maybe, as the UNDP would have it, "humanize," globalization and (by extension of the argument presented here) the earlier technocratic, prescriptive elements of the WC (UNDP 1999).

Given that the PWC holds a sanitized view of the sociopolitical dimensions of the development process, why is it an important break with the past? Because *it is a recognition that politics matters* – a recognition that has been absent from the economistic analyses of the impact of globalization over the last two decades. Along with the works of the more astute economists such as Stiglitz, Rodrik, and Krugman, it demonstrates a sensitivity to some of the political complexities inherent in the reform processes (although it has to be said that the PWC and the economic literature show little *understanding* of politics). Nevertheless, conceptual understandings of power and interest, although underdeveloped in the PWC, offer a starting-point for thinking about justice under conditions of globalization that did not exist until the end of the twentieth century.

Theorists are still groping for a universally acceptable definition of "social and economic justice." However, while that continues, we are now fairly sure that globalization, in its unadulterated form, results in unequal treatment for some states and, more importantly, exacerbates poverty for many sections of the weakest members of international society, and thus puts justice at risk. Poverty alleviation seems to have a stronger claim than equality in prevailing definitions of justice.[16] Thus the important normative questions are those that ask to what relevant community or society "social justice" pertains and in what domains the question of justice should be addressed. These questions have traditionally been understood in the contexts of the values that actors attach to their behaviour within market structures. However, markets are not the only sites of action; the domain issue is at the core of the "global governance" question. As the next section suggests, governments are no longer the only domain of policy-making or implementation.

Politics, domains, and actors in a post-Washington Consensus era

NGOs, GSMs and international organizations play important roles. They form part of a wider global governance agenda that, both in theory and practice, trails the integrated and globalizing tendencies in the world economy. As a consequence, the prevailing anarchical order of the state system is inadequate to the task of managing most of the agenda of globalization. While this may be well understood, the prospects of a post-anarchical, yet non-hierarchical, order remain more aspirational than real at this time.

As global governance is an imprecise term, one normative question for students of international relations over the next few years must be how much authority we should invest in the concept, given the wide-ranging way in which it is used. Currently, understandings of global governance can range along a continuum from basic, informal processes to enhance transparency in interstate policy coordination through to the somewhat grander, although still essentially liberal, visions of a rejuvenated system exhibited in the Commission on Global Governance's publication *Our Global Neighbourhood* (1995).

However, if we accept the argument that the transnationalization of market forces is exacerbating inequality, then the avenue for mitigating this gap lies with a reformist agenda for the global rules and norms that underwrite the current international institutional architecture. Currently driven by "northern" agendas, it is those states most disadvantaged by globalization that are "rule takers" (Hurrell and Woods 1999). As a result, such rules lack legitimacy even where states actually possess the necessary governmental effectiveness to enforce them, should they wish to do so. Either way, these processes have negative implications for a consensual evolution of global-governance norms.

A starting assumption for the analysis of global governance is that it, and the continuance of a state system, are not inimical. Nevertheless, to recognize that state power will not go away is not to cling to some Westphalian legend; rather, it is to recognize that states, and interstate relations, remain the principal sites of politics. As a result, the research agenda on global governance is complex. Before proceeding to think of global governance as the development of a PWC, it may help to identify those three interconnected elements of the debate that have developed to date and that are essential precursors to understanding the development of the PWC.

Global governance as the enhancement of effectiveness and efficiency in the delivery of public goods

This is a fashionable policy concept, especially in the international institutions which see their role as consolidating or institutionalizing the "gains" made by the processes of global economic integration. However, it fails to recognize that the successful internationalization of governance can, at the same time, exacerbate the "democratic deficit." This approach forgets that states not only are problem solvers but also the members of their policy élite are strategic actors with interests of, and for, themselves. Thus, much collective action problem-solving in international relations is couched in terms of effective governance; it is rarely posed as a question of justice, responsible or accountable government, or democracy. These latter questions are the stuff of political theory, but it is the political theory of the bounded sovereign state. Thus, we need to think beyond these confines. It is central to the understanding of the relationship between the PWC and global governance, but it also leads to a wider, second understanding of the concept of global governance.

Global governance as enhanced democracy

Paradoxically, the language of democracy and justice takes on a more important rhetorical role in a global context at the same time as globalization attenuates the hold of democratic communities within the confines of the territorial state. Indeed, as the role of the nation-state as a vehicle for democratic engagement becomes more problematic, the clamour for democratic engagement at the global level becomes stronger. However, these are not stable processes. Understanding of, and attention to, the importance of normative questions of governance and state practice as exercises in accountability and democratic enhancement must catch up with our understanding of governance as exercises in effectiveness and efficiency. The debate is largely divided between theorists and practitioners.

The current theoretical debate over what Tony McGrew calls the prospects for "transnational democracy" is fought between sceptics and protagonists. It is lively and, in parts, very sophisticated; however, it cannot be discussed here, save to note that it mirrors many of the wider debates in contemporary political theory over the nature of democracy in the twenty-first century.[17] Unsurprisingly, the debate within the policy community (and the principal focus of this chapter) is more narrowly focused. A key issue in the policy community is the identification of those agents who can advance the cause of greater accountability and transparency in the management of the international institutions while not undermining the overriding goal of effectiveness and efficiency. In this context, the greater incorporation of selected non-state actors into the deliberative process of these organizations is the principal instrument of contemporary policy reform.

Certainly, the incorporation of civil society actors into the policy process is a necessary condition for the legitimation of the liberalizing agenda. Despite increasing efforts, most international institutions are not good at reaching out to NGOs and GSMs and often see these non-state actors as both boon and bane (Simmons 1998). Once they are accepted as legitimate actors in the policy process, these organizations may well behave in a manner that challenges the global governance functions of these institutions. Thus, there is still a reluctance in the economic policy community to recognize the manner in which markets are sociopolitical constructions whose functioning (and legitimacy) depends on their possessing wide and deep support within civil society.

Global governance as the emergence of an international managerial class

Although often using different terminology, realists, liberals, constructivists, and Marxists alike identify individuals or groups of individuals from the corporate, bureaucratic, and intellectual-cum-research communities as increasingly significant strategic actors in transnational relations. For those of a critical Gramscian persuasion, these groups represent the key players in the development of a global market civilization (cf. van der Pijl 1998). Alternatively, representations of this phenomenon can be seen in the burgeoning literature on epistemic communities and policy networks.[18]

The globalization of the informational and technological élite is seen as an essential part of the process of economic globalization more generally. Without the advances in communications and technology and the development of these sources of knowledge and information it would be impossible to talk of a notion of global governance. Global data are a prerequisite of global governance structures. Multilateral and regional institutions identify enhanced policy coordination as one of their major goals, and this can be undertaken only if knowledge is enhanced and available for sharing. The role of international institutions as instruments of coordination for the mitigation of the risks attendant on a more open and deregulated global economy – especially in the financial domain – is becoming increasingly important.

Financial crises have demonstrated how feeble these instruments have been in some areas. International regimes and regional organizations, of greater or lesser effectiveness, are the obvious indicators of global governance of this kind. However, not only have the managerial class or transnational policy communities (pick your metaphor) flourished with the development of these technologies (especially Internet technologies), so, too, have NGOs and GSMs. The prevailing top-down view is far too technocratic and misses the major normative questions about how to reverse the inequality that is perceived to have been generated by globalization over the last few decades.

Global governance: From the WC to the PWC

If the WC was an attempt by an international managerial-cum-policy élite to create a set of global *economic* norms to be accepted by entrants to the global economy under the guidance of the existing international institutions, is the PWC an attempt to induce support for a new set of *sociopolitical* norms to legitimize globalization by mitigating some of its worst excesses? If so, then there is some danger in seeing global governance as a "progressive" concept. If captured by the existing international institutions (claiming that they are the only available sites of global governance) then, reflecting the ideology of globalization in its neo-liberal guise, the first definition (effectiveness and efficiency) will become the dominant mode of understanding global governance. Democratic accountability, the second definition, will be, *at best*, a secondary component.

Democracy in global governance systems

Given the open, loose, and institutionally deficient nature of a "global community" in which the agents of global governance might be held accountable, prospects for increased cosmopolitan democracy of the kind espoused in the works of Held and Linklater, for example, do not, at present, offer much encouragement.[19] The principal impediment to cosmopolitanism is that its liberal conception of the individual is unlikely to flourish in the absence of a constructed common civic identity. Globalization may have rapidly generated a set of technological and economic connections, but it has yet to generate an equivalent set of shared values and sense of community, even amongst those agents actively involved in discussions about greater global participation. Indeed, much of the policy-prescriptive work on governance currently being undertaken in or around the international institutions treats governance as a neutral concept in which rational decision-making and efficiency in outcomes, not democratic participation, is privileged.

In this regard, the debate on global governance within the international institutions (the United Nations, World Bank, IMF, and WTO) remains firmly within a dominant liberal institutionalist tradition; discussions about democracy beyond the borders of the territorial state are still largely technocratic ones about how to enhance transparency and, in some instances, accountability. They fail, or in some instances still refuse, to address the asymmetries of power over decision-making that characterize the activities of these organizations. The essence of the liberal institutionalist view remains avowedly state-centric and pluralist and is, perhaps not surprisingly, captured nicely by an American institutionalist, Robert Keohane, who would define global democracy as "voluntary pluralism under conditions of maximum transparency."[20]

The liberal institutionalist view is also essentially the reformist view held for the international institutional leaders by senior global decision makers from US Treasury Secretary Lawrence Summers to UN Secretary-General Kofi Annan. Annan called for better accountability to improve global governance after the abortive multilateral trade negotiations (MTN) ministerial meeting in Seattle in November 1999, and Summers called for greater transparency and accountability for the IMF at its Spring 2000 meeting.[21]

Global public policy versus global governance

Indeed, the preferred term in international policy circles is "global public policy" (Reinicke 1998), not global governance. The aim is to make provision for the collective delivery of global public goods (Kaul, Grunberg, and Stern 1999). "Public policy" has none of the ideological and confrontational baggage present in the notion of "politics." Institutional analysis, with its concerns for understanding the mechanisms of collective choice in situations of strategic interaction, is similarly "de-politicized." This is not to deny that recent rationalist theorizing of cooperation has not been a major advance on earlier realist understandings.[22] However, the problem with rationalist and strategic choice approaches is not what they do, but what they omit: they make little attempt to understand governance as an issue of politics and power. This has implications for the operational capability and intellectual standing of the international institutions.

In essence, the governance agenda as constructed by the international institutions in the PWC era has largely stripped questions of power, domination, resistance, and accountability from the debate. To the extent that the international institutions recognize that resistance is a legitimate part of the governance equation, it is something that is to be overcome by governance, not something that is a perpetual part of the process. In this regard, for many key players, global governance is not about politics. There are no problems that good governance cannot contain or "govern away." In effect, governance, in its effectiveness and efficiency guise, is "post-political." Agendas are set and implementation becomes the name of the game. Notwithstanding the fragmented and disaggregated nature of political community in a global era, there is no place outside the rubric of the existing formal governance structures for autonomous action on global policy issues.

The PWC view of "good governance" implies the universalization of an understanding of governance based on efficiency and effectiveness, in which democracy is a secondary component. Indeed, much of the prescriptive work on governance currently being undertaken in or around the international institutions treats governance as a neutral concept in which rationality in decision-making and efficiency in outcomes is uppermost. Nowhere is this better illustrated than in the efforts of those around the World Bank and the UNDP to develop public–private partnerships and policy networks for the collective provision of public goods (cf. Reinicke 1998). Such work is innovative, certainly by the standards of the international institutions, but it is also limited by the political implications of its "top-down" intellectual origins.

As a consequence, a case can be made that the PWC is likely to be as challenged in the long run as the WC. It cannot constitute a template for an emerging "global governance" agenda, nor even an emerging policy agenda. It suffers from the same failings as its predecessor. The PWC is no less universalizing, and attempts to be no less homogenizing, than the WC itself. Global policy debates, in this way, remain reliant on a set of "generalizable," but essentially Western and liberal, principles and policy prescriptions. Even while they offer a more subtle understanding of market dynamics than in the early years of global neoliberalism, these prescriptions still demonstrate a penchant for earlier hyper-globalist universalizing notions of a "one-size-fits-all" convergence for policy reform under conditions of globalization. Such prescriptions may well be resisted in the developing world as but a new form of Western hegemony.[23]

The participatory gap in global governance

To deny the governance implications of a strategy to develop the collective provision of global public goods is clearly an exercise in semantics.

To date it has allowed little or no provision for the extension and expansion of "democratic" participation. As is also apparent from activities within the various international institutions – such as the World Bank's "Global Development Network Initiative" (GDNI) and other efforts to engage civil society in the global policy debates – this situation cannot long prevail (cf. Stone 2000). Civil society in this sense is becoming to global governance what international markets are to economic globalization. However, for a range of reasons, closing the "participation gap" (Kaul, Grunberg, and Stern 1999) by incorporating non-state agencies into this process is not without its own problems. Nor does it corrode the importance of sovereign states, with their resources and rule-making capacities, at the base of any strategy to develop the provision of a public goods agenda. This is for at least three reasons.

The first is that, despite their visibility, NGOs and other non-state actors cannot approximate the legitimacy of the national state as the repository of sovereignty and policy-making authority, nor its monopoly over the allegiance of the society(ies) it is supposed to represent. Second and related, despite the appeal of expanding the parameters of participation to include these important actors, it is widely recognized that they are often less democratically accountable than the states and interstate organizations they act to counter and are invariably less democratic in their internal organization than their outward participatory activities would suggest.[24] Third, implementation of resolutions taken in "global" negotiations, or often by international organizations, remains primarily the function of national states, or at the very least depends on their compliance and complementary activity at the national level for their implementation (Higgott 1996).

These observations point to significant anomalies in the system. The expansion of participation to non-state actors such as NGOs and GSMs does not solve the problem of the under-representation of developing states in the more formalized policy processes. "Global" governance issues are dominated by the powerful states and alliance constructions and interest representations which feature in the structures of international organizations and groupings such as the G-7. Various calls for the expansion of the G-7 into the G-16, G-20, or similar, recognize that, in order to be effective, global economic leadership needs diversification, and that collaboration in the provision of public goods depends on an extended participation. There is a widespread recognition that the institutional constructions of key global policy forums are insufficient for the generation of meaningful "global" collaboration on a range of policy issues. Most importantly, the provision of those public goods identified as crucial to the construction of a fairer global order is complicated by the unequal nature of the negotiation processes and, as seen in Seattle, by the marginalization of developing states within these processes.

The roles of states in global governance systems

What the "global governance" agenda associated with the PWC implies (in theory at least) is an understanding of governance that transcends the national state. However, the practice of the PWC governance agenda builds, at first sight, on the idea that states have important functions in a market-based economy, especially when the concerns for governance centre on social equity and justice questions. If we accept that states continue to engage in (at least) two-level games (Putnam 1988), then effectively these conceptions of governance marginalize the international bargaining role of developing states (through the privileging of civil society and the structures of international organizations) while attempting to enhance the position of states as mediators between the forces of global change and the societies they are supposed to represent. For many members of the policy élite in the developing world (representative of their populations or otherwise), attempts to introduce a dialogue with non-state actors represent an alternative to giving them a larger voice in the global policy debates and are thus something to be resisted.

Thus, the international institutions may find themselves in some sort of wasteland between market economics (in which the state is inactive) and a raging debate about the significance and appropriate functions of state institutions. For example, in the "good governance" and the social capital state debates, the World Bank seeks, on the one hand, to plug the "developmental gaps" and close the "participation gaps" by engaging civil society. On the other hand, it seeks to dictate what states do and how they do it, as it attempts both to downplay the centrality of the state in global bargaining and to offset societal opposition to the state's continued pursuit of neo-liberal economic coherence. A similar disjuncture can be seen in attempts by the WTO to secure greater NGO input into the deliberations on the continued reform of the trading system, while at the same time fearing the potentially disruptive effect that any such widening of the deliberative process might have on the traditional highly structured nature of trade negotiations.

These fears were realized at Seattle, where members of the Asian and Latin American policy élite were not in accord with their counterparts in the developed world as to what are mutually agreed public goods. Whereas there is a widely held view amongst the economic policy and corporate élite of the developed world that the WTO and extension of its remit is a public good, this was not a view widely shared in the developing world at the end of the twentieth century. Many developing countries do not have the technical ability to keep pace with the current WTO "Built-in Agenda" from the last round, let alone the desire and political conviction to take on board a range of new agenda items (in the areas of investment, competition policy, labour standards, transparency) currently being pushed by the developed countries in general and the United States in particular. This lack of enthusiasm for further liberal reform of the global economy has been exacerbated by the crises at the close of the twentieth century.

A new normative agenda?

The critique of the preceding sections is not a plea to reject a major role for the agents of global governance (international organizations and regimes) in developing a global justice agenda; rather, it is a suggestion that we need to look beyond an understanding of these simply as agents of order. Notwithstanding their critics, and the ups and downs in their fortunes, international organizations and regimes are not faddish, but represent a continuous theme of development in international governance within the context of an international system of states throughout the twentieth century (cf. Kratochwil and Ruggie 1986; Rittberger 1993). The key characteristic of regimes as instances of international governance is that they are invariably issue specific in their agendas. In this regard, they contrast with domestic systems of government which, although having issue-specific competencies, also have overarching briefs of national welfare and order within confined, territorial contexts.

Under realist conceptions (or, indeed, international relations in general), international regimes and organizations have "no independent effect on state behaviour" (Mearsheimer 1994: 7). Through neo-liberal lenses they have had slightly more room for manoeuvre, but are still contained by the preferences of states. Their role is to act as agents of transparency, reducers of transactions costs, and mitigators of market failure. Nevertheless, this does not give them an independent capability to bring about change. We need to look beyond these explanations in an era of globalization. It is here that a constructivist agenda offers important normative (if not necessarily explanatory) lessons for scholars and practitioners of global governance under conditions of globalization.

If, as in a constructive perspective, social and strategic relationships are not merely the aggregate of self-interested calculation (as both realist and neo-liberal approaches would affirm), then international institutions will not simply reflect the preferences of states; they must also be vehicles for moulding and adapting state preferences. If this is the case, then they will become much more important actors under globalization than in the past. This is not to suggest that international organizations will become more important than states or, indeed, than multinational corporations; this is unlikely. In contrast to states or, indeed, firms, international organizations (be they international financial institutions [IFIs], the WTO, or functional organizations of the United Nations such as the World Health Organization) have no natural constituencies with primary loyalties. Economic life may be increasingly global, but everyday socio-political life for most people, as proponents of "glocalization" tell us, remains firmly embedded in national and local settings.

However, we must focus on the major international organizations and regimes as potentially greater sources of the promotion of social justice than may have been the case in the past. For example, while the principal aim of the IFIs has been, and remains, the promotion of economic liberalism, it is quite clear that there is now an understanding in even the most hawkishly liberal corridors of the IMF about how not paying attention to the question of social justice on a global scale could bring the whole edifice down. Furthermore, at the World Bank, with the greater attention it now pays to the development of civil society, it is clear that a "justice" agenda is an increasingly important aspect of its remit. Given that it has been traditional to see these organizations (especially the IMF) as nothing other than the promoters of free market liberalization, this represents a degree of change.

Mood swings are important in international politics, and we may be seeing one occasioned by the financial instability of the late 1990s. James Wolfenson at the World Bank, and even Michel Camdessus towards the end of his period at the IMF, regularly (if somewhat rhetorically in Camdessus' case) acknowledged the dangers of globalization without equity. As Wolfenson noted in an address to the Board of Governors of the Bank (October 1998) "... [i]f we do not have greater equity and social justice, there will be no political stability and without political stability no amount of money put together in financial packages will give us financial stability." As Ethan Kapstein has recently demonstrated, an economic system widely viewed as unjust will not long endure (Kapstein 1999).

Even Washington at the end of the century recognized that the push for capital liberalization, as part of its wider ideological shift in favour of freer markets, fostered the vulnerabilities that were the underlying cause of the economic crisis in Asia and Latin America. Senior figures in the first Clinton Administration (Mickey Kantor, the former United States Trade Representative and Commerce Secretary, and Laura Tyson, the former chair of the Council of Economic Advisers) conceded that they were insensitive to "the kind of chaos that financial liberalization could provoke" (*International Herald Tribune*, 16 February 1999). Perhaps more important in the longer term, economic theory is beginning to accept that early capital-account liberalization has been a mistake and that crisis prevention requires the minimization of short-term lending to poorer countries (Eichengreen 1999). Moreover, other post-crisis theoretical work, from within the IMF, demonstrates the manner in which short-term capital controls not only are effective in reducing the vulnerability of emerging markets to financial crises but also may even increase capital inflows (Cordella 2000).

Unlike the more zealous free-marketeers of the last two decades, the scientific communities that currently walk the corridors of the IFIs may be developing a more sensitized understanding of the manner in which markets need to be socially and institutionally anchored and how, if they are not, they may undermine any chances of legitimate recognition from within the wider reaches of global civil society. It is not impossible to envisage a situation in the future where even their role becomes increasingly challenged by the more aggressive elements of hyper-globalization. I do not want to oversell this case. We may not be witnessing a revolution in thought but we are seeing a stylistic and policy change from the assertiveness and hubris characteristic of WC days. In short, the financial crises shook, however briefly, the IMF's belief in the idea that there may be some "universal knowledge" of best practice in macroeconomic and financial management.

The PWC that is emerging from the end-of-century crises may not represent radical reform but it does represent a recognition of the limits of the market fundamentalism of the 1980s and early 1990s. It is a recognition that global markets are likely to remain open only in the context of an efficient regulatory environment. Nevertheless, there is no common shared global morality or sense of value underlying the PWC; indeed, it may turn out to be nothing but a sticking-plaster with no alternative shared global discourse – despite, for example, the best efforts of many to globalize a "sustainable development discourse." In such a context, the prospect of transformation is slight.

It is in this context that the development of an understanding of global governance as a mobilizing agent has important normative implications. It offers the best opportunity of reinstating a Keynesian compact (albeit by another name, certainly) or globalizing "embedded liberalism" as a way of recivilizing capitalism after the period of a neo-liberal hegemony that shattered it. Why is this important? Because the renewal of such a compact appears to be the most progressive *economic system* of wealth production, distribution, and exchange that is compatible with the prevailing realities of an *international political system* in which, notwithstanding the increasing role of new actors, the state remains the key decision-making actor.

This leads to two ironies. The first is that, in rejecting the Keynesian compact in the first instance (and especially the role of governments in fighting recession and stimulating demand when necessary), free-market fundamentalists attacked and reduced the effectiveness of those very structures that have allowed them to operate so successfully and profitably over the last quarter of the twentieth century. Second, in calling for the development of a new global Keynesian compact, reformers may be trying to reinstate a system that may well be necessary to ensure the survival of open liberalism, thus saving free markets from their own excesses.

Let us not forget that, at the time of its inception, the initial Keynesian compact was not just the current state of economic theorizing; it was also an exercise in normative political theory. It represented a bargain struck between the state and capitalism that would allow for the continuance of free markets accompanied by mechanisms that would prevent repeats of the Great Depression of the interwar years and provide compensatory support systems for those most dispossessed by free markets. The policy instruments for managing recessions in the developed world under this system were invariably stimulatory and consisted of dropping interest rates, cutting taxes, and raising government spending if necessary. By and large they worked; however, they were the policies of a pre-neo-liberal market fundamentalist, state-centric (essentially embedded-liberal) era.

The ideology of the 1980–1990s was increasingly ill-disposed to such measures and strongly in favour of the global financial market deregulation. However, what the crises of the late 1990s demonstrated was that the international financial system cannot be left to its own self-correcting devices. Inadequacies in individual domestic economies (usually identified as "crony capitalism") do not alone provide satisfactory explanations of the financial crises of the latter part of the 1990s. To prevent these crises recurring we must also start with a recognition that the global system is also a factor, especially to the extent that it does not treat all actors equally. Markets, as Paul Krugman (1999) has noted, "operate double standards."[25] Rich countries, when they stray from the straight and narrow of "market fundamentals," tend to get the benefit of the doubt that allows them to pursue reform policies at a pace, and with a freedom, that is never extended to the developing world by the global markets – or, indeed, the IFIs, for that matter.

As a consequence, a key normative goal must be an agenda for mitigating the market vulnerabilities of the weaker members of the international system. This might seem a reformist agenda but, in the context of a neo-liberal hegemony, it is a radical one. The globalization of modern financial markets, especially "innovations" such as hedge funds, have raised again the spectre of financial panics of the type associated with the interwar depression. A normative agenda that has any chance of being taken seriously must focus on building institutions and regulations – in short, on constructing an architecture of global governance that is more than simply a new financial architecture, but one that minimizes the prospect of a return to such crises.

Conclusions: Putting "politics" into global governance

This chapter addresses the relationship between globalization and governance by focusing on globalization defined, in a narrow sense, as the process of global economic liberalization and the emergence of an agenda for global governance as a response to this process. The chapter, somewhat artificially, attempts to capture the flavour of this relationship in an examination of a shift from the WC to the PWC. In the former, market-dominated consensus, no conception of governance was present; in the latter, it is argued, a limited understanding of governance is emerging. For obvious reasons, the trigger point in this transition was the financial crises of 1997.

The approach adopted in this chapter is, of course, restricted. Globalization is more complex than simply economic liberalization and global governance. It is not suggested that the PWC and global governance are synonymous; rather, it is suggested that the development of the PWC reflects the current way of thinking about economic governance questions within the mainstream of the international economic policy community. More generally, global governance has a much wider intellectual history and policy agenda than merely the management of the international economy at the close of the twentieth century. Throughout the twentieth century, notwithstanding failed attempts to build institutions such as the League of Nations, the growth of multilateral and regional institutions reflects an evolving "constitutionalization" of world order (Elazar 1998). However, enveloped in the language of a PWC, the new global-governance agenda is clearly a response to the backlash that followed the financial crises that have hit the emerging markets of Asia, Latin America, and Central Europe since 1997.

It stems from a recognition within the international policy community that, without a more humanized and equity-driven development strategy for the world's poorer countries, global economic liberalization may contain within it the seeds of its own demise. Although this agenda represents a qualitative change from the pre-crisis days of the WC era, the chapter argues that it is, nevertheless, likely to be constrained in the successful provision of what it sees as the collective provision of global public goods such as enhanced transparency, a continued liberalization of the international trading regime, and so on. In capsule form, at least four reasons were advanced to explain this judgement.

First, there is no settled view on what constitutes an agreed basket of public goods. It is quite clear that their identification is driven from the North. Southern policy communities involved in the global-governance debates, consisting of the state and regional policy élite as well as the increasingly articulate and forceful NGO communities, feel that the in-

terests of their societies are deemed secondary to northern corporate interests. The question is about how to reverse the inequality that is perceived to have been generated by globalization over the last several decades. This was a point recognized within international institutional circles of Washington prior to the Seattle Ministerial Meetings of late 1999 (Wolfenson and Stiglitz 1999) if less so in the corporate world at the other end of the Washington–Wall Street corridor.

The obvious response of those who advocate modest issue-specific definitions of public goods has been that there has to be a reality check on what is feasible and what is practical. This response is not without value, but it misses the larger political point. For developing countries buffeted by the financial markets, any strategy that attempts to cope with lesser-order problems while leaving the fundamental structures that they deem responsible for their plight untouched is unlikely to secure their tacit acceptance, let alone their positive support. Transformation, not reformism, is what they seek. Moreover, if the policy élite in those countries badly affected by the financial crisis have a conception of public goods, it is a reactive one, aimed at the mitigation of public bads rather than a proactive one for the advancement of public goods. In addition, any approach adopted by the policy élite of Asia and Latin America is, in the current climate, likely to be atomized and fragmented on a state-by-state basis rather than collective or coordinated at the regional (let alone interregional) level. The financial crisis has rendered ineffective many of the nascent exercises in regional policy coordination that had appeared to be developing throughout the 1990s prior to the crises.[26]

Second, the top-down agenda has been driven by a limited understanding of governance as simply the effective and efficient provision of public goods. Although this is no bad thing of its own, it denies the limited nature of such a strategy. The improved provision of public goods via enhanced transparency and reduced transaction costs is a necessary, but not sufficient, condition for improved global governance. Insufficient attention is paid to the democratic deficit inherent in this approach and the absence of legitimacy of the approach in the eyes of would-be recipients. This is, in large part, attributable to the limits of a liberal institutional approach to understanding global governance, with its emphasis on process and procedure, that currently dominates the international policy agenda.

Moreover, the chapter argues, a weakness with a liberal institutionalist approach, driven by rational actor models, is that it frequently exhibits a deficient understanding of the way in which politics can derail such processes. In effect, governance, defined as effectiveness and efficiency, operates with a very old-fashioned understanding of the distinction between politics and public policy. It aspires to governance without politics and, as such, appears doomed to failure. To "depoliticize" – that is, to place at one step remove the effects of globalization on the world's citizenry – is to misunderstand the manner in which it is the *practice* of politics that creates the structures of communities (cf. Crick 1962: 24). The current governance agenda emanating from the international policy community, largely because it is driven by members of a de-territorialized transnational policy élite, has no conception of the residual strength of identity politics, the importance of social bonds within communities, and, indeed, the manner in which globalization appears to be picking many traditional social bonds apart without creating new sources of solidarity (cf. Higgott and Devetak 1999).

In this context, effective and legitimate global governance, without a sense of global community, would appear a remote prospect. This is sham governance. Real governance is about political contestation over issues such as distribution and justice; it is concerned with the empowerment of communities from the bottom up rather than just the top down in the promotion of the public good. Both of these issues, in other than rhetorical fashion, still fall into the "too hard box" for the international policy community. They are either ignored, or assumed away as "policy questions" in which the global distribution of wealth and poverty, as currently constituted, is not part of the agenda for consideration. Nevertheless, governance is about making choices, while most specialists at the international institutions advancing a governance agenda have a conception of international relations that sees the global economy in de-contextualized fashion and their tasks as de-politicized and technical.

This is not an argument against the importance that liberal institutionalism places on international institutional reform; it is, rather, a recognition of the need to move beyond this to create a global public domain in which a deliberative dialogue between rule makers and rule takers, of the kind envisaged by cosmopolitan theorists, can take place. As we know well, politics within states would not function if the same rules and styles of operation applied in the domestic public sphere that institutional actors are trying to put in place in an emerging global public sphere. However, the scaling-up of a democratic system from the national to the global level is not going to be easy. It is difficult enough for citizens to contest governmental decision-making within states. As perhaps the leading theorist of (pluralist) democracy has recently argued, it is always going to be harder beyond territorial borders (Dahl 1999; see also Höffe in this volume).

The key difference between the domestic and international levels is that important background norms and private arrangements that are the stuff of politics and that lead to difficult issues and questions being placed in the "too hard box" at the international level, are more difficult to avoid at the domestic level. The Laswellian questions of who gets what, when, and how (Laswell 1958) have been removed from the international politics of the global economy and this is occurring at the very time when the disaggregation of the state and the geographical expansion of the economy is creating new intersecting relationships between local and global actors that will make these issues and questions the stuff of international politics in the next century. In denying them, or at least in failing to address them seriously, the international institutions, as significant sites for policy-making, are merely staving off the day when they will have to be confront them in other than token fashion. As one critic notes:

We should judge the global market, like the global political order, by the distribution it affects among today's overlapping cultural, political and economic groups. The issue is not how to repress or manage ... claims, containing them within the private or national domain, but how we can engage them internationally.[27]

Third, there is a further way in which the drive for effectiveness and efficiency is a politically inadequate strategy. This drive is, of course, accompanied by a range of devices to engage users – especially concerted and, indeed, genuine attempts to incorporate civil society into the policy process. But these are also problematic; they, too, are driven by a facile understanding of politics as "anti-politics," the prevailing assumption of which appears to be that resistance and opposition will be "managed away" by incorporation. As protests at international meetings such as the Seattle Ministerial Meetings and the joint meetings of the IMF and the World Bank attest, this is an untenable reading of the emerging relationship between civil society and the international policy communities.

Although the policy communities located within the various international institutions have clearly had no choice but to engage with NGOs and GSMs in current times, they have unleashed a series of tigers that will not remain easily within their control. The increasingly articulate and forceful critiques of globalization that emanate from these non-state actors are changing the nature of negotiating processes and the agendas of multilateral bodies such as the WTO, the World Bank, and regional bodies such as the Asia-Pacific Economic Cooperation (APEC). Strategies range from besuited, brief-cased experts striding the corridors of the institutions to the organization of the massive "off-Broadway" productions and festivals or resistance that now accompany these annual meetings. It is too early in the life of these interactions to tell how they will develop. The scenarios range across those of positive and fruitful engagement that legitimizes and advances the global policy agenda of the international institutions, at one end of the spectrum, through to a scenario where the international policy process finishes with the worst of both worlds – paralysis and an absence of legitimacy – on the other.

As even some influential economists now note, it may well be necessary to constrain the free market to save it. Scholars of international politics with a feel for governance and questions of accountability, legitimacy, and sovereignty have understood the importance of these sentiments for a long while. The softening and widening of the WC to include those elements of a PWC might represent one step on the learning curve for the international policy community, but it does not address the justice and poverty questions on the international agenda. The absence of a wide-scale acceptance of the "legitimacy" of any top-down agenda in the developing world remains, for quite appropriate reasons, a major challenge for the international policy community under conditions of globalization. These are issues of politics, not just of governance.

Notes

1. Thanks go to Professors Volker Rittberger and Michael Zürn for their helpful comments on a first draft of this chapter. Special thanks go to Professor Rittberger, Tanja Brühl, and Dr Albrecht Schnabl for their unfailing patience in the revision process.
2. Nowhere is this argument more forcefully articulated than in the work of Susan Strange. See especially Strange (1996, 1998).
3. Perhaps the most comprehensive text on the subjects is Held et al. (1998); a good definition is to be found in Scholte (1997).
4. A term originated by John Williamson to reflect shared opinion within the Washington international financial community that included not only the US administration, but also the major international financial institutions and think-tanks such as the Institute for International Economics, see Williamson (1990); for a discussion see Paul Krugman (1995): 28–29.
5. For critical reviews of the convergence hypothesis see the essays by Suzanne Berger and Ron Dore (1996).
6. Kenichi Ohmae (1995), cf. also Ohmae (1990). Nor is there anything new about this point: Charles Kindleberger (1969) argued a similar case.
7. To be fair to Williamson, he merely described a set of policy prescriptions for financial adjustment in developing countries and called it the "Washington Consensus." He cannot be held accountable for the pejorative connotations that have been attached to the epithet by other observers of these processes.
8. For a review of this literature on the Asian crisis see Higgott (1998).
9. See, for example, Dani Rodrik (1998), Paul Krugman (1999), Jagdish Bhagwati (1988), and Joseph Stiglitz (1998, 1999).
10. Cable (1994); see also Wes (1995).
11. For an elaboration, see Higgott (2001).
12. See the pioneering essays in Czempiel and Rosenau (1992); see also Rittberger (1993).
13. See Cynthia Hewitt de Alcántara (1998).

14. See UNDP (1997) and Kaul, Grunberg, and Stern (1999).
15. "Business Leaders Advocate Stronger UN and Take up Secretary General's Global Compact." New York, UN Press Release, 5 July 1999; "The Global Compact: Shared Values for a Global Market." New York, The United Nations, Department of Public Information, DP1/2075, October 1999. See also Ruggie and Kell (1999).
16. See the excellent paper by Ngaire Woods (1999).
17. But see the excellent review by Anthony McGrew (2001).
18. Most notably see Peter Haas (1992).
19. See David Held (1995) and Andrew Linklater (1998).
20. Robert Keohane (1998): "International Institutions: Can Interdependence Work?" Cited in McGrew (2001).
21. See Kofi Annan (1999) and Lawrence Summers (2000).
22. See Robert O. Keohane (1984) and Helen V. Milner (1997).
23. For an elaboration on this point see Richard Higgott and Nicola Phillips (2000).
24. See Cecilia Lynch (1998), Leon Gordenker and Thomas G. Weiss (1995), and the essays in Higgott, Underhill, and Bieler (1999).
25. For a discussion of what he calls the "double standard" and the "confidence game" in international financial markets, see Paul Krugman (1999), 104–117.
26. On the limits of Asian regionalism exposed by the financial crises, see Richard Higgott (1998); on Latin America see Nicola Phillips (1999).
27. This is well discussed in David Kennedy (1999): 57.

REFERENCES

Annan, Kofi. 1999. *Renewing the United Nations*. New York: United Nations.

Beddoes, Zanny M. 1999. "The International Financial System." *Foreign Policy* 116: 16–29.

Berger, Suzanne and Ron Dore, eds. 1996. *National Diversity and Global Capitalism*. Ithaca, NY: Cornell University Press.

Bhagwati, Jagdish. 1998. "The Capital Myth: The Difference Between Trade in Widgets and Trade in Dollars." *Foreign Affairs* 77(3): 7–12.

Bluestein, Paul. 1998. "Financial Crisis May Stall Capitalism's Global March." *International Herald Tribune*, 7 September 1998, 13.

Cable, Vincent. 1994. *The World's New Fissures: The Politics of Identity*. London: Demos.

Commission on Global Governance. 1995. *Our Global Neighbourhood. The Report of the Commission on Global Governance*. Oxford: Oxford University Press.

Cordella, Tito. 2000. "Can Short Term Capital Controls Promote Capital Inflows?" Social Science Resource Network Electronic Paper Collection, ⟨http:// papers.ssrn.com/paper.taf?⟩ abstract id'139633.

Cox, Robert. 1999. "Civil Society at the Turn of the Millennium: Prospects for an Alternative World Order." *Review of International Studies* 25(1): 3–28.

Crick, Bernard. 1962. *In Defence of Politics*. London: Penguin.

Czempiel, Ernst-Otto and James N. Rosenau, eds. 1992. *Governance without*

Government: Order and Change in World Politics. Cambridge: Cambridge University Press.

Dahl, Robert. 1999. "Can International Organisations be Democratic?" In: *Democracy's Edge*, eds Ian Shapiro and Christian Hacker Gordon. Cambridge: Cambridge University Press, 19–36.

Eichengreen, Barry. 1999. *Towards a New Financial Architecture.* Washington, DC: Institute for International Economics.

Elazar, Daniel. 1998. *Constitutionalizing Globalization.* Boston, MA: Rowman and Littlefield.

Garrett, Geoffrey. 1998. "Global Markets and National Politics: Collision Course or Virtuous Circle." *International Organization* 52(4): 787–824.

Gordenker, Leon and Thomas G. Weiss. 1995. "NGO Participation in the Global Policy Process." *Third World Quarterly* 16(3): 543–555.

Haas, Peter, ed. 1992. "Knowledge, Power and International Policy Coordination." *International Organization* (Special Issue) 46: 2.

Held, David. 1995. *Democracy and the Global Order: From the Modern State to Cosmopolitan Governance.* Cambridge: Polity Press.

Held, David, Anthony McGrew, David Goldblatt, and Jonathon Perraton. 1998. *Global Transformation.* Cambridge: Polity Press.

Hewitt de Alcántara, Cynthia. 1998. "Uses and Abuses of the Concept of Governance." *International Social Science Journal* 155: 105–113.

Higgott, Richard. 1996. "Beyond Embedded Liberalism: The International Trade Regime in an Era of Economic Nationalism." In: *Globalisation and Public Policy*, ed. Philip Gummett. Aldershot: Edward Elgar, 18–45.

Higgott, Richard. 1998. "The Asian Economic Crisis: A Study of the Politics of Resentment." *New Political Economy* 3(3): 333–355.

Higgott, Richard. 1999. "Economics, Politics and (International) Political Economy: The Need for a Balanced Diet in an Era of Globalisation." *New Political Economy* 4(1): 23–36.

Higgott, Richard. 2001. "Taming Economics, Emboldening International Relations: A New Normative Agenda for International Political Economy." In: *Ten Years After the Wall: A New Agenda for International Relations*, ed. Stephanie Lawson. Cambridge: Polity Press, 91–108.

Higgott, Richard and Richard Devetak. 1999. "Justice Unbound? Globalisation, States and the Transformation of the Social Bond." *International Affairs* 75(3): 483–498.

Higgott, Richard and Nicola Phillips. 2000. "After Triumphalism: The Limits of Liberalisation in Asia and Latin America." *Review of International Studies* 26(3): 359–380.

Higgott, Richard, Geoffrey Underhill, and Andreas Bieler, eds. 1999. *Non-State Actors and Authority in the Global System.* London: Routledge.

Hoagland, Jim. 1999. "Is the Global Economy Widening the Income Gap?" *International Herald Tribune* 27 April 1999, 8.

Hurrell, Andrew, and Ngaire Woods, eds. *Inequality, Globalization and World Politics.* Oxford: Oxford University Press.

International Herald Tribune. 1999. 16 February 1999, 1.

Kapstein, Ethan. 1999. *Sharing the Wealth: Workers and the World Economy.* New York: Norton.

Kaul, Inge, Isabelle Grunberg, and Marc A. Stern, eds. 1999. *Global Public Goods: International Cooperation in the 21st Century.* New York: Oxford University Press (for the UNDP).

Kennedy, David. 1999. "Background Noise: The Underlying Politics of Global Governance." *Harvard International Review* 21(3): 57–71.

Keohane, Robert O. 1984. *After Hegemony: Collaboration and Discord in the World Economy.* Princeton, NJ: Princeton University Press.

Kindleberger, Charles. 1969. *American Business Abroad.* New Haven, CT: Yale University Press.

Kratochwil, Friedrich and John Ruggie. 1986. "International Organization: A State of the Art on an Art of the State." *International Organization* 40(4): 753–775.

Krugman, Paul. 1995. "Dutch Tulips and Emerging Markets." *Foreign Affairs* 74(1): 28–44.

Krugman, Paul. 1999. *The Return of Depression Economics.* London: The Allen Lane Press.

Laswell, Harold. 1958. *Politics: Who Gets What, When, How.* Cleveland, New York: World Publishing Co.

Linklater, Andrew. 1998. *The Transformation of Political Community.* Cambridge, Polity Press.

Lynch, Cecilia. 1998. "Social Movements and the Problem of Globalisation." *Alternatives* 23(2): 149–173.

McGrew, Anthony. 2001. "From Global Governance to Good Governance: Theories and Prospects of Democratising the Global Polity." In: *The Global Polity*, eds Morten Ougaard and Richard Higgott. London: Routledge, 251–286.

Mearsheimer, John. 1994. "The False Promise of International Institutions." *International Security* 19(3): 5–49.

Milner, Helen V. 1997. *Interests, Institutions and Information: Domestic Politics and International Relations.* Princeton, NJ: Princeton University Press.

Ohmae, Kenichi. 1990. *The Borderless World.* New York: Fontana.

Ohmae, Kenichi. 1995. *The End of the Nation State: The Rise of Regional Economies.* New York: Free Press.

Phillips, Nicola. 1999. "Rethinking Regionalism? Governance After Financial Crisis." In: *Globalisation and Regionalisation After the Crisis*? Third Annual Conference of the ESRC Centre for the Study of Globalisation and Regionalisation, University of Warwick, 16–18 September 1999 (unpublished paper).

Polanyi, Karl. 1994. *The Great Transformation.* New York: Beacon Press.

Putnam, Robert. 1988. "Diplomacy and Two Level Games." *International Organization* 42(2): 427–460.

Reinicke, Wolfgang H. 1998. *Global Public Policy: Governing without Government.* Washington, DC: Brookings.

Rittberger, Volker, ed. 1993. *Regime Theory and International Relations.* Oxford: Clarendon Press.

Rodrik, Dani. 1998. *Has Globalisation Gone Too Far?* Washington, DC: Institute for International Economics.

Ruggie, John. 1995. "At Home Abroad, Abroad at Home: International Liberalisation and Domestic Stability in the New World Economy." *Millennium: Journal of International Studies* 24(3): 507–526.

Ruggie, John and Georg Kell. 1999. "Global Markets and Social Legitimacy: The Case of the 'Global Compact'". Paper presented to an International Workshop "Governing the Public Domain: Redrawing the Line Between the State and the Market." Roberts Centre for Canadian Studies, York University, Ontario, November 1999.

Scholte, Jan Aart. 1997. "Global Trade and Finance." In: *The Globalization of World Politics*, eds John Baylis and Steve Smith. Oxford: Oxford University Press, 429–448.

Scholte, Jan Aart, Robert O'Brien, and Marc Williams. 1998. "The WTO and Civil Society." Working Paper No. 14, Warwick University, ESRC Centre for the Study of Globalisation and Regionalisation, July 1998.

Schwartz, Peter and Peter Leyden. 1997. "The Long Boom: A History of the Future, 1980–2020." *Wired* (July): 116.

Simmons, P. J. 1998. "Learning to Live with NGOs." *Foreign Policy* 112: 82–96.

Stiglitz, Joseph. 1998. "Towards a New Paradigm for Development: Strategies, Policies and Processes." The 1998 Prebisch Lecture, Geneva, UNCTAD, 19 October 1998. ⟨http://www. worldbank.org/html/etme/jssp101998.htm⟩

Stiglitz, Joseph. 1999. "More Instruments and Broader Goals: Moving Towards a Post Washington Consensus." The 1998 WIDER Lecture, Helsinki, 7 January 1999.

Stoker, Gerry. 1999. "Governance as Theory: Five Propositions." *International Social Science Journal* 155: 17–28.

Stone, Diane, ed. 2000. *Banking on Knowledge: The World Bank's Global Development Network*. London: Routledge.

Strange, Susan. 1996. *The Retreat of the State*. Cambridge: Cambridge University Press.

Strange, Susan. 1998. *Mad Money*. Manchester: Manchester University Press.

Summers, Lawrence. 2000. Statement to the International Monetary Fund Financial Committee, Washington, DC, 16 April 2000.

UNDP. 1997. *Governance for Sustainability and Growth*. New York: United Nations.

UNDP. 1999. *Globalization with a Human Face: The UN Human Development Report*. New York: Oxford University Press (for the UNDP).

van der Pijl, Kees. 1998. *Transnational Relations and International Relations*. London: Routledge.

Wes, Marina. 1995. *Globalisation: Winners and Losers*. London: Institute for Public Policy Research, Commission on Public Policy and British Business.

Williamson, Jeffrey G. 1996. "Globalization, Convergence and History." *Journal of Economic History* 56(2): 278.

Williamson, John. 1990. "What Washington Means by Policy Reform." In: *Latin American Adjustment, How Much Has Changed?* ed. John Williamson. Washington, DC: Institute for International Economics.

Woods, Ngaire. 1999. "Order, Globalization and Inequality." In: *Inequality, Globalization and World Politics*, eds Andrew Hurrell and Ngaire Woods. Oxford: Oxford University Press, 8–35.

Zuckerman, Mortimer. 1998. "A Second American Century." *Foreign Affairs* 77(3): 18–31.

5

Pressing ahead with new procedures for old machinery: Global governance and civil society[1]

Diana Tussie and Maria Pia Riggirozzi

Introduction

Rising international citizen activism seems to be posing a serious challenge to the essentially intergovernmental patterns of international relations. Old questions regarding state–market relations are re-emerging in a new context. Two decades ago, however, the object of concern was to see how transnational corporations clipped at the borders of the interstate system (Keohane and Nye 1972). The analytical framework today is much less monistic, emphasizing the interplay of governmental and non-governmental forces in meeting economic, political, and social challenges. Approaches to international organizations have veered from the study of formal institutions focused on state power and national interest (Krasner 1983; Keohane 1984) to the study of collective action dilemmas (Baldwin 1993). Not only the boundaries between state and market but also those between state and civil society have shifted. The nation-state no longer has a monopoly of legal force over its subjects nor does it seem to command people's loyalties at all times. Global activism demands global representation bypassing traditional nation-state politics. Moreover, global markets are challenged more by a set of oppositional social forces identified as "globalization from below" (Falk 1998) than by governments. The endemic problem of cooperation and coordination in international policy-making has increased in both frequency and intensity and has become all the more difficult.

In this context, global governance has come under severe strain. Political and social activists vigorously advocate the democratization and accountability of international organizations, seen as instruments of US dominance during the cold war. International organizations born of the interstate system have picked up the glove, making efforts to deflect the pressure and reform their practices. In short, as was rather tempestuously expressed at the 1999 World Trade Organization (WTO) ministerial meeting in Seattle, multilateralism is no longer the sole result of interstate interests, or can no longer be seen as the sole preserve of states huddled under a technocratic mantle. The relationship between global governance and multilateralism requires deeper rethinking.

The concept of governance implies the making and acceptance of formal and informal norms, which apply to decision-making as well as policy implementation. Borrowed from American business studies, it owes its recent surge in international relations to its ability to bring non-governmental actors to centre stage and to explain patterns of interaction among governmental and non-governmental actors. Governance implies a system of checks and balances in which stakeholders, both public and private, cooperate and compete both vertically and horizontally to achieve a collective decision. The thrust of the concept lends itself to examine three configurations or spheres of interrelated authority defined by different norms, rules, and decision-making processes: these are global governance (encompassing the relationship among markets, intergovernmental organizations, and individuals as active citizens rather than as subjects of the state); institutional governance (encompassing relations between the bureaucracy and the stakeholders within international organizations); and, finally, governance at the national level (encompassing interactions between governmental agencies, non-governmental actors, and civil society organizations at the national level of policy-making) (Tussie and Casaburi 2000). All three are undergoing a process of radical change in relation to the activism of civil society. Economic and political interdependence complicates the issue of drawing clear boundaries between each level, but at the same time these spheres of authority create a range of opportunities for civil society organizations to undertake multilayered action. In effect, transnational social movements are contributing to redefine norms and patterns of collective action and consensus-building at the three levels of governance. A wide range of activities carried out by NGO campaigns have opened many opportunities for success in terms of agenda-setting, raising new issues, influencing standard-setting on human-rights norms, and providing surveillance and enforcement capabilities (Keck and Sikkink 1998; Smith, Chatfield, and Pagnucco 1997).

Against this backdrop, this chapter is an attempt to address the questions posed by emerging tensions and the readiness of international organizations to respond to new demands for participation, transparency, and accountability in global policy-making, raised by global citizen activism. Key international organizations such as the United Nations system, the World Bank, the Inter-American Development Bank (IDB), the International Monetary Fund (IMF), and the WTO, were selected to analyse how they have responded to these challenges. Ultimately, we hope to use our analysis to cast light on a number of empirical and normative questions related to the way in which the responses of international organizations and the rearrangement of actors provides a genuine contribution to global governance.

This chapter first examines the prospects of Northern non-governmental organizations' (NGOs') demands for democratizing global politics; it focuses on how these demands have discreetly targeted international organizations in a one-by-one procedure and have reduced the issue of global governance to the treatment of issues with an antistate bias. In the second section, following the seminal work of Cox and Jacobson (1973), selected international organizations have been gathered into two broad categories – service organizations and forum organizations. This framework was chosen to analyse how the international organizations perform their functions according to their missions and mandates, as well as the way in which they relate to each other. Stemming from this categorization, the third and fourth sections analyse how service organizations – the World Bank, the IDB, and the IMF – and forum organizations – the United Nations and the WTO – have reacted to the new challenge by opening channels of dialogue with civil society. These sections focus on the organizational and conceptual differences that mark the nature of NGO involvement. Finally, some concluding remarks are offered to address questions not only of institutional governance but also of global governance more broadly.

Global civil society and international organizations: Building new ties

The end of the cold war has not meant a mere adjustment of East–West, North–South relations. Together with the turn to market-oriented policies and democratization in many parts of the world, the interaction between state, market, and civil society is caught up in a process of transition. This process has several implications, not only at the domestic level but also at the global level, where social movements, mostly originating in the developed world, have stepped-up demands for more inclusive and democratic global governance. International organizations are adjusting their *modus operandi* to cope with these pressures. The IMF, the WTO, the United Nations, the World Bank, the regional development banks (including the IDB), have all undergone a paradigmatic shift that affects mandates, procedures, and decision-making processes. In fact, within the constraints of their intergovernmental character, these organizations have instituted new mechanisms for opening a dialogue with non-state actors who claim to represent the interests of losers in the globalization process (Higgott and Reich 1999). These procedural reforms are part of the *aggiornamiento* of the traditional state-centred accountability towards an increasing acknowledgement of civil society actors as legitimate global players. In fact, international organizations have been inclined to reform the conditions attached to their operations in a broad array of policy arenas. As large bureaucratic structures, international organizations are also under siege as to whom they are accountable. In many quarters the idea that the nation-state is the ultimate actor in development-related arenas is no longer tenable. UN Secretary-General Kofi Annan has probably gone furthest at the 1999 General Assembly, telling his audience that "states must serve their peoples. If they fail to do so and permit serious human rights abuses," he said, "they open themselves to justified intervention by the international community in the form of the UN itself" (*Financial Times* 1999: 4).

The increasing role of non-state actors – firms, business associations, NGOs, social movements – in the international scene is certainly the consequence of the impetus of NGO networks for democratizing global policy-making (Weiss and Gordenker 1996). Global activism has succeeded in incorporating protective labour conditions, and environmental, consumer, and gender considerations into international negotiations. In the same vein, many NGOs have attacked the operational procedures of international organizations, demanding more participation in proceedings and decisions, and greater public release of information (Scholte 1998a). However, the scrutiny of civil society has taken a one-by-one approach to international organizations without seriously questioning the division of labour among them. For example, since the 1990s, the distinctive character of the agenda of the international organizations towards developing countries is closely associated with "good governance" (modernization of the state, consolidation of democratic institutions, strengthening of local governments, protection of human rights and the environment, and reform of social policies), which, in turn, imply a profound transformation in societal relations at the national level. These new areas of intervention give rise to interwoven conditionalities and a new division of labour among the organizations. Illustrative is the case of Argentina's Judicial Reform, in which the IDB and the World Bank set the agenda for long-term judicial reform and disbursements, while the IMF tied its macroeconomic targets to those sectoral reform exigencies

(Acuña and Tuozzo 2000). Likewise, but in the issue area of labour rights, little has been said about the flexibilization of labour markets which comes as part and parcel of the conditionality in World Bank and IMF lending programmes and tends to pull labour standards and wages down. In contrast, the increasing of labour standards in developing countries is a core claim *vis-à-vis* trade agreements and the WTO. Ironically, when a trade agreement is finalized, this is the end of the process; very often, labour market flexibilization is already under way as part of financial packages. The demand of northern civil society is blind to the quiet *ex ante* transformation – if the dogs don't bark, the flock is well managed. The issue reaches the radar screen of international civil society when the after-effects spill onto Northern markets, in the form either of competing exports from developing countries or of capital moving abroad in search of lower labour costs. This discreet approach to issues has allowed each organization to respond by taking up a path and pace of its own. Global civil society has reduced the issue of governance to the provision of social and environmental public goods by international organizations. Lobbying is undertaken *vis-à-vis* the global system in order to shape an agenda that is, on the one hand, issue oriented and, on the other, self-defined as representative of the needs and aspirations of the dispossessed and the oppressed.

The contribution of transnational actors through mobilization and campaigns in promoting compliance with international norms by state actors should not be underestimated. At the same time, the thrust of an overly people-centred agenda might carry a bias against domestic policy processes and national institutional arrangements that are the context in which decisions are taken. The tendency to bypass national politics runs the risk of dismissing too lightly the role of the state in national policy processes. Through this lens, two key issues of global governance are overlooked. First, short-term capital flows, which are an essential and increasingly important element of the global economy, move in a rather ad hoc and footloose fashion. As long as capital flows remain largely uncontrolled by national governments as well as by international financial institutions, "the international economy will be hostage to spectacular boom and bust cycles" (Rodrik 1999: 3). Indeed, complacency on short-term capital flows, while focusing instead on internal structural reforms in the developing world, runs the risk of increasing rather than reducing systemic risk. As put by Rodrik, an unappreciated irony is that the conditionality of the international financial institutions is being propped up at precisely the moment when these flows are out of the reach of government control (Rodrik 1999). How to bring more of the global economy into the ambit of the international financial institutions cannot be ignored (see Higgott in this volume).

Second, another neglected issue of concern regarding how developing countries fare in the global economy is connected to the distribution of power and, specifically, to the decision-making processes in the organizations themselves. Currently, the G-7 countries hold a combined total of 45 per cent of the votes in both the IMF and the World Bank. In practice, these shareholding structures have had the effect of inhibiting the discussion of issues that are clearly in the interest of developing countries, such as the conditions attached to access to international liquidity and the consequences for democratic governance (Buira 1995). The new environment inclined to opening up participation to non-state actors irrespective of the distribution of power within these international organizations is a quicksand. It risks increasing the influence of US- and European-based groups. Surely (some) governments still have a role to avoid personal preferences masquerading as core thrusts (Woods, 1999)?

If international organizations are to become democratic, the rules of representation are the cornerstone. Creating a balanced representation of the global civil society requires the incorporation of Southern NGOs in addition to Northern NGOs. This view is not shared by all Northern NGOs, some of which argue that they are entitled to speak on behalf of Southern civil society at all times, since the latter cannot become engaged in the international arena – a tendentious argument, no doubt. True, some Northern NGOs have offered invaluable help in humanitarian relief, debt relief, and rectification of human-rights abuses; however, in the longer term, such intervention must be seen as a "fire brigade" that, in due course, should give way to proper empowerment of Southern NGOs.

Since global governance encompasses a wider range of actors – governmental and non-governmental – and is defined by multiple and heterogeneous agendas, the central question discussed in this chapter is how international organizations are adapting their own governance structures to the new requirements of global governance. The following sections paint in broad brushstrokes how key multilateral organizations have reacted to the pressure and interests of organized civil society in the North without changing the terms in which the problems of global governance are framed.

The evidence is that international organizations have initiated a process of opening-up toward NGOs with varying implications both for the involvement of global (mainly Northern) civil society and for global governance. The path, quality, and degree of openness, however, are all a product of each organization's mandates, constituencies, practices, rules, and norms – in short, the nature of its own institutional governance (Woods 1999), which now reflects contradictions in terms of to whom they are accountable. Although all international organizations are still constrained by their formal structure of state-centred ownership, not all of them have followed the same pathway towards civil society. This dilemma of accountability is overcome in different ways according to the character of the organization.

Sketching patterns of openness to civil society: Service and forum organizations

To analyse the patterns of decision-making within international organizations and their openness towards civil society, it is helpful to group these international organizations into the two broad categories that, nearly thirty years ago, Robert Cox and Harold Jacobson applied to dissect the anatomy of influence – namely, service organization and forum organization. On the one hand, service organizations, exemplified by the international financial institutions, provide specific in-country services and disburse funds to "clients." On the other hand, forum organizations are established to provide a venue or framework for negotiations and collective decision-making, ranging from consultation to binding commitments. Governments also often use forum organizations for the collective legitimization of their individual policies. Paradigmatic among these are the WTO and the UN system. In short, this distinction among organizations relates to the way in which multilateral organizations perform their functions (Cox and Jacobson 1973). It offers a conceptual framework to study the approaches of international organizations to civil society as well as the way they relate to each other. As a classification, it will not allow for blurred boundaries and hybrid forms of international organizations, but it provides a useful frame to highlight differences in organizational principles, core mission, and mandates, as well as the resources that each organization has at hand to cope with civil society participation.

Service organizations

The first to reach the radar screen of global civil society were service organizations as the prime movers of economic adjustment with the neglect of effects on the poor. The World Bank and the IMF came under siege in the "Fifty Years is Enough" campaign in the early 1990s. With funds to disburse, the World Bank began to set up liaisons not only with global networks but also with NGOs on the ground as managers of projects and consultants. The regional development banks and, very particularly, the IDB followed suit. Here, the NGOs serve as intermediaries, deliverers of services, and consultants in the joint implementation of programmes at the national level. Hence the basis for cooperation and even co-optation in service organizations is quite broad and fertile in comparison to that in the forum organizations. Funds always allow a measure of co-optation and provide opportunities for "clientelism" by engaging a wider range of actors in the delivery of services as well as room for adaptable bargaining strategies with those affected by the implementation. International financial institutions seek to lower the risk of their loan portfolio and to maximize the impact of their projects. Although this is to be expected from the start, the fact that the World Bank, the IDB, and, to a lesser extent, the IMF are considered to be service organizations leads to some particular considerations that, in turn, mark their specific differences from forum organizations.

As Miles Kahler has pointed out, "since agreements with the international financial institutions do not have the status of international treaties, either internally or externally, breaches of such agreements do not carry the same reputational consequences as do the breaches of other international agreements" (Kahler 1993: 364). However, the fact that disbursements of funds are attached to specific conditions allows global civil society an opportunity to inject social or environmental considerations into such agreements, which in turn opens a window for domestic civil society. In contrast to forum organizations, conditionality results in a different balance of power between member states and affected civil society.

The World Bank and IDB: Championing the agenda of civil society

Development banks and, in particular, the World Bank and the IDB appear to be the standard-bearers of a strategy promoting civil society participation in the field through lending operations that target minorities and vulnerable groups. The inclusion of NGOs has been an iterative process initially undertaken to improve the poor performance of their portfolios.[2] However, the trickle became a flood, and, since the early 1990s, multilateral development banks (MDBs) have undergone a paradigmatic change in their missions, mandates, and operations including new mechanisms to engage civil society in a wide array of operations.

Implicit in this shift is the idea that sustained economic development cannot be achieved without compensating the effects of adjustments with social programmes, political legitimacy, an adequate institutional and regulatory framework, and political and economic decentralization (Casaburi and Tussie 1997). In this view, the task of development is seen more and more as a participatory endeavour rather than a simple transfer of capital to developing countries (Tussie 1995). There are two strands to this shift. First, the focus of lending is placed on government intervention and public administration, which require a massive overhaul. Prominent issues on the agenda are state reform and modernization of public administration, consolidation of democratic institutions, decentralization, reform of social welfare policies, and protection of human rights and the environment. Second, the development banks have made great strides toward self-reform by adopting new procedures to enhance transparency, accountability, and participation as part of their operational guidelines. The mechanisms that were adopted sought to involve civil society through consultations and the joint implementation of social projects.

Within this common overall approach, there are noticeable differences in the thrust of the World Bank and the IDB. The discrepancy stems from their institutional cultures and characteristics – that means, their institutional governance. Whereas the World Bank's engagement with civil society is market-centric, the IDB's participatory agenda dovetails with the reform of the state. In fact, the World Bank leans on an "apolitical" (Nelson 2000) and "technocratic" conception of civil society, biased toward voluntary associations. The World Bank has often treated NGOs as a proxy for civil society. Consultation with an NGO or contracting with an NGO to implement a project is often assumed to promote effective participation – an assumption that can be interpreted as an effort to undercut, rather than support, the state. In contrast, the IDB views civil society within the context of the need to modernize the state. The World Bank contends that the strengthening of civil society will ultimately lead to improvements in the quality and efficiency of government. In contrast, the regionally rooted IDB has explicit commitments to borrower governments as part of a more complex strategy that views the state as a necessary pillar to strengthening civil society (Nelson 2000). These contrasting strategies stem from their respective institutional governance.

The IDB's institutional governance, and thus its decision-making procedures, is shaped by a voting structure in which the Latin American governments represent 50 per cent of the votes. Management can thus find nourishment not only in the Anglo-Saxon tradition of political participation and collective action based on voluntary associations that inspires the World Bank; the IDB struggles with a state-centric approach to civil society more akin to the regional traditions, advancing the liberal *economic* agenda but not totally buying into the liberal *political* agenda (Higgott and Reich 1999). To put it crudely, the World Bank sees the market as the defender of civil society and the state as the "oppressor." It promotes civil society to provide checks and balances to state intrusiveness and it pursues reform of the state to allow free markets to function. The IDB promotes the modernization of the state in order to open up spaces for the strengthening of civil society. The IDB is much more closely scrutinized by the governments of Latin America, which have a significant control over decision-making. This makes the IDB's overtures to civil society apparently more timid or cautious than those of the World Bank. At the very least, the nature and the extent of consultations *vis-à-vis* governments are still much greater.

These institutional and conceptual differences mark the nature of the dialogue with NGOs. In addition, the IDB is not in the line of fire of NGOs as is the WB. Global (Northern) civil society, having by nature a telescopic view of the field, takes it for granted that changes in the World Bank will in turn lead to changes in the regional development banks. Thus the World Bank has been hit harder and has become in the process more permeable to global civil society. Collaboration with NGOs covers broadly defined demands in consultations, meetings, and conferences carried out by working groups that discuss policy frameworks and operational strategies. The WB–NGO Committee, a joint forum for dialogue on World Bank policy, allows global civil society to establish a critical dialogue with the World Bank and to engage in lobbying activities concerning projects and procedures. This liaison poses challenges to national political authorities as many NGOs work hand in hand with the World Bank to push policy guidelines in "pet" issues. Thus, the receptiveness of the World Bank to global civil society in the policy process risks becoming more rather than less complex over time, rekindling North–South cleavages in a new guise. Conversely, the approach of the IDB, opening up to civil society by modernizing the state, may do little to enhance meaningful and autonomous citizen participation in order to put limits to the realm of necessity (Walzer 1980) and to curtail an absolutist tradition of state power in Latin America. Both MDBs, however, skirt contracts with trade unions and interest groups with long-standing presence in the region. This feature of the relationship between MDBs and civil society raises questions of representativeness and thus of the restricted nature of the participatory schemes. Even leaving aside the issues of NGOs representativeness, it is still important to indicate the bias, and to bear in mind the inclination to narrow down the dialogue to NGOs' constituencies. Ultimately, participatory mechanisms are used in a selective way and their application depends, largely, on the political sensitivity of the loans or on the ability to use the loans for electoral purposes (Tuozzo 1999: 15–16), reinforcing embedded patterns of "clientelistic" relations. However, national experiences reveal that the incorporation of mechanisms of transparency, accountability, and participation has opened, at least to some extent, the nature of the operations of the MDBs. The implementation of participatory projects in the region shows a very irregular picture characterized by islands of participation in social projects. None the less, negotiations restricted to governments and the MDBs belong to the past.

The IMF: Still an outlier

The fiscal crisis of the welfare state followed by the financial crises in emerging markets placed the IMF at the centre of the stage. NGOs, especially those based in Washington, demanded greater transparency and accountability in the implementation of adjustment. Unprecedentedly, the demands found an echo in conservative or orthodox groups in the United States. The opportunity for action was provided by the need to obtain congressional approval for a capital increase. This "unholy alliance" has led to a pragmatic response from the IMF which, despite internal resistance, has adopted access to information policies and initiated contacts with civil society organizations.

As in the case of World Bank and IDB reforms, the transformation of the IMF's operations was carried out by incorporating new guidelines and policy recommendations under the label of *good governance*. Good governance requirements were defined by the IMF, as in the case of MDBs, as necessary conditions for economic growth and equity in those national contexts characterized by weak judiciaries, obsolete legal norms, and highly corrupt and inefficient systems of public administration (Camdessus 1997). In this vein, recommendations of a wholly political nature for institutional modernization, administrative transparency, and sectoral reforms at the national level were added to the traditional objectives of macroeconomic stability and adjustment.

However, unlike the World Bank and the IDB, the IMF does not have participatory operations, even when IMF programmes directly or indirectly affect society at large. In contrast to the World Bank and IDB, the IMF is not tied by operational directives calling for civil society participation. In any case, the IMF's operational agenda leans toward making markets work, and its approach to civil society favours business associations above other forms of association. Although informal contacts have been developed with organizations traditionally neglected, they are centred on business and academic groups that share the IMF's broad philosophy.

Nevertheless, in recent years there has been evidence of increasing ties between the IMF and labour organizations. Since 1992, the IMF has held several meetings with labour groups, at the same time that trade union representatives have visited the IMF headquarters. More concretely, in 1995 the IMF's staff and resident missions received instructions to establish contacts with labour organizations in the countries where they were assigned. Even though these contacts are pragmatic in nature, they constitute an advance in terms of opening up to new international actors (Scholte 1998b).

Relations with other social organizations are generally lacklustre. Global NGOs, for their part, seem better equipped to deal with the World Bank than the IMF, although recently they have raised demands for substantive and operational reforms at the IMF. These "reformist" NGOs articulate themselves primarily in networks based in Washington and are demanding transformation of the IMF's rules, procedures, and policy direction. Their demands and lobbying activities are aimed at obtaining greater transparency in programmes negotiated between the IMF and governments, as well as in the design and implementation of the conditionality that accompanies these programmes. These demands are complemented by parallel activities such as the lobbying of legislatures in donor countries. The NGO movement shows two strands: one is mainly focused on human rights, the social impact of macroeconomic reforms, and the role of the IMF in highly indebted countries; another segment calls for drastic reductions in the activities of the international organizations or their abolition (Scholte 1998b).

Neither the new contacts nor the instances of opening described here modify the decision-making structure of the IMF, the priorities of its agenda, and conditionality, which continue to be negotiated with governments. Measures to increase openness and transparency show only an interest in addressing the contradiction between the confidentiality embedded in its institutional governance and the need for providing greater legitimacy to its operations. Conditionality has not been modified with compensatory mechanisms to take care of the "good causes," as in the case of the MDBs. Nevertheless, there are strong incentives within the IMF bureaucracy to open a policy dialogue with determined civil society organizations. The need for consensus building as a condition for successful implementation of programmes follows the logic of other service organizations, thus auguring well for further institutional changes.

Forum organizations

In contrast to service organizations, the approach towards civil society in forum organizations has so far been a piecemeal process couched in technocratic language and conditioned by the fact that operational agendas do not directly engage or benefit civil society with funding. Moreover, the resemblance of "parliamentary" negotiations in the UN General Assembly and WTO placed states as the main actors, leaving civil society organizations with a secondary role in the process of negotiations and decision-making. None the less, piecemeal "dialogues" consisting of informal contacts with certain citizen groups on specific issues have been stepped up in both organizations.

The United Nations system

The United Nations as a whole was established to provide a venue for interstate negotiations and decision-making, subordinating interests and procedures to a government-driven agenda. However, special programmes, such as the UN Development Programme (UNDP), provide funding for in-country (technical assistance) projects in a way similar to that of service organizations. In effect, while core policy debates in the General Assembly are conducted by government representatives, global UN conferences and programmes tend to amalgamate government interests and citizens' agendas.

This twin role of being both a forum and a service organization is reflected in a multiple agenda towards civil society participation. In other words, the UN system has moved on two tracks to engage civil society. Whereas the UN specialized agencies and special programmes, which finance and carry out projects in developing countries, call for the direct involvement of civil society in consultations about, and the joint implementation of, social and development programmes, in the General Assembly the involvement of non-state actors is either ad hoc or indirect, mainly as observers. Therefore, whereas the UN specialized agencies and special programmes share some features with service organizations, the General Assembly is a forum in which the main players are the member states.

The first interaction with NGOs took place at an early stage, at the time of foundation of the United Nations. The San Francisco conference was attended by several NGOs as observers. Their calls for incorporating human rights concerns were translated into the UN Charter, so that it encompasses the pursuit of human rights in addition to world peace and development.

There is no single UN agenda for interaction with civil society organizations. Instead, the different specialized agencies and special programmes have established their own arrangements, although the starting point for all has been Article 71 of the UN Charter. Article 71 states that the Economic and Social Council (ECOSOC) may make suitable arrangements for consultation with NGOs to pursue matters of its competence. A 1948 resolution established three different categories of NGOs, with special rights to interact with the UN system. Modifications over time notwithstanding, this threefold categorization remains in force today. A committee of ECOSOC consisting of 19 members (five representatives from African countries, four from Asia, two from Europe, four from Latin America and the Caribbean, and four from other countries) decides on the accreditation of NGOs and their respective consultative status (Willetts 1999).

The relationship between the United Nations and civil society has been neither linear nor progressive. Rather, it has been marked by cycles of greater and lesser tension in the context of the cold war. Not until *détente* in the 1970s did NGOs become real protagonists in defining programmes other than those of ECOSOC, at which point arms control and decolonization also came under their purview. The efforts and campaigns of the various NGOs – particularly those related to feminism, nuclear disarmament, and the environment – came of age at that time as well. In this context, the United Nations opened its agenda further to include new topics being thrust upon it by the NGOs. Meanwhile, the specialized agencies and special programmes – especially those associated with development and human rights issues such as the Food and Agricultural Organization (FAO), the UN Educational, Scientific, and Cultural Organization (UNESCO), the International Labour Organization (ILO), the UN Children's Fund (UNICEF), and the UN High Commissioner for Refugees (UNHCR) – were also admitting NGOs as consultants and implementers of programmes. More importantly, various NGOs and minority representatives, such as indigenous peoples, took advantage of UN agencies to make demands and expose the abuses of the states.

A turning point was marked with the prominent role of NGOs at the 1972 Conference on the Human Environment in Stockholm. The conference offered new opportunities for NGO participation. The goals of the 250 NGO participants included not only the broad incorporation of human development concerns but also the granting of observer status for NGOs at future UN conferences.

In many respects, there is a "before and after Stockholm." First, the conference laid the foundation for widening the participation of civil society in global policy arenas. Second, it redefined relations among the NGOs themselves, which, at the same time, were asserting more encompassing demands. As the NGOs formed international networks they emerged as new forms of global activism. Feminists set an important precedent by forging North–South linkages. Although the resurgence of bipolar hostilities in the 1980s slowed down such initiatives, it did not hold it back. NGOs began to direct their exhortations at the closed nature of debates and decision-making processes within the UN General Assembly and the Security Council, two bastions of state power. Demands for democratization of the UN system were translated into efforts to monitor the activities of the General Assembly, although it was not possible to acquire and exercise the kind of effective influence that had been achieved with the specialized agencies (Donini 1996).

With the waning of the cold war, a global agenda with real influence on international organizations was born. In successive global conferences – on environment and development in Rio de Janeiro in 1992, on human rights in Vienna in 1993, on population in Cairo in 1994, on social development in Copenhagen in 1995, on women in Beijing in 1995, and on habitat in Istanbul in 1996 – active NGO participants regained their former ground and expanded it further (Clark, Friedman, and Hochstetler 1999). Partly as a response to the importance of the NGOs as international actors, almost all the organizations of the UN system augmented the scope of their External Relations departments and NGO-liaison officers.[3]

These actions became trend-setters. Many NGOs began to turn their efforts toward opening and reforming the international financial institutions, which attach conditionality to their lending programmes in developing countries. This opened up a whole new chapter in relation to the in-country governance structures and the use of a controversial instrument for a "good cause."

In stark contrast to the international financial institutions, the UN system has remained less questioned. Not besieged as the World Bank and the IDB, the UN system has used its double nature as a forum and a service organization to incorporate civil society in a double movement. On the one hand, the activism of NGOs was oriented towards attaining a place in international conferences, which in turn contributed to an opening of the General Assembly to new voices, if not to new votes. The UN General Assembly is quickly becoming citizen-oriented, but states and citizens still compete for primacy. On the other hand, the UN specialized agencies and special programmes implement projects in much the same way as the service organizations described above.

The WTO: The failure of public relations

With regard to public relations the WTO, a club-like organization without access to hand-outs, is in a particularly vulnerable position *vis-à-vis* the demands of NGOs. An ironic circle of deceit occurred with the trade-opening processes in both developing and former communist countries associated with globalization. These processes were not negotiated, and hence cannot genuinely be attributed to the organization; nevertheless, WTO bureaucrats hailed them as an accomplishment and the beginning of a new era of global reach extending beyond Europe and North America. NGOs reacted accordingly and cast the WTO as the nerve-centre of globalization. Turning it into their object of anger was just the next small step ahead, as if there were a single recognized world authority for the world market economy. In response to civil society demands, the WTO has not been able to adopt a new guise to "seduce" civil society in the way that service organizations do with funding. Caught without money for projects, and hence deprived of hand-outs to co-opt NGOs, and at the same time providing a revenue for trade agreements leading to winners and losers, the WTO has quickly come under siege.

The transformation of the General Agreement on Tariffs and Trade (GATT) from a low-key "traders club" (Curzon and Curzon 1973) into a grander construction changed the agenda of trade negotiations and, at the same time, put the institution "on the spot." Although NGOs have been interested in the GATT since its inception in 1947, since the creation of the WTO the multilateral trading system has come under unprecedented scrutiny to the point of vociferous attack. Less obvious is whether NGO demands will lead to a more participatory and transparent negotiation process.

The WTO today covers a wider range of themes than those traditionally associated with lowering tariffs and dismantling non-tariff trade barriers. The agenda of the Uruguay Round (1986–1994) made room for the consideration of new issues such as intellectual property, services, and trade-related investment measures (TRIMs). More recently, following the North American Free Trade Agreement (NAFTA) precedent, the WTO has been asked to include discussion of labour standards, the environment, and human rights.

With an apparently politically less-sensitive agenda and narrower membership, the GATT never established formal channels of interaction with civil society groups. It was taken for granted that the fundamental responsibility for responding to public interest demands lies at the national level and that national governments should bear the task of developing greater ties with civil society groups in the formulation of trade policies. None the less, after the wave of internal reforms carried out by other international organizations, the WTO's incipient contacts with civil society established grounds for cooperation, primarily with NGOs and labour organizations that focus their demands on two fronts: these are, on the one hand, certain issues of substance such as the impact of trade on the environment, or labour standards; on the other hand, there is the process of trade dispute settlement itself. The WTO's intergovernmental structure and the nature of its operations have made for a half-hearted process of opening. Demands were articulated almost exclusively by Northern-based NGOs that have also incorporated gender and equity concerns. For their part, Southern civil society organizations share similar concerns but place priority on the income-distribution effects of trade liberalization, targeting what they perceive to be excessively rapid processes without reciprocity of access to Northern markets and safety nets for losers, be they poor countries or poor people.

On a short leash from member states, the WTO's initial response to civil society has been technical rather than political. In contrast to service organizations, the WTO has no services to deliver; thus, participation was narrowed to the disclosure of information rather than extended to an effective incorporation of civil society actors into WTO policy processes (O'Brien et al. 2000). The WTO's *Guidelines for the Adoption of Arrangements on Relations with Non-Governmental Organizations*, adopted by the General Council in 1996, outlined the function and roles that NGOs were allowed to play as observer without voice or vote. The arrangements are an excessively timid and overcautious framework for opening up the institution in the new scenario. Although accepting the need for increasing the dissemination of information about activities in order to improve transparency and dialogue, member states wished the demands away and did not seriously consider a strategy for the incorporation of civil society into its policy debates beyond some confidence-building measures. Prominent among these was the convening of five ad hoc symposia since 1996 on topics of concern to civil society: of these, three were on trade and the environment, one was on trade and development, and one was on trade facilitation. These symposia provided NGOs with the opportunity to hold informal discussions on specific questions with representatives of WTO member states.[4] Similarly, conversations and meetings were held with the councils and committees of the WTO. These meetings remained unofficial unless the corresponding council or committee chose otherwise.[5]

In sum, the WTO felt besieged, but civil society participation was largely confined to an exercise in public relations. The centralized bureaucratic structure of the WTO and the more government-driven dynamic contrasts sharply with the requirements for accessibility. Whereas the nature of programme delivery in service organizations of necessity involves other key members beyond governments, the agenda and procedures of the WTO rest squarely on governments. This cautious strategy backfired in the Seattle ministerial meeting where, for better or for worse, the tightly closed compartment of trade negotiations was seriously challenged; what this may mean in terms of democratizing the WTO in favour of levelling the market-access problems of developing countries remains uncertain. However, ignoring ethical claims such as labour standards, environment, and human rights may lead to the standstill of multilateral negotiations, and even to institutional paralysis and decay.

Implications for global governance

The picture we have drawn shows that the undertow has become a tide. Nevertheless, we are caught today between two modes of thinking about, and of handling, many international problems, gradually and erratically moving from one to the other and back. None the less, the era of restricted state-driven negotiations is seriously challenged. The enthusiastic arrival of civil (mainly Northern) society as new players at the table of global governance will draw welcome new lines of accountability in international policy-making. NGOs have kicked at the doors and wriggled deftly into the closed rooms of international negotiations. Chipping in at the sides of state power, in many instances they have altered daily operational procedures and priorities. Moreover, the "core issues of the liberal internationalist agenda" (Murphy 1994: 222) are now more widely accepted by different actors all along the ideological spectrum. However, the movement faces many weaknesses, not least of which is the question of representation. Moral absolutism leads to exhortative encounters, where NGOs in beguiling or condemning tones make efforts to be heard for the greater good of humanity, issue by issue.

The agendas and procedures of international economic organizations now combine the persistence of old, top-down practices with the new demands of transparency, participation, and accountability hailed by organized civil society. It is in this context that international organizations manage to capture an almost monopolistic role in development issues and policy recommendations. This gives them an unparalleled capacity to coach economic and social policies in a myriad of developing nations, shaping the way that they participate in the global economy.

Norms and rules in international organizations impose limits on their civil society agendas; these limits are in the process of erosion, no doubt. In service organizations analysed in this chapter, the existence of funded projects, as well as the more decentralized processes that flow from the executive board via the chief executive to the resident representatives in field offices, allows greater receptiveness to the interests and demands of civil society organizations. Thus, after years of closed negotiations and neglect of Northern NGOs' calls for reforms aimed at greater opening and accountability, and at more equitable and less environmentally damaging development strategies, by the 1990s the World Bank, the IDB, and the IMF have adopted mechanisms for including NGOs in their policy dialogue and procedures. This last point appears central to the execution of poverty alleviation and development programmes (World Bank 1996; Inter-American Development Bank 1996). However, resource allocation still remains, at worst, highly discretionary and, at best, subject to the needs of the iron-clad external financing gap which, in turn, requires measures of austerity. Although the World Bank and the IDB – and, to a lesser extent, the IMF – have adapted their institutional procedures to consider civil society to be clients and direct beneficiaries, similar results cannot be reached in forum organizations without altering forms of representation.

In comparing the two forum organizations addressed here, the United

Nations has been able to go further in reforming its traditional procedures. In fact, there is an official inclination to enhance NGOs' legal status
beyond the currently consultative status enjoyed in ECOSOC. NGOs
have been widely recognized by UN organs and programmes as vital to
the work of the United Nations.[6] However, as in the case of the WTO,
the character of these political debates is still subordinated to the interest
of the member states. Although NGOs have demonstrated that the multilateral trading system is being scrutinized by public opinion as never
before, the prospects of NGO demands for democratizing the WTO are
less obvious. In fact, the WTO has no means to co-opt them as in the
case of the international financial institutions, which made dialogue with
NGOs a central component of their institutional governance. In fact, the
WTO and the UN system still attribute an auxiliary instrumental role to
civil society in their policy negotiations. In these instances, the opening
up to civil society is more an exercise in public relations.

In short, the relationship between civil society groups, on the one
hand, and the World Bank and the IDB, on the other, is characterized by
cooperation and coexistence; relations with the IMF reveal distrust and
misgivings on both sides. It is important to note that, by and large, demands from NGOs that operate in developing countries target not the
procedures of the international financial institutions but, rather, the consequences of economic adjustment programmes. In this case, the agenda
of the organizations of civil society in the South partially diverges from
the priorities of Northern NGOs. All in all, the relationship between
Southern civil society organizations and international organizations remains undeveloped for at least two reasons: first, international organizations are sometimes seen as a "tool of imperialism," particularly because of the asymmetrical voting structure; second, Southern NGOs
also criticize the NGO movement itself, in which Northern NGOs tend
to control the funds, set the agendas, and move the processes (Vianna
2000).

The governance conditionality advocated by foreign NGOs can raise sensitive
foreign and domestic policy and security issues and create obstacles to implementation inside the borrowing country (...) Often such NGOs seek to super-
impose their own cultural values on societies subscribing to different ethical and
spiritual values. Consequently, such governance conditions are seen as imposing
the ideological or cultural preferences of advocacy groups in the industrial countries on borrowers, thereby inviting the charge that the MDBs are being made to
serve as instruments of rich-country paternalism, specially in their dealings with
poorer member countries, who must depend on concessional windows of the
MDBs for funding. (Aziz Ali 1996: 4)

Participation of Northern civil society may have been a good spark to
ignite the process of making international organizations more account-

able but it cannot substitute participation of organized civil society from the South. If the process of expanding global participation in global governance is to be successful, the initial advocacy of "the proxy" must contribute to building the stage for its own gradual demise. At the very least, "the proxy" must retreat into the safeguard of last resort that intervenes only when gross abuses must be stopped or avoided and national civil society is muted.

Democracy is, in essence, a way of distributing responsibility. Global governance, institutional governance, and national governance have a common normative and political denominator: extending the scope of inclusiveness depends on a political decision, which in turn relies on embedded structures of state-centred ownership. Thus, the challenge ahead is twofold: first, to move beyond an incremental incorporation of issues that affect the dispossessed; second, to shape intergovernmental relations in a democratic way. This approach to global governance does not require that we abandon citizen movements in favour of governments, but it does suggest the importance of placing governments within a wider political and economic context. To what extent have international organizations and the rearrangement of international actors – both governmental and non-governmental – contributed to global governance processes? The answer is Solomonic. The recent dialogue with civil society organizations has opened up wider interaction with unheard or previously silent voices, thus increasing the range of actors involved in the broad issues of international bargaining. Although the process has become more complex, little has been achieved to institutionalize these new avenues and modes of intervention properly. Moreover, how much global market forces have come under control, or how much these actions benefit the losers of globalization, remains open to question. While we muddle through without taking an overly pessimistic stance, an analysis of the relationship between global markets and international organizations remains on the "to do" list of our theoretical enquiry in international political economy.

Notes

1. This chapter draws inspiration from the seminal book edited by R. Cox and H. Jacobson, *The Anatomy of Influence: Decision-Making in International Organizations* (1973). This study was for long overshadowed in mainstream international relations. It was one of the first attempts to open up the "black box" of international organizations with a decision-making approach. By the time that the book was published, however, the discussion on influence within international organizations in international relations changed focus to the study of the influence of international organizations on states' behaviour and, by extension, to the study of international regimes as part and parcel of US hegemony/imperialism. The study of decision-making in international organizations, then, fell into the "black box" again. The recent "discovery" of international organizations by civil

society movements brought back the significance of Cox and Jacobson's insights. (See *Global Governance*, Special Issue, October 2000).

The authors gratefully acknowledge inputs from Nora Rabotnikof, William C. Smith, and Maria Fernanda Tuozzo.

2. Two internal evaluations, the *Wapenhans Report* (World Bank 1992) and *Tapoma Report* (Inter-American Development Bank 1993), reveal the difficulties of implementing MDB programmes and the low rate of returns on their loans. See Paul Nelson, 1997.

3. See United Nations Non-governmental Liaison Service, *NGLS Handbook* at http://ngls.tad.ch/english/pubs/hb/hb1.html (retrieved 10 August 2000).

4. See http://www.ictsd.org/html/review2-3.7.html (May 1999).

5. See *WTO Guidelines for the Adoption of Arrangements on Relations with Non-governmental Organisations*, at http://www.org/wto/spanish/ngosp/162.html (May 1999).

6. See United Nations Non-governmental Liaison Service, *NGLS Handbook* at http://ngls.tad.ch/english/pubs/hb/hb1.html (retrieved 10 August 2000).

REFERENCES

Acuña, Carlos and M. Fernanda Tuozzo. 2000. "Civil Society Participation in World Bank and Inter-American Development Bank Programs: The Case of Argentina." *Global Governance* 6(4): 443–456.

Aziz Ali, Mohamed. 1996. "Note on MDB Conditionality on Governance." G24/96/September.

Baldwin, David. 1993. *Neorealism and Neoliberalism: The Contemporary Debate.* New York: Columbia University Press.

Buira, Ariel. 1995. *Reflections on the International Monetary System. Essays in International Finance No 195.* Princeton, NJ: Princeton University Press.

Camdessus, Michel. 1997. "Toward a Second Generation of Structural Reform in Latin America." Presentation at the Annual Conference of the National Banks Association, May, Buenos Aires, Argentina.

Casaburi, Gabriel and Diana Tussie. 1997. "Governance and the New Lending Strategies of the Multilateral Development Banks." Working paper. Buenos Aires: FLACSO.

Clark, Ann, Elizabeth Friedman, and Kathryn Hochstetler. 1999. "Sovereignty, Global Civil Society and the Social Conferences: NGOs and States at the UN Conferences on Population, Social Development and Human Settlement." Paper prepared for presentation at the 40th Annual Meeting of the International Studies Association, Washington, DC, February 16–20.

Cox, Robert and Harold Jacobson, eds. 1973. *The Anatomy of Influence. Decision-Making in International Organizations.* New Haven and London: Yale University Press.

Curzon, Gerard and Victoria Curzon. 1973. "GATT: Traders Club." In: The Anatomy of Influence. Decision-Making in International Organizations, eds Robert Cox and Harold Jacobson. New Haven and London: Yale University Press.

Donini, Antonio. 1996. "The Bureaucracy and the Free Spirits: Stagnation and Innovation in the Relationship Between the UN and NGOs." In: *NGOs, the*

UN and Global Governance, eds Thomas Weiss and Leon Gordenker. Boulder, CO: Lynne Rienner.

Falk, Richard. 1998. "Global Civil Society: Perspectives, Initiatives and Movements." *Oxford Development Studies* 26(1): 99–110.

Financial Times 1999. "People First." 22 September, 4.

Higgott, Richard and Simon Reich. 1999. "From Globalization to Glamourisation: The Rise of the NGOs in International Relations." Paper presented at the Annual Convention of the International Studies Association, Washington, DC, 16–20 February.

Inter-American Development Bank. 1993. *Tapoma Report*. Washington, DC: Inter-American Development Bank.

Inter-American Development Bank. 1996. *Resource Book on Participation*. Washington, DC: Inter-American Development Bank.

Kahler, Miles. 1993. "Bargaining with the IMF: Two-Level Strategies and Developing Countries." In: *Double-Edged Diplomacy. International Bargaining and Domestic Politics*, eds Peter Evans, Harold Jacobson, and Robert Putnam. Berkeley, CA: University of California Press.

Keck, Margaret and Kathryn Sikkink. 1998. *Activists Beyond Borders: Advocacy Networks in International Politics*. Ithaca, NY: Cornell University Press.

Keohane, Robert O. 1984. *After Hegemony: Cooperation and Discord in the World Political Economy*. Princeton, NJ: Princeton University Press.

Keohane, Robert O. and Joseph S. Nye, eds. 1972. *Transnational Relations and World Politics*. Cambridge, MA: Harvard University Press.

Krasner, Stephen D., ed. 1983. *International Regimes*. Ithaca, NY: Cornell University Press.

Murphy, Craig. 1994. *International Organisation and Industrial Change: Global Governance since 1850*. Oxford: Oxford University Press.

Nelson, Paul. 1997. "Transparencia, Fiscalización y Participación." In: Diana Tussie, ed. *El BID, el Banco Mundial y la sociedad civil: nuevas formas de financiamiento internacional*. Buenos Aires: FLACSO.

Nelson, Paul. 2000. "Whose Civil Society? Whose Governance?" *Global Governance* 6(4): 405–431.

O'Brien, Robert, Anne M. Goetz, Jan A. Scholte, and Marc Williams. 2000. *Contesting Global Governance. Multilateral Economic Institutions and Global Social Movements*. Cambridge: Cambridge University Press.

Rodrik, Dani. 1999. "Governing Global Economy: Does One Architectural Style Fit for All?" Paper prepared for the Brookings Institution Trade Policy Forum Conference on Governing in a Global Economy, 15–16 April 1999, Harvard University.

Scholte, Jan Aart. 1998a. "The WTO and Civil Society." Working Paper, Centre of Studies of Globalisation and Regionalisation, University of Warwick.

Scholte, Jan Aart. 1998b. "The International Monetary Fund and Civil Society: an Underdeveloped Dialogue." Working Paper, Centre of Studies of Globalisation and Regionalisation, University of Warwick.

Smith, Jackie, Charles Chatfield, and Ron Pagnucco, eds. 1997. *Transnational Social Movements and Global Politics*. Syracuse, NY: Syracuse University Press.

Tuozzo, M. Fernanda. 1999. *Opportunities and Limits for Civil Society Participation in Multilateral Lending Operations: Lessons from Latin America, Documento de Trabajo*. Buenos Aires: FLACSO.

Tussie, Diana. 1995. *The Inter-American Development Bank*. Boulder, CO: Lynne Rienner.

Tussie, Diana and Gabriel Casaburi. 2000. "From Global to Local Governance: Civil Society and the Multilateral Development Banks." *Global Governance* 6(4): 399–403.

Vianna, Aurelio. 2000. "Civil Society Participation in World Bank and Inter-American Development Bank Programs: The Case of Brazil." *Global Governance* 6(4): 457–472.

Walzer, Michael. 1980. *Just and Unjust Wars: A Moral Argument with Historical Illustrations*. New York: Pelican Books.

Weiss, Thomas and Leon Gordenker. 1996. "Pluralizing Global Governance: Analytical Approaches and Dimensions." In: *NGOs, the UN, and Global Governance*, eds Thomas Weiss and Leon Gordenker. Boulder, CO: Lynne Rienner.

Willetts, Peter. 1999. "Environmental Politics and Transnational Actors in the United Nations." unpublished mimeo.

Woods, Ngaire. 1999. "Good Governance in International Organizations." *Global Governance* 5(1): 39–61.

World Bank. 1992. *The Wapenhans Report*. Washington, DC: World Bank.

World Bank. 1996. *The World Bank Participation Sourcebook*. Washington, DC: World Bank.

6

A subsidiary and federal world republic: Thoughts on democracy in the age of globalization

Otfried Höffe

The challenges of our time

Most of the time, only economists and political scientists or specialists of international law and demographic specialists deal with the question of global governance. Yet their predominantly empirical considerations lack a normative counterpoint that, in many cases, should represent a tacit prerequisite: according to which criteria may we consider global governance as successful or even legitimate? Furthermore, do not these criteria require an extension of what has thus far been achieved with respect to global governance? Moral philosophy and, more precisely, the philosophy of law and political philosophy are required to answer such questions while avoiding either moral prejudices or even moral infantilism. Social scientists fear that such a philosophy, being disconnected from experience, constructs an unrealistic utopia which not only does not exist but, more significantly, could never exist at all. I reply to this fear with a normativism that is at once constructive, open to experience, and realistic. This normativism observes that there is a lack of law, democracy, and justice in today's global political reality and provides a constructive alternative model. Moreover, far from adjusting normative criteria to conform to reality, the issues concerning the economic and social sciences (i.e. the issues concerning efficiency and practicability) require a normative idea as premise.

Any political philosophy that is truly political addresses the challenges

181

of its time. In public opinion and at first sight, one of today's most important challenges seems to be globalization. The word "globalization," however, has become so amorphous from overuse that a new definition is now called for. To this end, I propose three perspectives by means of which I redefine the term "globalization."

Plural globalization

The word globalization is usually employed in the singular, as a term relative to economic changes in the contemporary world. If this picture were, indeed, accurate, economics would certainly be of primary relevance to any account of globalization, when supplemented by international law, the theory of international relations, and sociology. Yet, for at least two reasons, philosophy has also been brought into the arena. First, philosophy generally works on the very prerequisite for any form of globalization – the faculty of language and of reason shared by all human beings. Second, philosophy, being exclusively concerned with these very capabilities, rapidly became a global success story. After beginning in Asia Minor and then flourishing in the Athens of classical antiquity, philosophy spread across the Mediterranean area, from whence it expanded worldwide. Consequently, the classic masterpieces of philosophy – those of Plato and Aristotle, Hobbes and Descartes, Kant and Hegel – were read everywhere long before one could even imagine a situation of financial and economic globalization. Furthermore, long before computers belonged to the effects of educated households, Nietzsche, Heidegger, and Wittgenstein were already there.

The common notion of globalization as a mere economic process is based on a wider economic reductionism that reconciles two groups otherwise bitterly opposed to one another – orthodox Marxists and orthodox Liberals. Although both groups believe that the major forces at work in the world are economic, in fact even changes in this area are not exclusively economic: they are also based on political decisions – consider, for example, Bretton Woods, the World Trade Organization (WTO), and the Organization for Economic Cooperation and Development – as well as on technological innovation, whether military or civil. In addition, globalization is not confined to the world of economics and labour, supplemented by global leisure and tourism: in fact, in addition to these, there are many phenomena that have little or nothing to do with economics. The totality of globalization, including its economic components, may be subsumed under three dimensions.

A first dimension of globalization consists of a multifaceted "society of violence," namely in (a) war, which threatens to assume global proportions as a consequence of new weapons technology, (b) internationally organized crime (drug smuggling, traffic in human beings, terrorism), and (c) transnational environmental damage. However, this society of violence also shows an anamnesic side: a "critical world-memory" reminds us of all the significant outrages that have been committed, and if this world-memory were to show justice, reminding us of these atrocities in a non-selective way (contrary to what has hitherto been the case), it would help to prevent future disasters.

Fortunately, this widespread society of violence is complemented by a still wider-spread "society of cooperation." Even here, the economy and the financial world, the labour market, and the transportation and communication network play an important role, although not an exclusive one. Philosophy and all the sciences (not only the natural sciences, medicine, and technology but also human sciences), major aspects of culture and, finally, colleges and universities are also becoming global. Even our liberal democracy belongs to this second dimension, since it exerts pressure on globalization (as is shown by the fact that, even though human-rights violations are not yet punishable on a worldwide scale, at least they are forced to confront worldwide protest). A common – in fact, global – public opinion is emerging and can join the critical "world-memory." The development of international law (particularly the development of the international jurisdiction, which began with the permanent International Court of Justice founded in 1920 which has been followed by the International Court of Justice in the Hague after the Second World War and which development is continuing with the newly instituted International War Crimes Tribunal) and the growing number of globally active governmental and non-governmental organizations make this public opinion still stronger. In addition to such newcomers as the World Bank and Amnesty International, older examples should not be forgotten, such as international sports organizations, the Universal Postal Union (founded 1875), the International Labour Organization (founded 1919), the World Health Organization (founded 1948), and last but not least, the much older churches and other religious communities.

One ought not to confuse this global society of cooperation with "pure love and friendship"; on the contrary, competition predominates in all these domains. Competition not only stimulates the forces from which we expect collective wealth, effort, risk-taking and creativity, it also involves costs that are sometimes internal to the economy (e.g. unemployment) and sometimes external to it (e.g. environmental pollution). It introduces us to the third dimension of globalization, the "community of shared destiny," in a narrower sense – the community of need and pain. This includes natural catastrophes, famine, poverty, and economic as well as cultural and political underdevelopment. It also includes civil wars, which are often not only the later consequences of colonization and decolonization but also the explosive answer to corruption and mismanagement. Finally, there are numerous immigrants and refugees with their sometimes religious, sometimes political, and sometimes economic background.

My first perspective on globalization is that all three dimensions announce a global need for action which, in turn, qualifies the dominant paradigm of political philosophy from Plato and Aristotle through Hobbes and Hegel – the nation-state or, more generally, the individual political community.

Two qualifications

Even understood as in this extended diagnosis, globalization does not qualify as the sole distinguishing mark of our time. There are actually important counterpoints – the growing self-confidence of certain regions and the formation of new territorial authorities, as well as the fragmentation of some mega-cities into separate ethnic and cultural groups and the strengthening of national sentiment among young democracies. In any case, a variety of languages, customs, morals, and religions exist. Even if humankind develops into a global community of fate, fate itself occurs in many respects at the regional, local, or completely individual level. This provides sufficient reason to consider the expression "global village" as an oversimplification and also to think that it is possible to escape the frequently conjured danger of an unavoidable uniformity of our way of life.

A closer diagnosis proceeds to a second qualification, which is a historical one. International trade routes such as the Silk Road were developed long before the modern era. In Hellenistic times there emerged what may be considered an approximation to a world trade area with world market pricing and even world trading centres such as Alexandria and the Mesopotamian city of Seleucia. Further, certain religions – such as Buddhism, Christianity, Islam, and Judaism – began to spread; thus they are called world religions, in which international pilgrimages to holy cities, such as those to Bodh-Gaya, Rome, Mecca, and Jerusalem have developed. Besides the religious pilgrimages there are also "epic" pilgrimages. The fables and tales of the sort depicted in Boccacio's *Decameron* are, in fact, a kind of international flotsam and jetsam coming from oriental and occidental influences, much of which can be traced back over Persia to India. But first of all, globalization concerns the forms of natural reason, i.e. philosophy, science, medicine, and technology.

Inventions such as the compass, telescope, gunpowder, and printing press preceded a second phase of globalization, the early and mid-modern period, i.e. the era of discovery and then later colonization, as well as the age of enlightenment.

The third historical phase of globalization, that in which we live at present, is similar in this respect. Both peaceful inventions (such as radio-technology and electronic media) and military inventions (first the long-range bomber, then the intercontinental ballistic missile) play a role. Political decisions come into play with respect both to the liberalization of financial and trade markets and to international organizations such as the United Nations or the World Bank. These practical and historical qualifications constitute the second of my three perspectives on globalization. They show us at once a twofold overvaluation of the notion of globalization: it is neither the only characteristic of our time nor is it an absolutely new phenomenon; it is a dominant feature with some fairly new aspects. Globalization is a strong force that requires us to qualify the nation-state as the only object of political philosophy.

Two touches of scepticism

Before attempting to respond to the realities of globalization, I would like to add two touches of scepticism to the usual contemporary discussions.

My first touch of scepticism consists in the observation that today's globalization is actually nothing especially new. Indeed, from the historical perspective, the element of today's globalization considered especially impressive (i.e. the internationalization of finance and currency markets) in part appears as mere repetition. In other words, European modernity seems content to indulge in the illusion that every generation surpasses the preceding one. However, at the time that the gold standard was still in place (i.e. from 1887 to 1914), trade between developed countries was on a level similar to the one we know today. In this respect, it is only today that we are returning to the status quo of the period prior to the First World War, the financial crises of the 1930s, and the Second World War. The fact that information is transmitted by cable under the ocean or by digital electronics is certainly not trivial, but the overall impact on global trade has been less extensive. With respect to the politics of peace, its impact is hardly discernible. Consider, for example, the peace treaty of 1648 which ended a period of great terror for Germany – the Thirty Years' War. Because it took a month for a letter to reach Madrid, the addressee had to wait about three months for new instructions from Spain, which is one reason why peace came only after four years of negotiations. Yet neither aviation technology nor electronic information transfer have been able to speed up the peace process in the Middle East or in the former Yugoslavia.

The second touch of scepticism results from the fact that even today's global economy is global only in a limited sense. Statistically, global trade occurs primarily (in fact, almost exclusively) between the European Union, Japan, the United States, and a couple of the so-called "emergent" countries. For the first three, exports do not amount to an excessively high share of commerce; exchange is probably more important in other areas. Again, globalization in the fields of science and culture is no less important than that in the economic sphere.

Two visions

How should humankind best respond to the challenges of globalization? In general, humankind knows of two fundamental models of social organization. Both contain a certain visionary power; some might call them utopian. On the one hand, common rules and public powers remove subjective will and privately held power. We consider it a moral imperative to replace violence by the rule of law and justice and, for this purpose, to establish public powers and to organize them within a democratic structure. Let us call these universal legal and political imperatives and an equally universal democratic imperative.

Liberal democracy, in particular, provides the conditions for the free play of human capacities, which, in reality, leads to hard competition. In return, it expects the greatest wealth in the form of goods and services as well as the highest results in the fields of science, medicine, technology, music, literature, and art. This second vision of a multidimensional well-being, the vision that a very old dream of humankind will become reality, complements the vision of peace and justice. Consonant with the words of the prophet Isaiah – "They shall beat their swords into plowshares, and their spears into pruninghooks" (Isaiah 2: 4) – physical violence should be transformed into economic and cultural forces and, wherever there is peace, something more than mere material well-being also ought to be achieved.

In both visions we have a situation in which everyone stands to gain. In a less ideal situation collective gain can be accompanied by individual or group loss. If this should be the case, it is necessary to do more than merely compensate for such loss. However, this is a secondary problem. First, we must ask whether that which is true within a political community may also be valid on a global scale? Should there not (1) be an order of peace and law, in which (2) by means of economic, scientific, and cultural competition the societies and, above all, the individuals flourish? For no society is an end in itself: what ultimately counts is the individual, and not the isolated human being.

Although legal and political philosophy endorses the second vision, it opposes its being made absolute by a second kind of economism that ousts politics through the market. We sometimes hear the opinion that politics has not been ousted at all but "only" transferred from democratically elected officials to international corporations and entrepreneurs. In many places a form of economic fatalism predominates, which maintains that "the economy decides both the means and ends" of political action. With its means, the economy determines the goals to which politics can do nothing but react, so that, instead of organizing, politics is committed to adaptation.

In truth, no anonymous fate is at work. Globalization has its names, such as the previously mentioned political agreements concerning the liberalization of world markets. As the domestic market is submitted to general frameworks, an analogous frame for the global market is likewise not excluded a priori. It is politics itself – in this case, hardly national politics and, indeed, a truly international politics – that either submits to the powers of market forces or compels them to establish fair regulations for competition as well as to enforce minimum standards for social and environmental matters.

The world community should, and must, leave many matters to happen on their own: these include the creativity of individuals and groups, free competition, and contingent evolution. In many instances, however, the power of the global community is required. We must, therefore, ask the following question: if law and justice, instead of violence, are to govern the relations between individuals and groups, and both are to be organized democratically, must not the same be true at both a *supranational* and an *international* level? Is there not, then, a need for a global legal system committed to law and justice and grounded in a democratic organization? Does not the best political response to the age of globalization lie in the extension of democracy from the level of the single state to a world democracy (one might also choose to call it a "world republic")? A world republic is a qualified world state that has democracy as a necessary qualification, at least at the global level, while, at the same time, reserving the possibility for non-democratic states to participate at the level of the world state, at least for a transitional phase (unlike the United Nations, which does not put as a condition for membership a gradual process of democratization). Given the three dimensions of globalization mentioned above, any such world republic should be responsible even for all three dimensions: (1) against the global "community of violence," (2) for establishing the framework of a "global community of cooperation," and perhaps (3) for the community of need and pain, for a "community of shared destiny."

Five objections

This response to the age of globalization seems compelling. However, it entails such a radical break with political reality that objections must be raised. I now consider five of these which seem especially significant. All of them represent serious hindrances and formidable obstacles which either obscure the ideal of a global legal order or obstruct its path. By overcoming the objections, we obtain a more attractive and more realistic model. It concentrates on the basic idea of a global order and leaves the further task of defining a global civic society to further consideration (cf. Höffe 1999b, chap. 12).

Ungovernability?

The first objection was presented by none other than Immanuel Kant, the philosopher of a global order of law and peace: a world republic (Kant suggested) is a monster impossible to govern owing to its sheer bulk and the impossibility of supervising it efficiently. Is this a reasonable objection?

To the citizens of Liechtenstein with its 28,500 inhabitants, Switzerland with its 6.5 million inhabitants is gigantic, while the USA with 265 million is truly gargantuan (to say nothing of the 950 million in India and 1.3 billion inhabitants of China). If a political community of the size of the USA – almost 10,000 times the size of Liechtenstein and approximately 40 times that of Switzerland – can, none the less, be in some ways governed, the first objection may be right, but it does not represent a devastating or even final argument against the idea of a world republic. Instead of an absolute veto, we find a relative and at the same time a constructive one: the world republic is permissible, even morally required, provided that it is able to prevent its own ungovernability as well as an overcompensation of this ungovernability – namely, too much bureaucracy or even a police state.

At this stage, we remain content to make one constructive point. A world republic must not follow the pattern of the United Nations, bringing together vast countries such as India or China with tiny or miniature states such as Liechtenstein. Ought we not first to introduce political unities of continental or subcontinental size? According to the model of the European Union, most problems could be dealt with "domestically," leaving the few remaining problems for a global government. Let us call this the "principle of large intermediary regional unities."

The principle of subsidiarity

According to a second objection, a world republic places the great accomplishments of civilization at risk – namely, human and civil rights – for, so far, only single states have successfully guaranteed these rights. With this objection, not only the normative presupposition (i.e. the commitment to human and civic rights) but also the empirical statement is right, although only a third of the objection itself is true: undoubtedly, in countries of the West, human and civil rights are mainly protected by the respective states (in Europe, of course, these rights are also guaranteed by the European Human Rights Convention), whereas citizens of other countries, who at present can rely only on international organizations for this protection, are far worse off. The second third of the truth is that Western states first endangered these rights: France persecuted the Huguenots; the United States of America were founded because of a lack of religious tolerance in Great Britain; and, in the USA itself, slavery was an institution far into the second half of the nineteenth century. The last third of the truth is that, where human and civil rights are already protected (partly through the state and partly thanks to regional human-rights conventions based on the European model), the world republic remains in the background. Where enormous violations of human rights have been committed, however, the world republic should restrain itself only when intervention on humanitarian grounds would cause even greater damage. In principle, though, simply to stand by and do nothing is neither acceptable nor justifiable.

As with the first objection, the second objection to a world republic amounts not to an absolute refutation but to a constructive veto. The individual states remain accountable for enforcing the law. Only individual states have the rank of first-order states, while the world republic is no more than a second-order (or, in such cases in which there are intermediaries – continental or subcontinental unions – even a third-order) state. We shall call it the principle of world state subsidiarity (on the general principle of subsidiarity, cf. Höffe 1996). This principle is twofold. First, the world republic should not be established "from the top," but rather democratically (i.e. built by citizens and individual countries). It is not a centralized world government but rather a world federal government or republic. Second, the scope of its tasks is limited to issues that are not to be dealt with by the individual state. The federal republic is a complementary world republic that does not relieve the states of their authority. The issues related to civil and criminal law; to labour and social law; the law governing the right of languages, religion, and culture; and other such tasks remain within the jurisdiction of the first-order governments of the individual states. However, this is true only as a first step. Owing to the many aspects of globalization, the primary states must work with their fellow primary states. It is better for them to pass on certain responsibilities to the top, such as the coordination of the transnational war on crime and the adoption of a social and environmental regulation of the international market. As for subsidiarity, the relevant model is not the United Nations (although they include almost all countries) but the European Union, a continental entity that explicitly commits itself to the principle of subsidiarity as a binding guiding principle.

The world republic has not merely subsidiary, but also primary, responsibility for peace between nations and for its precondition, disarmament, the begining of which is the non-proliferation of atomic, biological, and chemical weapons. The United Nations have actively promoted treaties on the non-proliferation of such weapons, as well as a ban on atmospheric nuclear tests and on underground tests over a low level. Nevertheless, the United Nations should receive more enforcement powers if it is ever to become a true world republic.

The principle of subsidiarity is complemented by a principle of caution and prudence. The individual states and regional units are not authorized to place the degree of liberal democracy that they have already achieved in jeopardy. Besides subsidiarity, the world republic must develop gradually, so that one can try new possibilities, gather experience, and, first and foremost, develop such important preconditions of a world republic as a global public sphere in politics. It is well known that Europe is already experiencing difficulties with regard to the establishment of a public sphere, which suggests that there would be even more difficulties in the case of a world state. To achieve such a worldwide public sphere it is important (though not sufficient merely) to become outraged about human-rights violations occurring on some distant shore (Kant already calls attention to the fact that "a violation of right on *one* place of the earth is felt in all"; Kant 1795). We must also – as already happens all too infrequently in the case of European Union legislation – lead the type of debate common within each state that prepares parliamentary discussions and legislation, accompanies them, and comments on them afterwards – and, if necessary, introduces amendments. There should even be a clear connection between a common public sphere and common institutions; for as long as a global public sphere is not in place, the establishment of a complementary and federal world republic would be unreasonable and even dangerous. In any case, a global legal system should be established neither by surprise nor blindly. In this perspective, the United Nations, as the sole international institution of which nearly all states are members, has here a decisive role to play if it is able fundamentally to reform its institutions and procedures.

During the period of transition involving a provisional world legal system, international organizations as well as international law will be in demand. This is because international institutions provide international cooperation with structure and permanency (cf. Rittberger 1993), something that a world system with rudimentary elements of statehood would also create.

The school of political science sees international institutions as mere instruments of state diplomacy: individual states jump into the foray with and against each other in pursuit of influence and resources (cf. Keohane 1986). The truth is that these international institutions are not only an arena for a power struggle but also a political forum for states. Moreover, international organizations themselves have some power to set agendas and are even able to persuade reluctant states to participate in negotiations. In the best of cases, they even become an arbitration authority: states use them when the costs of a military solution to conflicts are too high. Their significance as organs of coordination suggests an anticipation of a world republic. Indeed, they help member states to articulate and realize their interests (within certain limits).

International organizations supplemented by corporate actors and functional units are capable of impartiality (which is the central, formal duty of public authorities) only to a certain extent. For instance, small countries try to do with their superior number what the great powers achieve with their power: they attempt to make international organizations the instrument of their interests. For years, the movement of the non-aligned countries, for instance, formed the largest group in the UN General Assembly. For this reason, international institutions (although they can prepare the organizations and the rules that provide for a progressive taming of naked power) help to establish a system of global governance in the sense of a horizontal self-coordination. However, in the long run, they cannot be a substitute for a world republic.

Are democracies inclined towards peace?

According to a third objection, there is a much simpler way to protect human rights – namely, the democratization of all states. In accordance with the thesis of "global peace through global democratization," a worldwide peace policy can be content with a worldwide policy of democratization, and a world republic becomes superfluous. In fact, liberal democracy already protects human rights within states. Certainly, there are many more arguments in favour of democracy. However, just as the European Human Rights Convention already controls the protection of human rights through the single states, it is advisable to establish a global human rights commission that has authority even over regional authorities. (The United States, for example, would not pass muster because of its death penalty, even in peacetime.) Nevertheless, first of all, individual states (more precisely, their territorial integrity and their political self-determination) are to be protected.

With regard to the danger threatening the latter, contemporary political science has taken up Kant's famous thesis that liberal democracies –

or republics, as Kant called them – have little proclivity towards wars of aggression (cf. Doyle 1983; Singer and Small 1972). Kant does not assume that citizens have a genuine propensity towards peace but, rather, refers to their enlightened self-interest. In a democracy "the consent of the citizens of a state is required in order to decide whether or not there shall be war" (Kant 1795). And "since they would have to decide to take upon themselves all the hardships war entails (such as doing the fighting themselves and paying for the costs of war from their own resources, painfully making good the devastation such a war leaves behind [...])" they will hardly ever begin "such a bad game."

Nevertheless, history calls for scepticism: the new French republic militarily overran Europe and persisted with its own imperial interests; a still older republic, the United States of America, spread itself westward, acting ruthlessly towards the native peoples. Moreover, the USA first annexed Texas and then incorporated the states of Arizona, Utah, and Nevada, as well as California and New Mexico. Similarly, Great Britain was not hindered from realizing its plans as a world power – namely, the extension of the Commonwealth – by its internal evolution towards a more democratic government. For this reason political scientists were obliged to weaken their thesis: democracies are not, in principle, peaceful and are so only when fulfilling additional conditions; their propensity towards peace exists only towards other democracies.

Yet, even with this moderate thesis, a number of doubts remain. On the one hand, it is right that early democracies were lacking important elements such as equality of rights for the working classes and women, a higher level of education for the general population, as well as parliamentary decision-making procedures for declaring war and preparing public debates. The decision to go to war often enjoyed such broad support among the population that "more democratic democracies" would have hardly decided the matter otherwise. On the other hand, enlightened self-interest certainly does not always speak out against war. Where the proximity of war is not felt, citizens experience fewer hardships, and even fewer hardships if the enemy is clearly at a disadvantage. Moreover, remote wars can distract from domestic political difficulties, and sometimes there is mass hysteria. Furthermore, wars outside the country can be very profitable. Moreover, the inclination towards peace could weaken as soon as most states become democracies. The potential for conflict has arisen today in relation to commercial policy and environmental questions, a potential that could intensify in the event of serious economic and social problems. Although liberal democracies are hardly aggressive, they must not become the opposite – namely, pacifist. The best they can become is enlightened rationalists, for whom, in general, military undertakings do not pay dividends, especially not at the price of "human lives." Last but not least, there are numerous legal problems below the level of war.

Consequently, the universal legal and political imperative remains the task of contemporary society, again in the form of a constructive veto. The protection and maintenance of rights and peace, which has already been achieved by a worldwide democratization, should be recognized. In the same way, we must assume that states suffering under either an autocratic or a semi-autocratic hegemonic regime would be happy if they were, at least, liberal hegemonic regimes. However, one cannot expect that the degree of liberty existing within the state also extends to the relations between states. At least, liberal states attempt to find a certain correspondence between their internal self-dignity and their external actions. This implies neither that this attempt is always taken seriously enough nor that it is always successful. Here, one may be sceptical. A prudent global governance cannot be confident that a liberal hegemonic regime is completely innocent of abusing democratic principles in its external relations – even at times significantly – and of employing its power to enforce its own self-interests or, at least, its own particular interpretation of international law and the global common good. But individual states have a right (just as individuals do) for possible conflicts not to be resolved by force but by law. Hence, in fact, a world legal system and, ultimately, a world republic, is needed.

A worldwide sense of law and justice

According to a fourth objection, a world legal system would be possible only if a certain precondition were fulfilled – namely, a sensitivity to the law common to all human beings – a worldwide sense of law and justice. We all know that such a common sense of law and justice is already lacking within the same legal sphere (e.g. among Western countries). Let us take a small example: those who read about US legal compensations, multimillion dollar pay-offs in cases in which, at best, German courts would pay US$10,000, must ask themselves if, in legal terms, they are actually living on the same planet. Greater differences appear in the attitude towards the death penalty, and even greater discrepancies with regard to corporal punishment in some Islamic states or treatment of dissidents in China, Cuba, and North Korea.

On the other hand, there are important things in common: the duty of equality and impartiality is as globally recognized in the application of law as are procedural rules such as *audiatur et altera pars* (to hear both parties) and the presumption of innocence or the burden of proof, *in dubio pro reo* (doubt must benefit the accused). Further, nearly every legal system recognizes the same basic object of legal protection: life and limb, property, and dignity. The United Nations human rights conventions provide further evidence of commonalities. The "only" thing lacking is the willingness to enforce these standards in an unbiased and effective way. For this reason, our constructive veto seems simple, almost trivial: it is true that more time is needed for a worldwide sense of law and justice to unfold. Here, the already emerging common ground is remarkably developed. After all, this common ground has already made world courts possible, including the International Court, the Maritime Court and, most recently (even though it is not yet ratified), the International Criminal Court.

A right to difference

According to the fifth and final objection, we are threatened in today's age of globalization – threatened by a cultural levelling, against which a strong counterpoint is needed. This counterpoint would consist in such a strengthening of peculiarities that the social and cultural wealth of the world – and, most importantly, the identity of the individual human beings who depend on it – are protected and preserved. The Communitarians, who recently became so prominent, plead for "good fences" and, thus, for national separateness instead of global unity. Clearly, Communitarians are not stubborn nationalists. Nevertheless, according to philosophers such as Alisdair MacIntyre (1981) and Michael Walzer (1983), for example, the state is the highest social unity in which moral and political concepts such as justice and solidarity still make sense and have any significance.

Indeed, the patrimony of humankind is manifest not only in common elements but also in the diversity of cultures, traditions, and aspirations. In particular, the different states have a shared though different history. Each of them has a particular tradition and culture, and either a language or specific multilingualism. They also follow a common set of values, such that the dissolution of all states within a global state would limit the wealth of humankind. Moreover, the identity of the only unit that ultimately matters, the individual (though not isolated) human being, would be endangered. Individuals belong to such "communities" in spite of their individuality (or, rather, often in order to promote their individuality). Furthermore, these communities strengthen one of the most significant sources of help, i.e. "solidarity." Above all, every community has a right to follow its own conception of the common good, provided that it is consistent with the requirements of liberal democracy.

Such a right to national particularities is part of a more general right to cultural diversity which supplements biodiversity. This right – let us refer to it as a "right to difference" – is already favoured by the inherent indeterminacy of the universal principles of right, which suggests that, initially, human rights operate only as second-order rules. Only their "application" to particular issues and types of situations leads to common rules, i.e. those covering concrete actions. Yet, neither particular issues nor types of situations admit of a single interpretation. At this point history, culture and tradition have a legitimate role to play.

Let us imagine, by way of a thought experiment, ideal lawmakers, i.e. on the lines of either an ideal Solon or (as discourse theories prefer) an ideal parliament. Let us now instruct such lawmakers to enact laws equally valid for all cultures. In contrast to an empirically existing lawmaker, ideal lawmakers have all relevant knowledge at their disposal: they are omniscient. Untainted by particular interests and passions, the lawmakers orient themselves exclusively toward the principles of justice, namely, human rights: the lawmakers are perfectly just. Although such omniscient lawmakers can establish the framework for just laws, from the standpoint of justice, they are, in practice, unable to find a single solution. No more than one can design an actual chair from criteria such as comfort and durability, can one derive a fully specified legal norm from the principles of justice. Cultural particularities such as history and tradition, including diverse preferences and emphases (or even mere conventions) belong to the many components required. Last but not least, economic and other circumstances also matter.

Thanks to their omniscience, the "ideal Solons" know of the particularities. Thanks to their perfect sense of justice, they intend to let justice prevail with regard to these particularities; thus, they recognize them equally. The result appears to be paradoxical only at first glance: the interculturally justifiable principles of justice open to different cultures and universal principles might be expressed in a particular form. Here, in a culturally open moral universalism, both an ideal Solon and an ideal parliament find their limits and, for this reason, a participatory democracy is required.

If democratic discourse seeks more than the establishment of universally valid human rights, if it recognizes historical heritage and political decisions, it is open to a "right to difference." Indeed, the two are inseparable: the more rights we wish to award participatory democracy, the more we have to recognize the lack of a full determination of universal principles and the more we have to grant the right of difference. Failing this, democracy would degenerate into an organ of enforcement for an ideal lawmaker.

Let us now take freedom of religion as an example of the principles of human rights. Freedom of religion demands religious tolerance with regard to the practice of religion: it refuses to prohibit any community the exercise of religion, of either "freethinking" atheism or a total withdrawal from all religious community. (A religion that declares apostasy to be a crime, or even a capital crime, commits a major violation of human rights.) Aside from this minimum (i.e. aside from the individual right to a negative freedom of religion), a minimum of a positive freedom of religion – of a freedom of the kind provided by the *association law* – is probably required, namely, the right to develop oneself religiously and to build a religious community for this purpose. This twofold requirement, as included in article 18 of the *Universal Declaration of Human Rights*, leaves many concrete legal provisions undecided.

Freedom of religion does not, for example, prevent a community from understanding itself as Christian, Islamic, Jewish, or Shinto. Human rights do not require the legal and constitutional system to be organized without any reference either to atheism or to any religion. Consequently, different institutional arrangements are justifiable, such as the laicism of France (enforced by anticlerical radicals at the beginning of the century), i.e. the unambiguous separation between church and state, of which it makes an exception in Alsace-Lorraine. Conversly, the USA, founded as a refuge for persecuted religious communities, practises "benevolent neutrality." Germany, like Austria and parts of Switzerland, allows for an institutional connection between church and state, although not extending to the core of its constitutional law or to its political nucleus. Defined by the reformed national church, Scandinavian countries and, in another respect, Great Britain have the character of state religions. Israel ensures Christians, Druses, and Muslims full religious freedom, even their own jurisdiction for personal, matrimonial, and family law and nevertheless grants far-reaching privileges to Jewish religion. For example, the costs of religion are born one-third by the state and two-thirds by the communes. In an officially multicultural state such as Malaysia, three fundamentally different legal systems coexist, although in a complicated form: these are an "autochthonous" customary law, the Islamic Sharia, and the British Common Law.

In addition to these provisions, there is the task of weighing-up rights which, once again, owing to their "indeterminacy," can be operated in different ways by different communities. A contemporary issue is the freedom of the press: should it allow one to film violations such as property damage, kidnapping, and perhaps even genocide for television broadcast rights, instead of prohibiting them as far as possible? Another example: should one be permitted to either diminish or violate the privacy rights of public personalities as demanded for everyone else? Evaluating conflicting rights is also necessary for deciding which evidence should be allowed in criminal proceedings. Here, the protection of the private sphere as required by human rights is to be weighed against the prosecution of crime equally required by human rights. Further, related to the scarcity of resources, within the sphere of positive rights to freedom we must think of how much resources the health service and the educational system should receive. Finally, perhaps one ought to weigh up the institutions of the welfare state against the incentive to self-responsibility and personal initiative.

Obviously, such an indeterminacy and openness of universal principles has far-reaching consequences. At the conceptual level, we must distinguish a real universalism as grounds for the justification of universally valid principles (i.e. human rights, as opposed to a particularism and relativism of principles) from a universalism that requires everywhere in the world the same rules and customs and is better called uniformism. Additionally, on the historical and political level, the indeterminacy of universal principles bestows to the states the right to difference, namely, a universal authorization to particularity in some way comparable to the right to individuality, which is not due to human beings *in spite of* but precisely *because of* universal morality. Furthermore, one ought to ensure a right to unique character, not only to particular cultures but also to larger cultural areas such as Black Africa, South America, and South-East Asia. Because of this right to difference, there can be no world republic flatly opposed to the singular states of the Communitarians. According to the view of political theorists such as Charles Beitz (1979), the global political system should be set up as a homogeneous world republic similar to that of a single state. In his conception, possible subdivisions result only secondarily, from the top down, whereas the particular states themselves, considered as an expression of particularity, lose their rights. Yet, the right to difference opposes this.

Our constructive veto against Communitarianism admits that its position is right, but only one-third right. Human beings do, indeed, have the right to particularities – to their history, tradition, and religion, as well as to their own language, culture, and shared ideas of the common good. It is because of the diversity of these particularities that the social and cultural wealth of humanity increases; humankind has an interest in the right of difference to be realized. The second third of the truth is that individual states are not ends in themselves, in which case they would deserve unconditional protection. As unities existing for the sake of human beings, they can be transformed by human beings and for the sake of these human beings. They can dissolve and construct themselves, and thereby achieve both lesser and greater unity. The last third of the truth is that neither states nor foreign citizens are relieved of the universal legal and political imperative. The constitutive principle that satisfies all three requirements of legal ethics is called "federalism," here understood in its broader sense to include both federal and confederate states. Only a federalist unity can be a morally dictated and legitimate world republic.

There are three possible strategies to legitimize the world republic democratically. According to exclusive legitimation by the citizens, the world state would be derived from the will of the entire world population, of the people of the global state, partly (but not only) through NGOs and global social movements (GSMs). It is customary for these latter organizations to care for corporate, professional, and minority interests, e.g. special-interest groups. Many of these are undemocratic, even by a weak definition of democracy. Even the UN specialized agencies are undemocratic structures, since their members are states, whether democratic or not, and some states have more powers in the UN structures than others (the most obvious example is the so-called veto right of the five permanent members of the Security Council). The malevolent view on states being ruthless power entities and the corresponding benevolent view of NGOs and GSMs – as being beneficient, enlightened, and public-spirited – does not always correspond to reality. Since individuals are the authority of last resort in matters of legitimacy, one could consider this first strategy to be appropriate. Indeed, the interests of states are legitimized by their citizens, so that one could eliminate the individual states as additional authorities of legitimacy.

Nevertheless, the right of particular statehood speaks against this, as does the fact that the interests of collective units cannot be reduced to the sum of the interests of their members. This suggests a second strategy of democratic legitimation. While single states represent both the distributive interests of the single citizens and collective interests of the people, one would wish to eliminate the first legitimation and defend a legitimation exclusively based on individual states, with the result that the collective will of single states would take all decisions alone. However, this contradicts the legitimate authority of last resort, i.e. that of the individual human being. To the latter belong religion, language, and professional life, demanding hobbies, or political and social interests for which there are specific agencies that cross the territorial boundaries of the nation-state. The same is true of human interests, such as those represented by organizations such as Amnesty International, Greenpeace, or Medicins sans Frontières (Doctors Without Borders), and further membership of a diaspora such as the Irish, Jewish, and Kurdish peoples.

If only for the sake of "membership across state lines," legitimation based exclusively on states is ruled out, so that only the third strategy remains, i.e. mixed legitimation. The world republic wins its democratic legitimacy through the connection of legitimation by citizens and legitimation by states. As a consequence, all power of the world state comes from its "double" people – from the community of all human beings and from all states. This double legitimation must find expression in the organization of a world state. The parliament, its most important organ, must consist of two chambers – one chamber for the citizens and another for the states. At this point in time, one need not think further about the specific constitution of these assemblies; clearly, Liechtenstein would not have the same weight as India or China. In any case, the large regional intermediary authorities could change the situation.

A final balance: Multilevel cosmopolitanism

The world state, which should exist according to the universal legal and political imperative, would be a *subsidiary* and, further, a federalist world republic. In it we would be citizens, understood here not as an exclusive but, rather, complementary citizenship. The exclusive conception of citizenship corresponds to that kind of cosmopolitanism which – along with Hegel's *Philosophy of Right* (1967) (§209, Note), "is crystallized, e.g. as a cosmopolitanism in opposition to the concrete life of the state." This cosmopolitanism, not without an air of superiority, often declares: "I am neither German, French, nor Italian but only a citizen of the world." Here, world government substitutes for the single states, and cosmopolitan civil rights replace national civic rights. In the globalistic world state, one is a world citizen and not a citizen of a particular state. The federal world republic avoids the flat alternative "national or global" and "particular state or cosmopolitism." Global civic rights do not take the place of national civil rights; rather, the former supplement the latter. The famous question on constitutional law concerning the competence to evaluate matters of competence (*Kompetenz-Kompetenz*) is of importance but in a systematically subordinate sense. Incidentally, federal nation-states are confronted with the same problem and are able to solve it. To a certain extent, this idea realizes a global variation of de Gaulle's world of separate "fatherlands" (*patries*) and large political regions although, unlike de Gaulle, it is one with a special and (until now unknown) multiple citizenship. In the coming years, the European democracies will have to decide whether their citizens are primarily German, French, or Italian or, rather, citizens of Europe. In all these cases, one is primarily either a citizen of a European state or a European citizen, and secondarily either of the two, which means both at the same time and in a hierarchical order. Thirdly, one is a world citizen, a citizen of the federal and subsidiary world republic.

The United Nations as a model?

In the existing network of international institutions, the United Nations plays a major role in the perspective of global legal ethics. The programme of the United Nations is close to the ideal of a global order such as the federal and subsidiary republic. Not only does it pursue its primary goal to promote a global legal order and a peace order but also its principles correspond to the normative principles developed above.

The similarity begins with the circumstances of the foundation of the United Nations and the circumstances that make a world republic necessary. After the obvious failure of the League of Nations, a new world organization was needed that was to preserve the world from future wars (see the preamble of the Charter of the United Nations and Article 1). The similarity also lies in the universal membership of the United Nations: now even both Koreas are members and only Switzerland and micro-states such as Kiribati, San Marino, and Monaco are still missing. Last but not least, the UN Charter amounts to nothing less than a world constitution guided by the relevant principles of legal ethics.

The UN Charter commits all states to the respect for human rights and dignity, for equal treatment of men and women, as well as for equal treatment of all states, whether large or small (preamble, Article 1). The member states commit themselves to solve their conflicts with peaceful means (Article 2.3) and to renounce the use of violence (Article 2.4). The integrity of the territory and of the people of each state is inviolable, and each state has one vote in the General Assembly.

The United Nations has been founded by sovereign states. However, by the ratification of the Charter, they renounced part of their sovereignty and headed towards a federal world republic. The recognition of human rights amounts to a self-limitation of their domestic sovereignty; the renouncement of violence limits the external sovereignty. Chapter VII even gives the Security Council the authority to take measures against states that are either a threat to peace or who commited aggression against another state. Article 25 obliges the member states to contribute to such measures by offering military support. Yet the United Nations has no monopoly of physical force, which corresponds to our idea of a multilevel sovereignty in which most of the power should belong to the individual states.

The United Nations is close to a world republic by another aspect, too: its organs are submitted to the principle of separation of powers. The General Assembly somehow resembles the legislative power. Admittedly, the General Assembly can adopt nothing but recommendations, most of which are not legally binding, excepting those on the budget and assessed contributions, for instance. The Secretary-General has certain (although narrow) executive powers. The Security Council has more executive power and is the only UN organ that has the character of a public enforcement authority. In its role of judging in which cases a threat to international peace and security has occurred and which state is the aggressor, and then of deciding to take action, the Security Council is at risk of being biased by the special status of the Permanent Members who are often inclined to promote their own interests and to protect their client states. Such extensive competences clearly contradict the principle of the separation of powers. The right of the Permanent Members of the Security Council to prevent the Council from reaching a decision also contradicts the very idea of democracy. Therefore, the UN Charter pursues two deeply contradictory goals – the universalist legal ethics of human rights and the legal solution of settling conflicts by privileging five Great (and not so great) Powers in the Security Council. In the United Nations, power has priority over the law.

Concerning the third power (the judiciary power), there is at least the International Court of Justice and further specialized tribunals. However, none of these tribunals disposes of any enforcement power. The compliance with the judgements by the parties involved relies on the voluntary submission to them. Since the time of the League of Nations, all attempts to establish the usual mandatory jurisdictions have been unsuccessful. There is no equivalent of the authority of the national tribunals to prosecute illegal acts. The states members of the United Nations have no possibility of lodging an appeal against the decisions of the General Assembly and of the Security Council. In addition, the parties that obtain a judgement in their favour can ask only the Security Council for enforcement, so that the enforcement of judgements belongs to a political, not to a judicial, organ – thus again infringing the principle of separation of powers.

Because only one of its organs is really a (public) power, the United Nations does not reach a high degree of statehood. Even if one would reinforce its statehood, it could not achieve the level of even a rudimentary world republic. Indeed, the privileges of the five permanent members of the Security Council contradict the principles of democracy and make out the world organization to be oligarchic. All states are equal only in the General Assembly; yet, in the General Assembly, each state has one vote, whether it has a large or a very small population.

In one more aspect the United Nations diverges from the ideal of a world republic: it has only an upper house – the General Assembly – and no lower house. There is an Economic and Social Council (chapter X of the Charter), but its members are elected by the General Assembly, which does not make it a second independent house. Thus, the United Nations fits only to the dimension of the law of nations, not to the dimension of cosmopolitan law. This may have been wise at the time of the foundation of the United Nations, because – among other reasons – peace had priority and there was no global civic opinion. Yet a global democracy would be needed, especially with respect to the goals declared by Article 1,3 and by chapter IX, Articles 55–60 of the Charter, i.e. international cooperation in economic, cultural, and humanitarian matters.

REFERENCES

Beitz, Charles R. 1979. *Political Theory and International Relations*. Princeton, NJ: Princeton University Press.
Doyle, Michael W. 1983. "Kant, Liberal Legacies, and Foreign Affairs." *Philosophy and Public Affairs* 12(3): 205–235 and 12(4): 323–353.
Hegel, Georg Wilhelm Friedrich. 1967. *Philosophy of Right*, trans. by T. M. Knox. Oxford: Oxford University Press.
Höffe, Otfried. 1996. "Subsidiarity as a Principle in the Philosophy of Government." *Regional and Federal Studies* 6(3): 56–73.
Höffe, Otfried. 1999a. *Gibt es ein interkulturelles Strafrecht?* Frankfurt/M: Suhrkamp.
Höffe, Otfried. 1999b. *Demokratie im Zeitalter der Globalisierung*. Munich: Beck.
Kant, Immanuel. 1795. *Toward Perpetual Peace* (1795), trans. by Mary Gregor. Works, vol. "Practical Philosophy." Cambridge: Cambridge University Press.
Keohane, Robert O., ed. 1986. *Neorealism and its Critics*. New York: Columbia University Press.
MacIntyre, Alasdair. 1981. *After Virtue*. Notre Dame, IN: University of Notre Dame Press.
Rittberger, Volker, ed. 1993. *Regime Theory and International Relations*. Oxford: Clarendon Press.
Singer, D. and M. Small. 1972. *The Wages of War 1816–1965: A Statistical Handbook*. New York: Wiley.
Walzer, Michael. 1983. *Spheres of Justice*. Oxford: Robertson.

BIBLIOGRAPHY

Halperin, Morton H. and Kristen Lomasney. 1993. "Toward a Global 'Guarantee Clause'." *Journal of Democracy* 4(3): 60–69.
Höffe, Otfried. 1995. *Political Justice*, trans. by Jeffrey C. Cohen. Oxford: Basil Blackwell.
Maoz, Zeev and Bruce Russett. 1992. "Alliance, Contiguity, Wealth and Political Stability: Is the Lack of Conflict among Democracies a Statistical Artefact?" *International Interactions* 17: 245–267.

7

Global governance and justice

Yash Tandon

The new men of Empire are the ones who believe in fresh starts, new chapters, new pages; I struggle on with the old story, hoping that before it is finished it will reveal to me why it was that I thought it was worth the trouble.

J. M. Coetzee, *Waiting for the Barbarians*

Introduction

In a framework paper informing this particular dialogue, three sets of actors were identified as having significant influence on public policy-making at the global level. These were:

1. States and intergovernmental organizations (IGOs);
2. Transnational corporations (TNCs) and business associations that operate in the market; and
3. Civil society organizations, including non-governmental organizations (NGOs), transnational social movements (TSMOs), and the media.

Then a question was posed to this writer: "Which actor (or triad of actors) is best able to strengthen justice in the world?"

Three preliminary questions need be asked before we begin. One, where is a scholar located in the total constellation of moral, social, and political forces? As Edward Said reminded us, no scholar can totally step out of history or his/her political and social conditioning (Said 1995); those who say that they are "objective," "universal," or "neutral" are fooling themselves as well as others. Two, how is the language of discourse crafted, by whom and why? Philosophers such as Wittgenstein tried to expurgate language of impurities of expression, but failed (Wittgenstein 1958). As we show, language continues to remain one of the most powerful forces of control and manipulation. Third, where is an alternative discourse going to come from? The hegemony of the dominant discourse is so pervasive and stifling that discordant voices are often dismissed as "not constructive," or "conspiratorial," or "not nuanced enough," or "Manichean." This is part of the perennial problem of constructing a critical ontology from one defined by hegemonic theory.

This chapter presents an alternative language of discourse created from the periphery of the contemporary global system of governance. It is in three parts.

In the first part (pp. 205–214), the chapter looks at the Real World. It argues that contemporary civilization has become pathological: it is devoid of both rationality and humanity. To use the Kantian metaphor, the dominant force behind the shaping of contemporary culture is the "crooked timber," the base aspect of human nature. Those who control the system use language and ideology to obfuscate reality and legitimize exploitation. International institutions (such as the United Nations, the World Bank, the International Monetary Fund [IMF], the World Trade Organization [WTO], among others) provide three things – ideologists who craft the language of mainstream discourse, rules of global governance, and sanctions. There are contradictions within and between them but, in the contemporary world, members of a hegemonic political and economic power bloc (the G-7/8 and the hundred or so megacorporations) use their control over these institutions to govern the rest of the world. The bulk of humanity are mired in poverty (not of spirit or of mind, but material poverty) and its concomitant effects, i.e. vulnerability to social and natural conditions. The system has spawned the growth of science and technology to unprecedented heights, but at the same time it has also spawned totally unjustified poverty to unprecedented depths. This contradiction is a product of the system's pathology.

In the second part (pp. 214–221), the chapter examines the concept of justice. It takes John Rawls' concept of justice as fairness as its point of departure. Rawls applied it only within a domestic context. The chapter argues that it can (and should) be extended to the global arena. It goes on to critique alternative concepts of justice that are based on welfare and charity. It also critiques those who argue that the world is already witnessing the emergence of a cosmopolitan or a Kantian global system.

In the third part (pp. 222–225), having worked the concept in the abstract, the chapter seeks to apply this to the real world. It asks which of the main actors in the global system have the capacity to advance the cause of justice, as defined. The chapter argues that this is a concrete and conjunctural question; it cannot be answered in the abstract. On this basis, it argues that only peoples' movements have the potential to advance the cause of justice in the contemporary world.

The real world of global governance

Civilizational tendency towards barbarism

Contemporary civilization has become barbaric, both as between human beings and in terms of relations with other species of life. It has become wantonly destructive. It is a norm among predatory animals to kill only when in need of food; at some time in the historic past, humans also used to kill mainly for food; hunting was part of food gathering. As "civilization" moved on, humans began to kill other animals for fun as well as for food. In the capitalist phase of our civilization, the dominant culture is for humans to kill other species, not for food but for profit. Food is only the medium through which to make profits; though millions may starve, profits must first be made.

Unlike animals, humans also destroy species that they do not eat. Thus, they kill weeds because weeds reduce the output of corn, or wheat, or what have you. They kill pests although they do not eat them. The wanton, and senseless, part is that the destruction has to be total. The cholera virus has to be annihilated for good, the cotton bollworm has to be eliminated permanently, and the stalk-borer grub has to be destroyed forever. Animals have to be put into zoos and parks, crop varieties into gene banks and laboratories; none must have free existence except at the dispensation of humans. This is the anthropocentric part of global governance.

Unlike animals, humans kill competitors. Lions do not kill cheetahs just because both prey on giraffes. Humans kill other human beings as well as other species in competition for land, for forests, for cattle, for fish, for water, for space, for pleasure. Competition may have been the impulse behind the development of science and technology, but it is also at the root of the barbarism of human beings. Our present capitalist period is the most competitive and also the most destructive. Millions of species are destroyed every day. Millions of human lives are wasted simply because they do not have the "market power" to buy food, shelter, clothing, or medicines. Ours must be the most barbaric period of human "civilization."[1]

Natural species are destroyed and manufactured products that yield profit to the capitalist offered in their place. For the loss of the microbe that filters drinking-water is offered the manufactured substitute with its "more efficient" filtration technology. For the loss of natural nutrients, fruity vitamin supplements are offered. However, consistent with man's anthropocentrism, nobody has replaced the sea snails on which the life of the Borneo hooded tern had depended. There is no profit to be made out of the hooded tern; unlike humans, they cannot buy sea snails from the market.

Much of the rise in consumer-product diversity is a direct result of the decrease in biodiversity. Consumer-product diversity now far exceeds biodiversity: 200 million new product options have been generated since 1993 in replacement of the millions of now extinct species. Half a century ago, Joseph Schumpeter had said that "creative destruction" was the necessary basis for the development of capitalism (Schumpeter 1943). If so, then its present phase is dominated by the destruction of Nature and its substitution by profit-seeking "creation."

The pathology of global governance

Global governance is ruled by profits. This is not an expression of reductionism. There are, of course, other aspects of globalism, such as art, music, culture, communications, football, Wimbledon tennis, white-water rafting, social welfare, acts of charity, and novel-writing. There are also large sections of societies that do not function in the market where profits rule. None the less, as broad generalizations go, profits form the basis of contemporary global governance and are also at the root of its pathological character.

Take global medical governance, for example. In 1977, the World Health Organization published the *Essential Drugs List* of some 306 drugs which, it said, "... should be available at all times in adequate amounts and in the appropriate dosage form." Nevertheless, the poor in the third world (and that means the majority of the population) wait for decades to have access to life-saving drugs, such as those against HIV/AIDS (for example) which is a deadly scourge in the South. A few large global corporations dominate the pharmaceutical industry and they will not allow these 306 or so drugs to be marketed at prices affordable to the people. In South Africa in 1999 the government introduced a system of compulsory licensing and parallel imports of patented drugs, but the multinational drug industry backed by the US government used all the power at their command to block this action. In the world of global governance, health is subordinated to the demands of profit, and the protection of patents takes precedence over the protection of human lives. This is only one instance of the pathology of global governance.

In 1992, during the Earth Summit in Rio, many countries signed the Convention on Bio-Diversity (CBD). This recognized the right of indigenous communities and sovereign nations to their biodiversity. However, this would have blocked the access to it of pharmaceutical multinationals. Instigated by the latter, the United States and its allies in the West succeeded in pushing through the Trade-Related Intellectual Property rights (TRIPS) agreement, within the agreements of the GATT Uruguay Round. This effectively took away the rights of governments and communities recognized under the CBD (Correa 2000). The companies secured the right under TRIPS to exploit biological resources, wherever these might be. Countries that would forbid this are subject to sanctions by the governments of countries in which the major pharmaceutical companies originate. In effect, this puts a great divide between the "North" (where these companies originate) and the "South" (where most of the biodiversity exists), or to use Samuel Huntington's pithy phrase, between "the West and the Rest."

The Huntington thesis revisited

In 1993, Huntington put forward the challenging thesis that the post-cold-war period would be one of "clashes of civilizations."[2] By making somewhat simplistic assumptions, and an even simpler classification of "civilizations" (never easy to categorize), he laid himself open to much deserved criticism. None the less, his thesis retains a kind of macroscopic validity, much like when historians make broad generalizations about history as "the age of reason" or "the romantic period." As generalizations go, then, what we are witnessing in the post-cold-war period is indeed the increasing dominance of one particular branch of human civilization – the Euro-Christian-Judaic-capitalist[3] – over other civilizations.

Contrary to all reified polarities, the reality is, of course, much more complex and contradictory. This polarity between the "North" and "South" is widening in our times.[4] Propositions that seek to qualify this broad division of the world – such as that there is a "North" in the "South" and a "South" in the "North" – strengthen, not weaken, the argument. The "North" and "South" are more than geographic constructs: they also refer to particular manifestations of certain cultural and consumerist attributes. The dominant North historically created and continues to nurture a minuscule class of its own kind in the South – those that rule and over-consume; the North also creates an impoverished and marginalized "South" within its own midst – those who do not rule, and who under-consume.

Modernization theories of the 1950s and '60s assumed that the South would "eventually" catch up with the North if they would only open up their economies to Western technology and science, and emulate the North's democratic institutions. Retrospective analysis indicates that those theories were no more than ideological expressions of the West's continued drive to dominate and conquer the "Rest." That drive continues to this day; however, it is now termed "globalization." Like the earlier concept of modernization, globalization is also presented by its ideologists as something driven by technological and economic forces that cannot be stopped – something "natural," inherent in history itself.[5]

Socialization of language

Language can obscure reality. It is often deliberately crafted to encourage a certain perspective, a certain mind-set. For example, in colonial times, a person from the colonized world did not have an individual identity: he was an Arab, an Asian, or an African. Their personalities were generalized, their individuality dissolved; that made the colonized easier to handle.[6] Racist polarity between "us" and "them" facilitated global governance during the colonial period.

Nothing describes the skilled use of language to create mind-sets more than the West's definition of what constitutes "barbarism" in our time. Nobody in his right mind would condone the bombing of American embassies in Nairobi and Dar es Salaam in August 1998. Whether that was the work of the "terrorist" Osama bin Laden remains an open question. The US Government believes that bin Laden was the culprit; on that basis, it bombed a pharmaceutical factory in the Sudan, alleged to be supplying biochemical weapons to bin Laden. Not a single country, not even the United Kingdom, supported the United States. If one were to be objective about the matter, then the American act qualifies as an act of barbarity no less than that of the bombing of its embassies. In the text of the West, however, only the latter is barbaric.

The United Nations Children's Fund (UNICEF) reported in 1999 that almost 600,000 children under 5 years of age perished in Iraq because of the West's sanctions. The infant mortality rate increased from 56/1000 before to 131/1000 after the sanctions (UNICEF 1999). If this is not barbarism, what is? And yet, in the vocabulary of the ruling circles of the West, this is no more than "collateral damage" that sanctions cause to the children. It is incredible how language can caricature a grotesque reality and "cleanse" it of evil and absolve the responsibility of its perpetrator. "Blame it on Saddam Hussein" is the West's outrageous and indefensible defence of this carnage.

The blame culture is deeply rooted in Western culture and the history. Blame the "collateral damage" against the people of Yugoslavia on Milosovic. Blame Fidel Castro for US sanctions on Cuba, isolate him, and, if possible, remove him from power. Blame the British atrocities against the Mau Mau on Jomo Kenyatta, lock him up; blame Nasser, bomb the Suez Canal; blame Lumumba for the chaos in the Congo in the 1960s, kill him; blame Gadaffi, bomb his home; blame Mugabe, he is a Marxist; blame Mahathir Mohamed, he refuses to conform. The demonization of the "rebellious" leader in the South has been an abiding feature of West's "justification" for its barbarism against the "Rest."

Language makes "acceptable" that which is inhuman and unjust. "Collateral damage" to civilians sanitizes bombing. The collective noun, "the African," dehumanizes the individual, objectifies him, and makes it easier to dispose of him. Demonization of the individual leader separates him from his people, his history, and his reason; casts him as irrational or simply mad (the gallant Somali fighter against British colonization was simply called "the Mad Mullah"), and therefore beyond the pale of "civilized" discourse.[7]

Socialization of ideology

Where language is a one-off description, ideology is a complex network of values, prejudices, and assumptions. Both serve the same purpose of obscuring reality and making "acceptable" that which is inhuman and unjust. The anthropocentric ideology puts humans at the centre of the universe, and "justifies" to himself the subjugation of all "lower" species of life to his control and abuse. The ideology of the "White man's burden" puts the White man (and woman) at the centre of the universe, and relegates all other human species to lower levels to be controlled and abused. The ideology of "Anglo-Saxon superiority" puts the Englishman and the Anglo-Saxon American at the centre of the universe. In an ever-decreasing circle of defining the "superior" being, it is finally the Anglo-Saxon MAN whose gender ideology puts HIM at the centre of the universe, so even Anglo-Saxon women are then relegated to a step below the top. Racist and sexist ideologies set the pecking order of human society.

Where language is descriptive, ideology is prescriptive: it shows the direction in which the universe must move at the behest of the "superior" beings. The communist ideology was teleological: it promised to lead to the classless society at the behest of the vanguard of the proletariat. The capitalist ideology is economistic: it promises unending "growth" at the behest of the owners of capital. Both are reductionist and presumptuous; both denigrate the role of the human spirit in the advancement of humanity.

Communism is no longer an issue today; capitalism is. As the ruling ideology of the moment, it has passed through many phases and modes, from the competitive phase to that of monopoly, from the state interventionist mode to that of privatization. However, its underlying ideology –

namely, that it is the profit incentive that promotes growth – has remained constant. Like all ideologies, it is a combination of truth and lie; in our period, the lie overshadows the truth. Speculative capital, which now forms over 90 per cent of the movement of capital, promotes growthless profit. Speculative capital disembowels the economy of industry and productive activity. It generates money with money without having to go through the process of production. It gives the lie to the capitalist ideology that capital generates growth. We have reached a stage in the development of capitalism where 90 per cent of capital generates only air – and profits. The tragedy is that this happens at the cost of the lives and livelihoods of millions of people, as happened in Thailand, South Korea, and Indonesia in 1997–1999.[8]

Another ideological tenet of contemporary capitalism is that those in the South must liberalize their economies to provide incentives to foreign direct investments (FDI) for the sake of their own growth; this is the lie of globalization. A fundamental aspect of globalization is a desperate effort by an overflow of capital in the West seeking profitable ventures in the South,[9] but the matter is presented as if it is the South that needs capital and they must therefore provide the best incentives for it.

Ironically, and that is the force of ideology, most governments in the South have taken the ideology for truth, so they vie with one another to offer most competitive terms to Western capital. In the process, they cheapen their resources and the value of their labour power. This sets a vicious circle of poverty and debt bondage from which it is impossible to escape. Those East Asian countries that were able to generate self-motivated growth in the 1980s and 1990s were forced by speculative attacks on their currencies in 1997 to roll back their gains and succumb to the power of Western capital. The currency crises forced the opening of their economies to ownership and control of foreign capital. Thus, for example, in South Korea, whereas formerly only up to 15 per cent of the shares of Korean companies could be owned by foreigners, after the crisis foreigners could own first 50 per cent and later up to 100 per cent. The result is that South Korea is now more foreign-owned than during its last fifty years of industrialization. Lawrence Summers, the former US Treasury Secretary, said that the IMF deal in Korea accomplished for the United States what trade could not in all the trade rounds.[10] The West is once more in command in the Pacific, both economically as well as militarily.

The UN system and global governance

At the end of the Second World War, the victorious powers had created two sets of institutions. One set related to economic matters: these were the IMF, the World Bank, and the General Agreement on Tariffs and

Trade (GATT). The second set consisted of the United Nations and its specialized agencies. These represented the more "visionary" aspects of global infrastructure, dealing with dispute settlement, health, welfare, labour, culture, education, trusteeship, and other such matters. The visionary part of the United Nations also paid homage to the idea of "We, the Peoples ..." as against "We, the Governments ..." although, in the Security Council, it congealed power in the hands of the large and powerful.

Over the decades, the vision and authority of the United Nations has diminished and the power and control of the Bretton Woods institutions have increased. During the cold war years, the peace and security dimension of UN work was used mainly by the United States and its allies to legitimize their global policies and interventions, such as in Korea, the Middle East, and the Congo. The peoples of the South were able to use the United Nations to effect and legitimize decolonization, but not without a price. Because of the nature of alliances that needed to be built, and because of Western hegemony in the United Nations, decolonization came with mixed baggage. Although the former colonial powers were eased out, in most cases the United States came out on top of the situation. In the Congo, for example, the United Nations became the means, under US hegemony, to neutralize nationalist forces led by Patrice Lumumba and to instal in power Mobutu Sese Seko, who ruled the country for 27 years as a bastion of Western interests in Africa. Where the West adamantly backed Portugal in its colonies and the apartheid regime in South Africa, a door was opened to Soviet influence and ideology. With the demise of the Soviet Union, the West is once again the dominant force in these countries. They can now pursue their interests directly – that is, without having to go to the United Nations. In fact, they have more or less lost interest in the United Nations as a mechanism for peace and security; the United States even refuses to pay its full dues to the United Nations.

The United Nations has thus become largely ineffective on issues of peace and security. In Africa, for example, it made half-hearted, ineffectual, interventions in places such as Somalia, Angola, and Rwanda.[11] This has led Africans to accuse the West of double standards. For example, when it comes to removing Jonas Savimbi from his position blocking peace efforts in Angola, the United Nations has been extremely parsimonious in the resources it has provided and half-hearted in the pursuit of the objective that it has set for itself. In contrast, the Western efforts to try to get Milosovic out of Bosnia and Kosovo were an entirely different story. This duplicity of the West has been observed by Africa, even in relation to issues such as the care of refugees. Once again, African refugees are treated to the minimum of resources, compared with refugees that came out of Yugoslavia.

The social and economic dimensions of the United Nations have suffered an even worse fate. The United States and some of its allies, especially the United Kingdom, have tried over the years systematically to destroy the role, influence, and justification of organizations such as the United Nations Educational, Scientific, and Cultural Organization (UNESCO), the International Labour Organization (ILO), the United Nations Industrial Development Organization (UNIDO), the United Nations Environment Programme (UNEP), and the United Nations Conference on Trade and Development (UNCTAD). UNCTAD, for example, is no longer what it used to be: it can provide technical assistance and undertake research but it is no longer permitted to give policy advice to developing countries. The Economic and Social Council of the United Nations, similarly, has been virtually disembowelled of its role and functions. Most of the economic functions of the United Nations have been effectively transferred to the Bretton Woods institutions and the WTO. These, in contrast to the United Nations, have become powerful institutions of global governance. It is now the World Bank, not UNESCO, that lays down educational programmes for developing countries. The weighted voting in the IMF and the World Bank puts decision-making powers effectively into the hands of the West. In the case of the WTO, decision-making is, in theory, by consensus; in practice, however, decisions are taken in small committees and they come out as negotiated settlements between its powerful members – the so-called "quad countries" (the United States, the European Union, Canada, and Japan) and without the participation of the developing countries. Yet these decisions bind these countries.

Global governance, the IMF, the World Bank, and the WTO

Ideology needs ideologists, paid servants of the ruling circles. These are located in the institutions that churn out globalist ideologies neatly expressed in elegant, "balanced," official language. Not all officials of the IMF, the World Bank, and the WTO are conscious peddlers of ideology; most of them, in their innocence or ignorance, have "faith" in what they preach. They are recruited to those jobs precisely because of their faith. They actually believe that developing countries must open their doors to capital to get out of the vicious circle of poverty. Since the Asian crisis of 1997, some of them are beginning to have doubts about the efficacy of their medicine, and most now make a distinction between "bad" speculative capital and "good" FDIs – in practice, an untenable distinction.

The problem is that, when ideology takes hold of one's mind, no amount of contradictory evidence will dislodge it. There is always that item in the complex set of assumptions that will "explain away" contradictory evidence. "If only the Governments in the South were to do as we tell them to, they really should not have problems." This is the escape route of all ideologists. Ideologies are, in the words of Karl Popper (1959), "impossible to falsify."

For over twenty years, the so-called "Washington Consensus" (WC) provided the ruling orthodoxy of "development" theory. Its "axiomatic" tenets were the basis not only of mainstream development economics at the academic level but also of the main policy directions for developing countries, especially those that had come under the World Bank's Structure Adjustment Programs (SAPs). Joseph Stiglitz, former senior Vice-President of the Bank, in a stinging attack on IMF bureaucrats, said that the sum total of their knowledge boiled down to six concepts: inflation, money supply, growth, interest rate, budget, and trade deficits (Stiglitz 1998).

At the political level, the minimalist state became part of the WC orthodoxy. Developing countries that were hostage to SAPs were forced either to privatize or to stand accused of "Soviet style" statism. Stiglitz was later to say that the focus of the WC on liberalization, deregulation, and privatization had grossly ignored the important role the state needs to play in regulation, industrial policy, social protection, and welfare. He said that the WC was "misguided."

Misguided or not, the WC had served its purpose for the West. Liberalization, deregulation, and privatization gave Western corporations a greater control over the economies of developing countries. The illusion that SAPs were creating conditions for growth is finally being shattered. However, the poor are now paying a heavy price: thousands have lost jobs and have joined the "informal sector" as the final refuge for survival; thousands have had their real wages slashed; and under "cost-sharing" imposed by the IMF, the poor are forced to pay cash for health services and education, or are taking children, mainly girls, out of school. Meanwhile, Western multinationals and speculators are piling on their profits.

In 1994, the WTO was created following eight years of intense negotiations between (mainly) the USA and Europe. Most developing countries joined later, because staying out might have been worse for them, but they had practically no say in the making of the WTO. The rules are backed by mandatory sanctions against those that fail to fulfil their obligations, even if they had no part in their making.

The WTO has potentially, and under pressure from the West, an ever-expanding agenda. Under the prefix "trade-related," all manner of issues are now brought under its sanctions-bearing authority. TRIPs, to which we referred earlier, should never have come into the WTO. In like manner, trade-related investment measures (TRIMs) have made serious inroads into the sovereign right of nations to regulate foreign investments.

Not satisfied, the rich countries of the OECD have pushed (so far without success) for a Multilateral Agreement on Investments (MAI) which would force developing countries to give "national treatment" to foreign investors. If this is successful, it would mean that foreign investors would be treated at least on the same basis as nationals; indigenization policies of the South would therefore become illegal and so subject to sanctions.

The West is now pushing into the WTO other issues. These include the environment, labour standards, e-commerce, competition policy, and genetically modified organisms (GMOs). These are all potential minefields. Successively more and more of our lives are being subject to market forces, from food production and entitlement to childcare, from water to education. Every time a new sector is privatized and brought into the market, the West introduces it into the World Bank or the sanctions-bearing WTO. This process not only undermines the ability of the developing countries to use policy tools for development but also puts beyond the pale of the market the poor and the vulnerable that do not have the means to secure their livelihood from the market. In the double-speak language of the neo-liberalists, these are merely "market failures." The ingenuity of linguistic gymnastics has reached quantum leaps of absurdity.

The world of justice in a globalized world

Justice as fairness

Justice is at the heart of the discourse of this chapter. It has been a hotly contested terrain throughout history,[12] and has many rival conceptions. This chapter takes as its point of departure the Rawlsian concept of "justice as fairness" (Rawls 1972).

Before we get into it, let us note that some of Rawls' propositions are derived from his specific condition as a scholar from a particular tradition – the Western liberal tradition. Hence, his views carry certain biases and prejudices that stem from this tradition. For example, Rawls gives priority to liberty over equality, and does not adequately address the question of inequalities in wealth and power leading to inequalities in the exercise of liberties, or what happens when basic liberties are in conflict. Furthermore, he has this strange notion that liberal states do not go to war or, if they do, it is when they are threatened by autocratic states! This is a highly biased and one-sided view of history.

No matter, for Rawls brings some interesting ideas to the concept of justice. One of them is a set of basic principles of justice that he derives from an imaginary condition of primordial equality that he calls the "original position." Second, is his notion of the "difference principle."[13]

In Rawls' imagined "original position," individuals are subject to a "veil of ignorance" so that, in devising principles of justice, they have practically no knowledge of the self – their sex, status, class, colour, religion, strength, intelligence, or their conception of the good.[14] As he explains:

The aim is to use the notion of pure procedural justice as a basis of theory. Somehow we must nullify the effects of specific contingencies which put men at odds and tempt them to exploit social and natural circumstances to their own advantage. (Rawls 1972: 136)

By this process, Rawls arrives at two principles of justice and two priority rules for institutions. It is important to quote him *in extenso*:

First principle
Each person is to have an equal right to the most extensive total system of equal basic liberties compatible with a similar system of liberty for all.

Second principle
Social and economic inequalities are to be arranged so that they are both: (a) to the greatest benefit of the least advantaged, consistent with the just savings principle, and (b) attached to offices and positions open to all under conditions of fair equality of opportunity.

First priority rule (the priority of liberty)
The principles of justice are to be ranked in lexical order and therefore liberty can be restricted only for the sake of liberty. There are two cases: (a) a less extensive liberty must strengthen the total system of liberty shared by all; (b) a less than equal liberty must be acceptable to those with the lesser liberty.

Second priority rule (the priority of justice over efficiency and welfare)
The second principle of justice is lexically prior to the principle of efficiency and to that of maximizing the sum of advantages; and fair opportunity is prior to the difference principle. There are two cases: (a) an inequality of opportunity must enhance the opportunities of those with the lesser opportunity; (b) an excessive rate of saving must on balance mitigate the burden of those bearing this hardship.

General conception
All social primary goods – liberty and opportunity, income and wealth, and the bases of self-respect – are to be distributed equally unless an unequal distribution of any or all of these goods is to the advantage of the least favoured. (Rawls 1972: 302–303)

Although the above principles appear to savour of egalitarianism, Rawls denies that this motivated his theory. What he is opposed to is institutionalized inequalities, unless these are "to the advantage of the least favoured."

What is attractive about Rawls is that, unlike nineteenth century utilitarians and present-day economists who define benefits in terms of welfare, he defines it in terms of "primary goods" – liberty and opportunity, income and wealth, and the bases of self-respect. Again, unlike natural law theorists (including Grotius and Locke), who argued that justice can be discovered through reason, Rawls' principles are based on fair procedure (justice as fairness), that individuals would agree to under a "veil of ignorance." Under these conditions, they agree to the "difference principle": social and economic inequalities are to be arranged "to the greatest benefit of the least advantaged." He sees natural talents of individuals as collective assets to be so distributed that they enhance "the opportunities of those with the lesser opportunity." In some ways, Rawls is even more radical than those who today talk about "Global Public Goods" or "the Global Commons" (Kaul, Grunberg, and Stern 1999).

However, Rawls' radicalism disappears when he steps beyond the borders of "liberal" states to that of international relations. In his book *The Law of Peoples* he argues that the difference principle does not apply between nations or in what he calls "hierarchical" societies (Rawls 1999). However, consistent with his liberalism, he would not brook intervention on the part of liberal states into the affairs of "hierarchical" societies, however much these offend liberal sensitivities.

We depart from Rawls in two significant ways: first, we disagree with his methodological individualism. We accept that part of liberal ethics which argues that basic human rights are inherent in individuals. However, to push this to the level that denies that societies are more than the sum of individuals is methodological individualism that cannot stand either empirical or ethical test. No individual is born outside society, nor can exist, materially or spiritually, outside the material or social production and reproduction of life. We would thus argue that, like individuals, communities and nations also have inherent rights. Implicit in Rawls' theory of non-intervention in *The Law of Peoples* is the notion of national self-determination, but he refrains from formulating it as an explicit principle. One consequence of this is that he is unable to extend, to stretch, the principles of justice obtained in an "original position" to the community of nations.

What Rawls is unable to do because of methodological limitations, we now do. Following from him, let us imagine an "original position," comprising nations. In this condition and under a "veil of ignorance" they seek to arrive at fundamental principles of justice. They are ignorant about their character, strength, location, religion, ethical norms, and all such attributes that would, in Rawls' words, "tempt them to exploit social and natural circumstances to their own advantage."

Placed thus, nations would then, I argue, agree to principles of justice as fairness along lines similar to those arrived at by individuals in Rawls' "original position." In other words, Rawls' two principles and two priority rules will apply as much between nations as they apply between individuals. Each nation will have "an equal right to the most extensive total system of equal basic liberties compatible with a similar system of liberty for all." Also, to quote directly from Rawls, "Social and economic inequalities are to be arranged so that they are both: (a) to the greatest benefit of the least advantaged, consistent with the just savings principle, and (b) attached to offices and positions open to all under conditions of fair equality of opportunity." Furthermore, "justice is lexically prior to the principle of efficiency and to that of maximizing the sum of advantages; and fair opportunity is prior to the difference principle." His "general conception" will also apply as between nations – namely, that "all social primary goods – liberty and opportunity, income and wealth, and the bases of self-respect – are to be distributed equally unless an unequal distribution of any or all of these goods is to the advantage of the least favoured."

Is this outlandish; is it "going too far" to extend principles of justice arrived at between individuals to nations? I suggest it is not. Already, even in the real world of today, there is a generally accepted principle that the least-developed countries (LDCs) should be treated to an "unequal distribution" of global social goods (tariff reductions, debt remissions, technical assistance, etc.) in their favour. Similarly, at the 1992 Rio Summit on "Environment and Development," the principle of "common and differentiated responsibility" was accepted as an allocative principle. The entire global community accepted a common responsibility towards the environment. However, the developing countries were to have a lesser degree of responsibility, and were to be assisted with finance and technology to meet their obligations. Also, under GATT the principle of "special and differential treatment" for the developing countries was accepted until it was undermined by the Uruguay Agreements and the WTO.

Our second difference with Rawls is the methodology he adopts in his work *The Law of Peoples*. Unlike his *Theory of Justice*, where he conceptualizes justice in the "original position," when he comes to writing *The Law of Peoples* he has in mind extant societies – his own and "the others," those that are "hierarchical." He has allowed himself to be influenced by concrete history; he now talks like a "real world" person and not one in the "original position." He violates his own norms that he had set in his "original condition."

The truth of the matter is that, in the real world of today, all societies are hierarchical. Liberalism is a product of a certain history and culture and contains generally acceptable values of human rights and respect for basic liberties. However, in the real world, liberalism has also become fused with capitalism. Within the domestic arena, even in the West, the individual is submerged under the weight of an order – the capitalist order – over which he/she has little control.

Indeed, one of the problems of the present epoch is the incomplete democracy (or democratic deficit) in the United States, the most powerful country on earth. The US Government is accountable more to its corporations than to its people. The US Congress is, in fact, a plutocratic powerhouse: without millions of dollars, there is no way of getting into it. With approximately 36 million people living below the poverty line (at last count), and with one individual (Bill Gates) owning assets more than the combined assets of the poorest half of the population, the United States has become as much of a "hierarchical" society as any.[15]

We were drawn into a discussion of the real world because of Rawls' departure from the imagined world of "original position" in his *Theory of Justice* (Rawls 1972), where he has much clarity, to the real world in his *The Law of Peoples* (Rawls 1999), where he loses his clarity. But let us return to the conceptual level and examine, very briefly, some alternative formulations of justice, and assess their comparative merit in relation to justice as fairness. We consider three of these, as follows:
1. Justice as charity;
2. Justice as welfare;
3. Justice as a teleological movement of current history.

Justice as charity

Justice as charity has a long and, in some circles, an honoured history. It has both a religious as well as a secular pedigree. Most religions believe in charity. As for the secular version, there is a respected tradition in the West, especially in the United States, for the rich to create charitable foundations for worthy causes (even if they do so mostly to avoid taxes).

Underlying charity are two basic assumptions. One is that inequality is an inevitable outcome of every social and political process; "It is a fact of life. The poor are always with us." The second is that the rich have a custodial responsibility towards the poor.

How do we assess justice as charity? In the absence of nothing else, charity may have some role to play; in terms of justice, however, it has serious problems. The biggest difficulty is that it clouds reality and prevents a critical examination of how and why the rich get richer and the poor poorer. The recipients of charity accept their condition as "natural," or "God-given," and they are placed in a position of permanent gratitude to the alms-giver.

At the international level, the ordinary people in the West genuinely believe that the "aid" their countries give to the developing countries is an act of charity. It blinds their sight to the real world of unequal exchange between nations, or to the fact that most of them became rich on a history of slavery and colonialism. They acquire a certain air of superiority and a condescending attitude towards those who receive "aid." Hence, charity, instead of ennobling the spirit, diminishes it. We would prefer Rawls' "bases of self-respect" as a significant "social primary good," rather than charity. As the earliest Western feminist, Mary Wollstonecraft, said in 1792, "It is justice, not charity, that is wanting in the world" (Wollstonecraft 1792).

Justice as welfare

Justice as welfare has a more recent history. It goes back, essentially, to the nineteenth century utilitarians, whose chief spokesman, Jeremy Bentham, laid the philosophical foundations for maximizing overall welfare level. In contemporary times, it is a favourite subject of a certain genre of economists (hence called "welfare economists"), of whom the best known are A. M. Polinsky, R. Rosner, and A. K. Sen. They have tried to bring a measure of "scientific" (econometric) sophistication to utilitarianism, and they deal with concepts such as efficiency, allocation and distribution, entitlement, the Gini coefficient, and, above all, Pareto optimality. A situation is said to be Pareto optimal if it is impossible to change it without at least one person feeling that he/she is worse off than before; it is Pareto superior if nobody is worse off but at least one person feels that he/she is better off than before.[16]

What do we make of welfarist concept of justice? There is no question that welfare economists have made a valuable contribution by introducing a normative side to economics. They have been influential in challenging Gross Domestic Product (GDP)-based notions of growth. A. K. Sen, for example, has directly influenced the conceptual underpinnings of UNDP's annual "human development" surveys, and the poverty-alleviation concepts of the World Bank.

However, as a principle of justice, the concept of welfare is quite inadequate. As a distributive principle it accommodates inequalities provided that the overall benefits (or welfare) exceed the cost, and provided that Pareto optimality is secured. This is not a satisfactory proposition; Rawls' idea that inequalities are acceptable only if they benefit the most disadvantaged is much more satisfactory from the point of view of justice. In the "welfare" model the rich could well grow richer, provided that they take care of the welfare of the poor. In the "justice as fairness" model, the "social primary goods" (liberty and opportunity, income and wealth,

and the bases of self-respect) are to be distributed equally unless an unequal distribution is to the advantage of the least favoured.[17]

As for welfare models that focus on allocatively efficient outcomes in
economistic terms, the words of C. G. Veljanosky are worth repeating.
Efficiency, he says, is "little more than technocratic principle of unim-
provability; there is no rearrangement of society's productive activity or
allocation of goods and services that will improve the economic welfare
of society given the distribution of wealth upon which market transactions are based" (Veljanovsky 1984: 22).

Justice as teleological movement of current history

There are many who believe that the world is already moving in the right
direction. In other words, the real is the ideal; what is, should be. Leading lights among these are political thinkers such as David Held, who argues that a "cosmopolitan" global order is already emerging, and international lawyers such as Ernst-Ulrich Petersmann, who argues that a
Kantian constitutional order leading to "perpetual peace" is looming on
the horizon.

David Held, to be fair, is aware of the iniquities of the existing global
system, and the limitations of the liberal state. He none the less expresses
what can only be described as a naïve faith in the movement of recent
history, especially in the space that, he claims, is opening for a "cosmopolitan" order to emerge out of the erosion of national sovereignty and
"global interconnectedness" (Held 1991).[18]

The fact of the matter is that both the erosion of sovereignty and the
emerging interconnectedness have specific characteristics. Sovereignty is
inseparable from power. It is primarily the power and sovereignty of
small and middle states, principally those in the South, which have been
eroded. The power and "extraterritorial sovereignty" of the US State
and of the European Union (the collective power of Europe) have increased phenomenally, mostly at the cost of the countries of the South.
As for global interconnectedness, that, too, is one-sided. Under the dual
impact of liberalization of markets and of concentration of power in the
hands of fewer and fewer corporations (through mergers and acquis-
itions), the power of those who control the means of communications and
finance has increased astronomically. What is emerging is not a "cosmopolitan" world order, but a "homogenized" world under the control of
one particular culture and power bloc.

Ernst-Ulrich Petersmann, on the other hand, is a self-proclaimed Kantian. Like a priest who sees goodness in every heart, Petersmann sees the
emergence of a Kantian constitutional order in every expression of the
Kantian imperatives. Thus, he says, "Article 1 of the 1949 Basic Law of

Germany, for instance, reflects Kantian legal philosophy" (Petersmann 1998). He argues that European integration law and the 1994 WTO agreement have "underlying Kantian legal theory" (ibid. 20). EC law and the WTO law, and their comprehensive guarantees of individual access to domestic courts, reflect another important Kantian idea (ibid. 21). Petersmann would have a "new UN" modelled after the WTO, with "strong leadership" provided by the United States and Europe.

Like the 1944 Bretton Woods Agreements, the 1945 UN Charter, GATT 1947, or the 1994 WTO Agreement, a new UN Charter will not come about without strong leadership and political pressures from the United States and Europe. In order to be politically acceptable, there is a need for a transitional period during which, like the temporary coexistence of GATT 1947 and the WTO, the new United Nations could coexist with the United Nations of 1945, in order to maintain orderly relations with non-democracies. However, in order to set sufficient incentives to join the new United Nations, and disincentive against "free-riding," the advantages of the new UN system, including the financial and development assistance from Bretton Woods institutions, should be focused on democracies joining the new United Nations, just as the advantages of the WTO law were not extended to member countries of GATT 1947 until they acceded to the WTO (ibid. 23).

Here is a recipe for an authoritarian global system imposed by a United States–European coalition under the guise of creating a Kantian "constitutional order." It is these kinds of prescriptions, made not by irresponsible but by respected intellectuals, that confirm the scenario of a world being globalized under the hegemony of one particular branch of human civilization (see above).[19]

Both Held and Petersmann are guilty of contingent thinking. Rawls had his individuals placed in a "veil of ignorance" in order to "nullify the effects of specific contingencies which put men at odds and tempt them to exploit social and natural circumstances to their own advantage." But while Held hopes for a new United Nations built on what he calls a "democratic international law" (Held 1992: 43), Petersmann models his new United Nations after the WTO and under the hegemony of the United States and Europe, a United Nations where there shall be no "free riders."

Whatever their differences, what Held and Petersmann do is link their ideas to the real world, and it is to this real world that we must return. It is not enough to remain in the conceptual world shrouded by a "veil of ignorance." And so we come to the last question: which of the three sets of actors identified earlier (states and IGOs, TNCs and business associations, or civil society and NGOs) are best placed to address the matter of global justice defined as fairness?

Demands of justice against those of power

The first point to establish is that, when it comes to the role of major actors, it is a concrete or contingent question, not one that can be analysed in a "veil of ignorance" or in the abstract. The veil needs to be removed. The concrete set of questions is: Which states? Which IGOs? What business associations? Which civil society?[20]

We have already described the real world in the first part of this chapter. The United States, as stated earlier, is not only internally "hierarchical" but also externally predatory. In the international arena the US corporate sector uses the power of its state to impose its order on the rest of the world.[21] The ordinary people in America are implicated in this powerhouse and its predatory character by the manner in which they cast their votes every two or four years, lured by the promise of jobs from their corporations and an over-consumptionist lifestyle. As President Clinton is reported to have said: "You don't have to be a genius to figure out that, if you want to keep 22 per cent of that world's income for 4 per cent of the world's people, you've got to sell something to the other 96 per cent" (USA Today, 26 November 1999). It is (he said) a question of simple maths: the over-consumptionist demands of the US (and generally Western) populations drive their corporations to overexploit the rest of the world. The super-profits of these corporations, in turn, keep their domestic populations materially satiated and ideologically co-opted.[22]

One serious consequence of this perversion is that even the rich heritage of the West in the area of human rights is fraught; it is corrupted. When Western states espouse the cause of, for example, child labour in the South, one is never sure whether this is a genuine concern for the children or a protectionist excuse to save their industries from competition of products of "cheap labour." When 20,000 trade unionists marched in the streets of Seattle on the eve of the third Ministerial conference of the WTO in November 1999, they wanted the issue of labour to be included in WTO's agenda. The US President supported this demand and went further: he said that those countries that would not abide by labour-standard requirements would face US sanctions.[23] Clinton was thus both protecting American jobs and buying votes for his party. The hypocrisy of the American state was only too apparent to the discerning South, who noted that out of the 10 core labour conventions passed by the ILO, the United States has signed only two of them.

By the same token, when North Atlantic Treaty Organization (NATO) countries bomb Iraq and Yugoslavia, it is not on some high moral grounds of defending "human rights": it is to protect their own vested strategic and economic interests. Western actions at the international level have debased the currency of human rights.

It should be clear, therefore, that the states (qua states) in the West are not among those that would administer justice as fairness in the global system. It is not their job to administer justice; theirs is to order and administer a global system that serves their own strategic and economic interests.[24]

It should be equally clear that Western TNCs are also not purveyors of justice. They might administer charity, even welfare. Indeed, from the viewpoint of justice as fairness, the motivations behind their charitable or welfare activities are questionable. In every ordered society, the ruling classes give handouts to those they oppress and exploit, as a way both of placating them and of salvaging their own conscience (Thompson 1991). Those who receive charity or welfare, however, are seldom fooled. They appear eternally grateful to the "master," but they know that there is no justice in their acts of charity/welfare. In the real world, the transnationals are part of the problem, not a solution. One major strand of peoples' movements globally is aimed at either liquidating the TNCs (an ideal), or at least making them more accountable to society.

As for states and business corporations in the South, they are both weak and dependent upon the powerful states and corporations in the Western world. In the contemporary dispensation, capital is dominant. With capital comes technology and with technology comes the knowledge of production. To secure these, the states in the South have to open up their markets to Western corporations and to vie with one another to provide competitive terms to capital. This raises the cost of capital for all. Since they cannot lower the cost of capital, and since the prices of their raw materials are, in any case, determined by market forces over which they have little control, the states in the South and their business companies can compete in the world market only by lowering the wages of the working classes. This is one of the fundamental reasons behind the impoverishment of the people of the South.

Furthermore, the purchase of capital- and knowledge-intensive products from the North, with constantly decreasing value of their exports, is the basis for the empirically verified phenomenon of long-term secular decline in the terms of trade of the South. These are conditions of unequal exchange embedded in the system.[25] This is fundamentally at the root of the increasing debt burden of the South. It has risen (in billions of US dollars) from 567 in 1980 to 1,086 in 1986, to 1,419 in 1992, to 2,030 in 1998.[26] The South is thus in the grip of the banks and the corporations of the North, in debt bondage. We have said that one major strand of global peoples' movements is to rein-in TNCs; another such strand is the global anti-debt campaign, backed by a vast alliance of NGOs, churches, and trade unions.

Thus, the states and business in the South have been guilty of swallowing Western ideologies, together with their capital and technology, and are responsible for perpetuating a system that has impoverished their people. And so, to the question of what role they play in effecting justice as fairness, the answer is that they play an ambiguous role. When they seek Western capital and technology and access to Western markets, they act like supplicants and come down hard on their own populations in enforcing SAPs and other dictates of corporate capital. However, when they feel they are not getting a fair deal from the North, they protest and fight back, as indeed happened at the Third Ministerial meeting of the WTO in Seattle in December 1999. For the states in the South to defend the interests of their people, they have to be constantly pressurized from below.

As for IGOs, there is a clear division between those where the South have some voice and those which are totally dominated by the North. As earlier stated, the Bretton Woods institutions and the WTO are largely creatures of the rich countries of the Organization for Economic Co-operation and Development (OECD). They provide the capital and the rules that regulate trade and the movement of capital. When their regulatory sanctions are weak or ineffective, the states of the West step in to impose these with economic and, if necessary, military means. Clearly, then, the IMF, the World Bank, and the WTO cannot be counted upon to administer justice as fairness; indeed, they are part of the problem, not its solution.[27]

However, there are, on the other hand, IGOs such as the ILO, the UNESCO, the FAO, the UNDP, the UNCTAD, and the United Nations University, in which the South have a certain space. Imperfect as they are, they none the less have an important role towards building a fairer system of global order. Often, however, they are schizophrenic: being intergovernmental, and funded largely by Western donors, they have to "balance" the equity demands of the weaker members of the international society with the demands of the West to conform to the peremptory rules of the capitalist order. Therefore, like states in the South, for the more democratic IGOs to defend justice they have to be constantly pressurized from below by those who suffer from the system.

That leaves us to consider the third major actor in the global sphere, namely, civil society organizations including the so-called NGOs, transnational social movements, the trade unions, and the media. We have already referred to two of these – the movements that seek to rein-in the TNCs and make them accountable to society and be sensitive to concerns of justice, and the anti-debt peoples' coalition against debt. There are literally thousands of such NGOs and peoples' movements that have in recent years come to play a significant role in reforming or challenging the global system.

Coming as they do from diverse backgrounds, cultures, and mandates, there have, of course, been many contradictions.[28] None the less, overall they seek a fair dispensation towards the weaker member nations of the international community and weaker and vulnerable groups within countries – such as women, children, immigrants, indigenous peoples, and ethnic minorities, and those important inhabitants of this universe that have no voice of their own, such as Nature and animals. Overall, and keeping in mind the many contradictions between them, they are the only agencies that can be relied upon to be agents of the Rawlsian concept of justice as fairness.[29]

On strategic and tactical issues, the NGOs and peoples' movements fall into two broad divisions: there are those that believe (and hope) that the system is reformable – they seek to work from within the system to try to change it; and there are those that have no faith in the system's ability to reform, whether from the inside or as a result of pressure from the outside. Even amongst these, their methods differ between those that resort to violence (a very tiny minority) and those who use various tactics of lobbying, advocacy, and civil disobedience at both local and global levels.

Concluding remarks

Anybody who works in the area of global justice has a challenging task. To start with, there are so many rival conceptions of it. Most of them are influenced by real-world situations where biases and prejudices are unavoidable. Rawls provides us with a helpful way out of it with his concept of justice as fairness derived from the "original condition" by individuals in a "veil of ignorance." In this chapter we have simply extended this to the community of nations.

Justice as fairness, we argue, is a better concept than justice as charity or as welfare. The welfarist notions that guide most contemporary thinking in agencies such as the World Bank and the UNDP have serious flaws, whereas justice as charity is humiliating. Both avoid the reasons why the poor are getting poorer and the rich richer. Indeed, they can accommodate inequality as long as the welfare of the indigent is taken care of. Following from Rawls, we argue that this is not good enough: if there has to be inequality, it has to be in favour of the least advantaged, the ones with the least opportunities.

The concept of justice as fairness also conforms to most ordinary people's understanding of justice. Most people would protest at being treated "unfairly." They also recognize when others are being treated unfairly. "Fair trade" is the demand of people not only from the South but also, increasingly, of those from the North. When the WTO takes decisions in secret (in the so-called "green rooms" where only the powerful meet), it goes against the grain of "fair" play. Thus, at the end of the 1999 Seattle conference of the WTO, it was not just the developing countries and their NGOs that revolted against the manipulations of the United States, its allies and the Secretariat, but also most NGOs and peoples' movements from the North: it is "not fair," they said, for the developing countries to be so manipulated and to be bound by rules in the making of which they were systematically excluded. So Rawls' concept of what he calls "procedural justice" has much merit. To quote him again, "The aim is to use the notion of pure procedural justice as a basis of theory." How rules are made is equally important as, if not more important than, the rules themselves. Fairness, above all, is fairness in the making of rules of global governance.

In this context, rule-making in IGOs should favour the weak and the vulnerable nations, communities, minorities, indigenous peoples, and the underprivileged sections within societies. Principles such as the "special and differential treatment" in the old GATT, and the "principle of common but differentiated responsibility" agreed at the Rio Summit, should be resurrected and re-confirmed as the guiding principles of justice as fairness in the global context. The Western countries have systematically sought to erode them.

So what are the challenges before those who struggle for justice? The first challenge is to recognize the injustices of the contemporary situation and to understand their causes. We have argued that these are essentially systemic in character. Capitalism that was progressive in its time when it challenged a feudal order or the remnants of slavery is now reaching a point of absurdity. When over 90 per cent of the movement of capital is engaged not in production but in pure speculation, then that should be hint enough to most reasonable people that, as a system, it is becoming counter-productive even by its own original tenets.

It should also be clear to most reasonable people that, if 20 per cent of the world's people in the richest countries compared with 20 per cent of the poorest in the poor countries had their incomes increased from 30 times in 1960 to 82 times in 1995 (see note 4), then there is something fundamentally wrong with the system; it is palpably unfair. It is also evidence that the theories of "development" peddled by "experts" not only have failed but also may have drawn the wool over the eyes of most people. As it turns out (in retrospect), these theories were, in essence, ideological justification for the captains of capital (the TNCs) to acquire control over the world's markets and resources.

Globalization, as defined by the "experts," is movement along the same route. Although presented as an "inevitable" process, what "experts" do not say is that it is not inevitable that it should be spearheaded by capital. We argue that it can, and should, be spearheaded by people, a globalization from below, not one from above. Thus, those working for justice need to be critical of the ideologies and the language used by the so-called "experts" who obfuscate reality. They should also be aware of the double standards that the Western governments apply when dealing with the South.

In this context, people should demand not just debt relief but its total cancellation. It was unjustly accumulated to start with, and it is one of the principal reasons for the continuing poverty of the South. Africa, for example, pays out more in terms of debt servicing than all the "development aid" it receives. Initiatives such as the Highly Indebted Poor Countries (HIPC) should be exposed for what they are – palliatives to placate public opinion. Similarly, TRIPS should be taken out of the WTO, and the right of peoples to their biodiversity recognized under the CBD should be confirmed. The WTO itself should be brought back to dealing with matters related to trade, narrowly defined as dealing with tangible goods; it should be stopped from extending its tentacles to matters that properly belong to other agencies of the UN system, such as the ILO, UNEP, UNCTAD, UNDP, UNESCO, and the FAO. People should demand that the original mandates of these organizations be reconfirmed and that they be provided with adequate human and material resources to carry them out.

The tasks of global governance are too critical and too important to leave to governments and to TNCs, who are part of the problem. The people of the United States and Europe have a greater responsibility than even those from the South; their countries suffer from a serious case of democratic deficit. Electoral democracy is only, as they say, "skin-deep." Furthermore, they have a responsibility to look seriously into their consumption habits and lifestyles. Besides straining the world's resources, these become an excuse for their corporations to overexploit the South and to co-opt the people of the North in perpetuating an unjust system. The world's resources ("public goods") should be so distributed that the least privileged have an "unequal" share of it, in their favour.

Finally, we end as we started. Human beings must question their anthropocentrism. They are the most conscious and the most deliberative beings on earth, but that gives them no right to inflict carnage on the rest of Nature's multiple species; on the contrary, it is their obligation to protect them and give them space. That, too, is part of justice and good global governance.

Notes

1. The rate at which global biodiversity is decreasing is one of the worst in the Earth's history, comparable to the "K-T Event" that ended the Age of Dinosaurs 65 million years ago with a loss of 76 per cent of the world's species. According to a study conducted in conjunction with the UN Task Force On Global Developmental Impact, "The planet Earth stands on the brink of one of the most devastating global extinctions in history. By the year 2040, nearly two-thirds of all current species will be extinct. Rainforest habitats that were once lush canopies of life, sustaining millions of highly specialized and interdependent species of plants and animals, have been reduced by upwards of 95 per cent in some areas." Because of the interdependent nature of systems such as the Amazon, the disappearance of any one species can lead to the death of countless others. "The extinction of the Borneo hooded tern was an indirect result of the disappearance of the native species of sea snails upon which it fed."
2. Samuel P. Huntington *The Clash of Civilizations?* (1993), in which he said that "the paramount axis" of world policies would be between "the West and the Rest," and that the central focus of conflict in the immediate future will be between the West and several Islamic–Confucian states.
3. This is a descriptive category, not evaluative. In terms of values, this civilization brings with it a mixed heritage. Broadly speaking, there are essentially two traditions dominant in this civilization. There is the "naturalist" or "rational" tradition that has a rich, humanist, and caring intellectual and cultural content. It is this tradition that has been, in the main, responsible for the contemporary human rights movement. There is, then, the "realist" tradition, linked with thinkers such as Hobbes and Machiavelli. For this tradition, politics is amoral; the name of the game is power. There is room for "virtue," but only in so far as it is necessary to legitimize power. One might say, generally, that the humanist tradition has been dominant within the domestic milieu of Western countries, and the realist tradition in the practice of their international relations. Overall, and not without foundation, the Euro-Christian-Judaic civilization is equated, for the last 500 years, with capitalism. There is also a third tradition, a revolutionary tradition, most popularly associated with Karl Marx. This tradition has had a profound impact on the course of history over the last 150 years. With the defeat of the Soviet Union in the cold war, this tradition has lost some ground (in the West), but it is still quite virile, especially in the so-called "third world," and is likely to re-emerge as a strong force. Marx's critical ontology and epistemology was based on an analysis of the capitalist system in an emancipatory project that is still on the historical agenda. Its future will have new form, even new content, and may not necessarily be in the way Marx projected it.
4. UNDP 1998: 29: "In 1960 the 20 per cent of the world's people who live in the richest countries had 30 times the income of the poorest 20 per cent – by 1995, 82 times as much income."
5. In a sense, globalization is part of movement of history itself. But capital-led globalization is not inevitable, and it can be resisted; indeed, there is a growing resistance to it.
6. For a scholarly analysis of the colonial text, see Said (1983).
7. It would be quite instructive for some researcher to catalogue the number of third-world "rebellious" leaders that have been, or are, described as "mad" in the Western press. In the case of Saddam Hussein, his image degenerated over time from Hitler, to "the butcher of Baghdad," and then in the words of Senator Alan Simpson, "the mad-

man." In recent months I have often encountered friends in Europe who innocently ask me whether Robert Mugabe has "really gone mad." A friend from Malaysia tells me that he is asked the same question about Mahathir Mohamed.

8. In South Korea, thousands of workers took to the street to protest against their mass retrenchment.

9. UNCTAD surveys on investments show the differential rates of return on capital between the North and the South. Typically, investment in Africa can earn 25–40 per cent profit compared with 5–6 per cent in the United States. The most volatile of this is speculative capital. One important source of it is pension funds in Western countries looking for higher profits in order to meet their future obligations. For details, see *Mutual Fund Fact Book* 1998.

10. "In some ways the IMF has done more in these past months to liberalize these economies and open their markets to US goods and services than has been achieved in rounds of trade negotiations in the region" (Summers 1998).

11. In a review of the United Nations' action (lack of it) in Rwanda, an independent commission singled out the United States and the present Secretary-General for their callous withdrawal of UN peace-keeping forces from Rwanda in full knowledge that this would lead to massacres of the Tutsis. A quarter of a million people were hacked to death.

12. For example, in Western philosophy, the debate goes back to Aristotle's Nicomachean Ethics, 350 BC; in ancient India, in the Vedas and Upanisads to between 4000 BC (Bal Gangadhar Tilak) and 1200 BC (Max Muller).

13. Needless to say, these ideas, too, have attracted much criticism. Among his most passionate critic is Robert Nozick, the arch-defender of nineteenth century *laissez-faire* capitalism.

14. I would contend that the device of "original position" to work out principles of justice in the abstract is preferable to other alternative ways of doing this, such as game theories and the prisoners' dilemma (PD) matrix. Game theories and PD matrices are devoid of normative content and can at best predict "rational" behaviour, rationality being defined in purely selfish or functional terms.

15. It is necessary to add that this is not a new argument. Unfortunately, since the end of the cold war and "the end of history" claimed by liberal triumphalists, the earlier debate on the nature of the Western liberal state has been all but forgotten. Political theorists such as C. B. Macpherson (1977) have cogently argued in the 1970s that the liberal pretensions of the capitalist state are fundamentally flawed, that the "liberal state" inescapably reproduces inequalities of everyday life, distorting decisions in favour of propertied interests. See also Carole Pateman (1985). In more recent times, the Communitarians, such as Charles Taylor, Stephen Mulhall, and Adam Swift (1995), have challenged liberalist assumptions from another angle: they argue that individualism and the acquisitive spirit is an invitation to man to behave in a socially irresponsible manner, and is the main cause of the crisis of our civilization.

16. The Pareto optimality is also at the basis of the more crude talk among social and environmental activists and trade negotiators about creating "win–win" situations.

17. For a critique of Rawls from a welfare perspective, see Amritya Sen 1984: 278–285.

18. See also Held 1993.

19. The fact that Petersmann, besides being a university professor, is the legal adviser to the WTO, makes his utterances even more ominous and scary for those from the South who see the WTO, as it is presently constituted and run, as a veritable instrument of domination and oppression.

20. I realize that some of the essays in this volume talk about the state and civil society in

the abstract, even when writing about this world. To each his/her own desert. But I have fundamental difficulty in dealing in the abstract with issues that are concrete and contingent.

21. For a comprehensive account of this, see David C. Korten (1995).
22. The North has 25 per cent of the world's population and 85 per cent of the world's income, and accounts for 80 per cent of world consumption of natural resources. It generates 75 per cent of industrial and municipal waste, and has contributed about 80 per cent of global CO_2 emissions since 1950. (Symposium on Sustainable Consumption, Oslo, January 1994, Opening Speech by Minister T. Bernsten.)
23. This was one of the major reasons for the collapse of the Seattle Conference of the WTO. The countries of the South came out collectively to oppose such an imposition of labour standards on them, using the sanctions machinery of the WTO.
24. It is commendably the merit of the "realist" school of International Relations in the West that it makes no bones about arguing that their states are motivated not by considerations of abstract justice, however conceptualized, but by considerations of *Realpolitik*. Unlike the "idealist" school, they do not pull the wool over the eyes of naïve observers of the international scene. We have cited Huntington above, but see also, for example, Hans Morgenthau (1973) and Hedley Bull (1977).
25. For a classical statement on this problem see, e.g. Samir Amin 1977.
26. Figures derived from IMF sources. See Dot Keet 1999: 2.
27. Indeed, at the WTO Seattle conference in November–December 1999, the key players within the WTO, led by the United States, became so blatantly manipulative of the processes of decision-making that the South repudiated the whole conference. See Yash Tandon 1999: "Blip or Turnaround." *SEATINI Bulletin* 2: December 1999.
28. Two such contradictions might be mentioned here. One is between NGOs' and peoples' movements, but the differences between the two are often exaggerated. Another is between those that come from the North and those from the South. Differences between these, although they exist, are also often exaggerated.
29. Questions are sometimes raised about their "representativeness," but that is a false issue. It is false to apply the electoral principle to them, just as it is to their adversaries, the corporate world.

REFERENCES

Amin, Samir. 1977. *Imperialism and Unequal Development*. Ness York: Monthly Review Press.

Bull, Hedley. 1977. *The Anarchical Society. A Study of Order in World Politics*. London: Macmillan.

Correa, Carlos M. 2000. *Intellectual Property Rights, the WTO and Developing Countries*. London: Zed Books.

Held, David. 1991. "Democracy, the Nation-State and the Global System." In: *Political Theory Today*, ed. David Held. Cambridge: Polity Press, 197–235.

Held, David. 1992. "Democracy: From City-states to a Cosmopolitan Order?" *Political Studies* Vol. XL (*Special Issue: Prospects for Democracy*, ed. David Held), 10–39.

Huntington, Samuel P. 1993. "The Clash of Civilizations?" *Foreign Affairs*, 72(3): 22–49.

Kaul, Inge, Isabelle Grunberg, and Marc. A. Stern, eds. 1999. *Global Public Goods*. Tokyo: United Nations University Press.

Keet, Dot. 1999. *The International Anti-Debt Campaign*. Cape Town: Alternative Information and Development Centre.

Korten, David C. 1995. *When Corporations Rule the World*. USA: Kumarian Press, Inc. and Berrett-Koehler Publishers, Inc.

Macpherson, C. B. 1977. *The Life and Times of Liberal Democracy*. Oxford: Oxford University Press.

Morgenthau, Hans J. 1973. *Politics Among Nations. The Struggle for Power and Peace*, 5th edn. New York: Knopf.

Mutual Fund Fact Book, 38th edn. 1998. USA: Investment Company Institute.

Pateman, Carole. 1985. *The Problem of Political Obligation: A Critique of Liberal Theory*. Cambridge: Polity Press.

Petersmann, Ernst-Ulrich. 1998. "How to Constitutionalize International Law and Foreign Policy for the Benefit of Civil Society?" *Michigan Journal of International Law* 20(1): 15–25.

Popper, Karl. 1959. *The Logic of Scientific Discovery*. London: Hutchinson.

Rawls, John. 1972. *A Theory of Justice*. Oxford: Oxford University Press.

Rawls, John. 1999. *The Law of Peoples*. Cambridge, MA: Harvard University Press.

Said, Edward W. 1983. The World, the Text and the Critic. Cambridge, MA: Harvard University Press.

Said, Edward W. 1995. *Orientalism: Western Conceptions of the Orient*. London: Penguin Books.

Schumpeter, Joseph A. 1943. *Capitalism, Socialism and Democracy*. London: George Allen & Unwin.

Sen, Amritya. 1984. *Resources, Values and Development*. Oxford: Basil Blackwell.

Stiglitz, Joseph. 1998. "More Instruments and Broader Goals: Moving Toward the Post-Washington Consensus." Speech delivered 7 January 1998 at the 1998 WIDER Annual Lecture, Helsinki, Finland.

Summers, Larry. 1998. "American Farmers: Their Stakes in Asia, Their Stake in IMF." Office of Public Affairs, US Treasury Dept, Washington DC, 23 February, 1998.

Tandon, Yash. 1999. "Blip or Turnaround." *SEATINI Bulletin* 2: 1–22.

Taylor, Charles, Stephen Mulhall, and Adam Swift. 1995. *Liberals and Communitarians*. Oxford: Basil Blackwell.

Thompson, E. P. 1991. *Customs in Common*. London: Penguin.

UNDP. 1998. *The Human Development Report of 1998*. New York: United Nations.

UNICEF. 1999. *Iraq Child and Maternity Mortality Surveys, 1999*. Geneva: UNICEF.

Veljanovsky, C. G. 1984. In: *Readings in the Economics of Law and Regulation, No. 22*, eds A. Ogus and C. G. Veljanovsky.

Wittgenstein, Ludwig. 1958. *Philosophical Investigations*, 2nd ed transl. G. E. Anscome. Oxford: Basil Blackwell.

Wollstonecraft, Mary. 1792. *Vindication of the Rights of Woman: With Strictures on Political and Moral Subjects*. London: Joseph Johnson.

Acronyms

(I)NGO	international non-governmental organization
AFRC/RUF	Armed Forces Revolutionary Council/Revolutionary United Front
AFTA	ASEAN Free Trade Area
APEC	Asia-Pacific Economic Cooperation
APSA	American Political Science Association
ASEAN	Association of South-East Asian Nations
CBD	Convention on Bio-Diversity
CFC	chlorofluorocarbon
CICC	Coalition for an International Criminal Court
CIS	Commonwealth of Independent States
CSCE	Conference on Security and Cooperation in Europe
DSB	Dispute Settlement Body
ECJ	European Court of Justice
ECOMOG	the ECOWAS Monitoring Group
ECOSOC	United Nations Economic and Social Council
ECOWAS	Economic Community of Western African States
EU	European Union
FAO	Food and Agriculture Organization
FDI	foreign direct investment
GATT	General Agreement on Tariffs and Trade
GCC	Gulf Cooperation Council
GDNI	Global Development Network Initiative
GDP	gross domestic product
GMO	genetically modified organism
GPP	global public policy (networks)

GSM	Global Social Movement
HIPC	Highly Indebted Poor Countries
ICANN	Internet Corporation for Assigned Names and Numbers
ICBL	International Campaign to Ban Landmines
ICC	International Chamber of Commerce
ICC	International Criminal Court
IDB	Inter-American Development Bank
IETF	Internet Engineering Task Force
IFI	international financial institution
IGO	intergovernmental organization
ILO	International Labour Organization
IMF	International Monetary Fund
IR	international relations
ISDSC	Inter-State Defense and Security Committee
ISOC	Internet Society
IT	information technology
ITU	International Telecommunication Union
LDCs	least-developed countries
MAI	Multilateral Agreement on Investment
MDB	multilateral development bank
MNC	multinational corporation
MTN	multilateral trade negotiations
NAFTA	North American Free Trade Agreement
NATO	North Atlantic Treaty Organization
NGO	non-governmental organization
OAS	Organization of American States
OAU	Organization of African Unity
OECD	Organization for Economic Co-operation and Development
OSCE	Organization for Security and Cooperation in Europe
PPP	public–private partnership
PRI	Institutional Revolutionary Party (Mexico)
PTTs	post and telecommunications companies
PWC	post-Washington Consensus
SADC	Southern African Development Community
SAP	Structural Adjustment Program
TCP/IP	Transmission Control Protocol/Internet Protocol
TNC	transnational corporation
TRIM	trade-related investment measure
TRIPs	trade-related intellectual property rights
TSMO	transnational social movement organization
UIA	Union of International Associations
UNCTAD	United Nations Conference on Trade and Development
UNDP	United Nations Development Programme
UNEP	United Nations Environment Programme
UNESCO	United Nations Educational, Scientific, and Cultural Organization
UNHCR	United Nations High Commissioner for Refugees
UNICEF	United Nations Children's Fund

UNIDO	United Nations Industrial Development Organization
UNITeS	United Nations Information Technology Service
UNTAC	United Nations Transitional Authority in Cambodia
USTR	United States Trade Representative
WB–NGO	World Bank–Non-Governmental Organization (Committee)
WC	Washington Consensus
WEU	Western European Union
WHO	World Health Organization
WIPO	World Intellectual Property Organization
WTO	World Trade Organization

Contributors

Tanja Brühl is a Research Associate at the University of Frankfurt, Germany, with a particular interest in international relations and international environmental policy.

Richard Higgott is Professor of International Political Economy and Director of the ESRC Centre for the Study of Globalization and Regionalization, University of Warwick, UK. His areas of professional interest include international relations (international theory and international political economy, especially Asia-Pacific economic cooperation), comparative politics, and comparative political development, especially in the Asia-Pacific region.

Otfried Höffe is Professor of Philosophy at the University of Tübingen, Germany. His areas of professional interest include political theory, moral philosophy, epistemology, ethics, Aristotle, and Kant.

Sorpong Peou is Professor of Political Science at the Sophia University, Japan. He is particularly interested in international security, international organization and law, international relations in East Asia, and comparative politics in Asia.

Maria Pia Riggirozzi is a member of the School of International Studies at the University of Miami.

Volker Rittberger is Professor of Political Science and International Relations and Director of the Centre for International Relations/Peace and Conflict Studies, University of Tübingen, Germany. His areas of professional interests are in the fields of German foreign policy, comparative foreign policy, theory of international relations, international institutions, and peace and conflict studies.

Yash Tandon is Director of the International South Group Network (ISGN) and Editor of SEATINI (Southern and Eastern African Trade Information and Negotiation Initiative). He lives in Harare, Zimbabwe.

Diana Tussie is Professor of International Relations, La Facultad de Latinoamericana de Ciencias Sociales (FLACSO), Sede Académica Argentina.

Michael Zürn is Professor of Political Science at the University of Bremen and the International Institute for Intercultural and International Studies, and is Director of the Centre of European Law and Politics at the University of Bremen (ZERP). His areas of professional interest include international and transnational relations, peace and conflict studies, international institutions, globalization, European integration, and international environmental policy.

Index